YOU KNOW *LESS* THAN YOU *DON'T* KNOW

TRANSFORMATION—NOT CHANGE—IS KEY TO SUCCESS

DR. PATRICIA ANDERSON

TRILOGY CHRISTIAN PUBLISHERS
TUSTIN, CA

Trilogy Christian Publishers
A Wholly Owned Subsidiary of Trinity Broadcasting Network
2442 Michelle Drive
Tustin, CA 92780

You Know Less Than You Don't Know

Copyright © 2022 by Dr. Patricia Anderson

All Scripture quotations are taken from the King James Version of the Bible. Public domain.

No part of this book may be reproduced, stored in a retrieval system, or transmitted by any means without written permission from the author. All rights reserved. Printed in the USA.

Rights Department, 2442 Michelle Drive, Tustin, CA 92780.

Trilogy Christian Publishing/TBN and colophon are trademarks of Trinity Broadcasting Network.

For information about special discounts for bulk purchases, please contact Trilogy Christian Publishing.

Trilogy Disclaimer: The views and content expressed in this book are those of the author and may not necessarily reflect the views and doctrine of Trilogy Christian Publishing or the Trinity Broadcasting Network.

Manufactured in the United States of America

10 9 8 7 6 5 4 3 2 1

Library of Congress Cataloging-in-Publication Data is available.

ISBN: 978-1-68556-901-3

E-ISBN: 978-1-68556-902-0

Transforming the world | One leader at a time

To my mother, Hyacinth:
Despite the complexities of what I encounter in life, she provides simple words of advice that work every time. She is that solid rock that is supportive and provides a space for me to sit in and just be at times.

To my grandmother Adlyn Cornwall who told me "get your education; no one can take that away from you."

Conventions

Throughout this body of work, I will use the acronyms ATL and PTL. The context of the sentence will inform you which definition is being used.

ATL stands for Authentic Transformational Leadership or Authentic Transformational Leader.

PTL stands for Pseudo-Transformational Leadership or Pseudo-Transformational Leader.

Contents

Introduction ix
Chapter 1. Change versus Transformation 1
Chapter 2. Transformational Leadership History 11
Chapter 3. Transformational Leadership Model 16
Chapter 4. Authentic Transformational versus Pseudo-Transformational Leadership................................... 25
Chapter 5. Transformational Leaders: Past, Present, Future 42
Chapter 6. Transformational Leadership During Crisis and Disruption 47
Chapter 7. Stakeholder Engagement................................. 58
Chapter 8. Lead, Learn, Level Up! 64
Chapter 9. Transformational Leadership and Organizational Change Management 94
Chapter 10. Walk the Diversity, Equity, Inclusion, Accessibility (DEIA) Talk 106
Chapter 11. Women in Leadership 114
Chapter 12. Leadership Playbook for the Future 125
Special Focus: Christian Leaders in the Metaverse 156
Appendix A: Conversations at the Top 161
Appendix B: Leadership Case Study 180
    Chapter 1. Introduction.. 182
    Chapter 2. Research Method 201
    Chapter 3. Research Methods 241
    Chapter 4. Data Analysis and Results 261
    Chapter 5. Discussion and Conclusion...................... 281
References 300

Introduction

*Superior organizational success
is boosted by positive leadership behavior.
Leaders' behaviors drive employee/follower motivation,
creativity, performance, and productivity.*

For many organizations, the question is how executive leadership has handled the sudden and multiple disruptions and crises that transpired, beginning with the global COVID-19 pandemic in 2020. How do leaders navigate the aftereffects? Did they simply change, or did leadership choose instead to transform?

The answer is transformation and not change. With or without pandemics, what businesses need in times of uncertainty is leadership that enables organizations to move through the crisis while maximizing efficiency and efficacy. Business disruption is the make-or-break point.

Stakeholder optics of change are often viewed as an untenable headwind: Conform to or else! On the other hand, transformation is an intentional, systematic, and incremental pursuit of better future states. It communicates a prescriptive communal approach where tailwinds guide progression and is so powerful that there is no path backward (ex.: butterfly to the caterpillar).

This leadership playbook teaches you how to efficiently optimize leadership during disruption and beyond. An increase in leadership EQ is imperative: understand yourself emotionally and extend that awareness to your followers, your employees, and your other stakeholders.

I began to practice this several years ago when I was experiencing challenges with new business ownership. One of my friends suggested that I read the book of Proverbs; there are thirty-one chapters (one for each day of the month). She felt (and was right) that as an entrepreneur, it guided every facet of business ownership (personal assessment/development, leadership, internal and external customer relations, and governance).

I am passionate about normalizing Authentic Transformational Leadership (ATL). As we witness The Rise of the Human, The Great Resignation, and the C-suite Purge, it is clear that the leadership status quo has been disrupted. Individuals in and out of the workspace are requiring leaders who are transparent, honest, and authentic and to be held accountable in ways that are profound and have deep social impacts.

Another passion as I endeavor to "transform the world one leader at a time" is to research and establish best practices for leading in the Metaverse. As we plunge further into the Internet of Things (IoT), leaders must exploit the convergence of people, data, and virtual tools in ways that deliver meaningful experiences to their internal and external stakeholders.

As a Christian and a leader, I know that I know less than I don't know. So I leaned into Romans 12:2 to gain knowledge about transformation, "be not conformed to this world: but be…transformed by the renewing of your mind…" It further states, "…that ye may prove what is that good, and acceptable, and perfect…"

This instruction is simple, clear, and imperative: Transform, don't conform! You transform by renewing your mind. Your mind has to arrive first! The establishing chapter in this book outlines the difference between change and transformation and positions you to move through good, acceptable, and perfect. This transformation is incremental, sustainable, and impervious to disruption and crisis.

CHAPTER 1

Change versus Transformation

Stop changing—it doesn't work! When you change, the tendency is to regress to the mean, but when you transform, that option is a non sequitur.

Change is not transformation; change is externally driven, while transformation is internally driven. For example, in Organizational Change Management (OCM), you may undertake a project to upgrade your existing software system; this change is driven by actions, meaning there is a focus on the activities and tasks of purchasing and implementing the software. The transformational aspect of the project is the approach to influencing users to adopt and use the new system. There has to be an internal mindset shift to accomplish this.

Another externally driven pursuit is the typical New Year's resolution. Many, like myself, choose to be healthier. Some choose to start a gym membership. Others engage in lifestyle changes such as a change of diet. Usually, these actions are short-lived, and there is a reversion to previous activities (or non-activities), indicating the binary aspect of change. That short amount of time that our typical New Year's resolution lasts is proof that the mind has to arrive first (as in transformation).

Your mind and belief system have to transform for you to be effective and have lasting effects. This premise is imperative because change is focused on tasks and processes. Transformation focuses on mindsets and beliefs, which in turn drive actions.

The methodology for change is tactical. I'm currently working with organizations on their digital transformation and OCM projects. The project's timelines are two to five years. The timeline is temporary since it has a beginning and an end to it. Transformation, however, is continuous. After the project ends, transformation enables it to stick and avoid reversion to past activities.

Change is focused on the current and the past states. Earlier, I used the resolution of going to the gym, but many may look at a past photo of themselves as their new goal weight. This past photo becomes the imagery or the vision to change their current body shape. The individual also acknowledges the reality of their current weight juxtaposed with their past ideal weight. The change, then, is prescribed by that vision. Like the software project referenced earlier, leaders deciding to upgrade their software is an example of change subscribing to a vision.

On the other hand, transformation prescribes a vision. This is similar to the view that God sees the end from the beginning. In that regard, you are not only establishing the pace but are also setting the stage. In transformation, you are progressing, as a caterpillar does, toward becoming a butterfly.

Change is focused on the problem that needs fixing. In the case of the software project, the software has run its course and is now outdated and processing information at a less than desirable pace; it's time to upgrade or change. Transformation, on the other hand, focuses on the solution. The difference between change and transformation is now evident, a problem-focused versus a solution-focused method.

Change is focused on the state of doing; this includes performing tasks and activities. Transformation focuses on the state of being. A mindset and belief shift occurs; it is now a matter of your believing and then becoming and doing. The drivers for change are our actions and visible steps. Comparatively, transformation is driven by our mindsets. The mind is the most powerful tool in our repertoire, and that's what we use to propel transformation. In change, you can move from state A to state B, i.e., going to the gym at the beginning of the year. You can also reverse that action—regress to not going to the gym. Change also involves your mental assent only. "New year, new me!" activities are based on mental assent only.

Transformation is a continuous evolution to future states. While transitioning to the next stage, you experience multiple states, making it difficult to reverse. This is due to an evolution of your foundational structure that enables you to move forward. You will go through a process of moving into "good," "acceptable," and eventually "perfect"—like a caterpillar transforms to become a butterfly perfectly poised to soar.

Moving through good, then acceptable, and to perfect causes a paradigm shift to occur. From that point, your infrastructure has shifted, your belief system has also shifted, your mindset has shifted, and therefore your behavior as a whole will shift.

Here's another example; think of the undo/redo button that you use in document editing. It also highlights the temporary aspects of change. The fear of mistakes is not as bad when there is a clear and easy option to simply hit the redo or undo buttons. However, undo does not work when transforming from a caterpillar to a butterfly. There is no way for the butterfly to simply decide that it is no longer satisfied with its new glow and revert to being a caterpillar. That, similar to transformation, cannot be reversed; there is no path backward. With change, there is a path backward since your evolution was solely driven by behavior.

At times, life provides perilous moments that result in our evolution as individuals. What happened at the onset of COVID-19? Pivot! Suddenly we had to pivot or perish. The crisis of COVID-19 represents the headwinds of change. Instantaneously it became imperative to not only change but to do so at a greater pace than usual. It was a moment that many struggled with, like an aircraft in a headwind.

On a similar note, you will sometimes run into resistance when you try to facilitate changes at an organization that encompasses varying mindsets. Some will strongly oppose any new directions or tools proposed. Others might even try to sabotage change for fear that they may be undervalued or replaced. The need to prove their valuableness can cloud their view on the needed change. This opposition epitomizes headwinds.

Contrastingly, transformation constitutes tailwinds. Tailwinds are not working against an aircraft; rather, they accelerate it. The tailwinds of leadership should include accountability, innovation, emotional intelligence, collaboration, creativity, and role modeling. When a crisis like a pandemic arises, these leaders are poised to move through it. There is less need to rethink leadership, your resources, or your talent; you are a transformative organization; you have the impetus to effectively lead through future disruptions.

Consider the change and transformation represented on your breakfast plate. Involvement (change) and commitment (transformation) are both symbolized. When a chicken provides its eggs for breakfast, it denotes one aspect of itself. However, the bacon represents a fully committed transformation. Let's try an exercise right now. Write your full name and title with your dominant, then non-dominant hand. Writing with the non-dominant hand represents transformation; you can continue to write with it until you gain proficiency or simply revert to writing with your dominant hand. The temporal aspects of writing with your non-dominant hand and then reverting to the dominant hand represents change, while the pursuit of proficiency with the non-dominant hand represents transformation.

Why is that? Well, it's uncomfortable, or perhaps it does not look as great, or maybe it takes a lot longer to write using the non-dominant hand. However, with transformation, you have to continue using your non-dominant hand to write until you are eventually adept at using that hand. Now, you have a promising two sets of writing tools to use as opposed to remaining the same using your dominant hand. Transformation is not comfortable, but it is valuable.

For Christians, the Bible also illustrates the differences between change and transformation. It contrasts the law with the dispensation of grace. Under the law, individuals are required to perform yearly sacrifices and observe 613 commandments. Why yearly? Because changes did not stick. The yearly sacrifices only helped change the behavior, not the mindset. The dispensation of grace, however, prescribed a one-time sacrifice that drives transformation from the inside out. The law is focused on what you do, while grace is focused on who you are, what you think, and what you believe.

Earlier, we discussed that change is observing the past and the present, while transformation targets the future. Consider an iceberg. What is visible is the tip that is much smaller than the larger mass below. Correspondingly to the imagery, the work involved in the mindset and belief transformation is much more extensive than the change.

Domains of Knowledge

Recently, I was in a meeting with various leaders of an organization. As the CEO was directing the conversation, several individuals were jostling for attention and asking questions. Many remained silent and chose to observe instead. If I were the CEO, I would be also interested in those not participating, as this may indicate there is valuable knowledge that is not being communicated.

Let's look at the four domains of knowledge: the known knowns, the known unknowns, the unknown knowns, and lastly, the unknown unknowns.

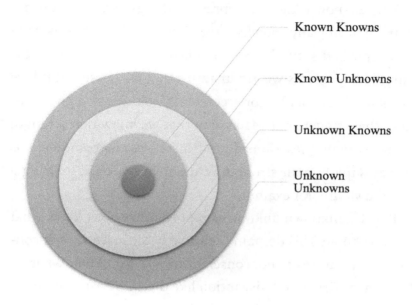

Image 1: Knowledge Domains

Let's analyze these domains to further elaborate on the change versus transformation subject. Debuting first is the known knowns, which constitutes the knowledge that you are aware of, that you know. This can easily be described as the basic knowledge of yourself, like your name, your date of birth, the number of children you have, etc.

The next domain is the known unknowns. What do you know that you don't know? For instance, if you're like me, you know that you do not know how to fly an aircraft or build a TV from scratch. Many of us are also very aware that we do not possess the knowledge to build our own homes. Do you notice that in the figure above, the known unknowns domain is bigger than the known knowns? You know less than you don't know.

The unknown knowns represent things that you are not aware of having any knowledge of. This knowledge may be buried deeply and securely in your subconscious. This can be exemplified as talents we are unaware that we possess until we are allowed to articulate or accidentally go through a pivot moment that triggers our realization that we know that strength or those capabilities. Consider the instances where individuals display superhuman strength in moments of crisis—lifting a car off a victim, for example.

Finally, unknown unknowns represent we don't know what we don't know. This domain is elusive because we are not conscious of what we are not conscious of. We don't know what we don't know. Crisis and disruption like the COVID-19 pandemic position us to leverage all four domains.

So, in theory and practice, we know less than we don't know. There is a greater amount of knowledge that we do not possess than what we do possess. This illustration is one that learning leaders recognize. They have ascertained that knowledge is provisional; knowledge is valid until there is new knowledge, which happens as we move through the four domains.

These domains further highlight the difference between change and transformation. When you are pursuing a change management endeavor, you are operating in what you know. From the project example given earlier, we know that the software is outdated; it is no longer effective or efficient.

As a result, we will obtain new software that we are aware of that is better. Change operates in the known knowns domain. Transformation, through progressive elaboration, instantiates all four domains: the collaborative, innovative, creative, and inclusive aspects of transformation tap into a greater source of knowledge.

When an apple changes from green to red, we say the apple is ripe; however, it is the transformation occurring on the inside of the apple that makes it ripe, not the change from green to red. To summarize, change is not transformation. The differences are illustrated in the table below:

 Change	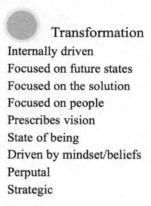 Transformation
Externally driven	Internally driven
Focused on current/past states	Focused on future states
Focused on the problem	Focused on the solution
Focused on progress	Focused on people
Subscribed to vision	Prescribes vision
State of doing	State of being
Driven by actions	Driven by mindset/beliefs
Binary	Perputal
Tactical	Strategic

Image 2: Change vs. Transformation

Reflective Discourse

1. What is your method for examining whether your leadership has transformed versus simply changed?
2. How do you gain the necessary insights to create an environment that is transformation ready?
3. What infrastructure do you have in place to maintain your company's transformation?

CHAPTER 2

Transformational Leadership History

*Transformation is not a "one and done" practice;
it is a continuous evolution to better future states.*

Let's take a look at how leadership has transformed over the years. The first theory we will investigate is the Great Man Theory. Introduced by Thomas Carlyle in 1888, it emerged as the standard for capable leadership. Carlyle purported that leaders, because of innate abilities, were great men. These innate abilities, seen in mostly white males, oversimplified the theory and resulted in two issues; one: once it was determined that you possessed abilities that no one else had, you were automatically a leader.

The second concern is the name indicated that only a man could be a leader. Wealth and money are a patina that some individuals use to present themselves as above the law and escape punishments. This skewed perception of the wealthy can also lead to a belief that the rich are automatically smarter than the average person. Critics of this model advanced alternate theories to support efficacious leaders who were nurtured versus possessing natural abilities as advocated by Carlyle.

The flawed Great Man Theory gave way to the Trait Theory (Allport 1937). The Trait Theory in part supported the Great Man Theory and its endorsement of natural-born leaders; however, Allport claimed that leaders are not necessarily born that way. Instead, Allport stated that individuals should be analyzed and tested for the presence of leadership traits.

Nature versus nurture was disputed. Critics of Carlyle's Great Man Theory gave credence to the concept that leaders who were nurtured could prove just as effective as those possessing the natural abilities advocated by Carlyle. The Trait Theory and previous Great Man Theory focused on the abilities of the leaders, which led to the Behavioral Theory. Leadership theorists acknowledged the need to study not only the traits of leaders but their behaviors and impact.

Behavioral theory, as advocated by B. F. Skinner (1945), showed that interactions with the environment influenced behavior. The more inclusive Behavioral Theory allowed more individuals the option and opportunity to learn the skills necessary to become leaders. The behavior and impact of leaders were in question and resulted in Skinner's advocacy that behavior was learned and not inherited. This, as a result, paved the way for learning leadership.

Do you notice a progression here? We are moving through the domains of knowledge (known knowns, known unknowns, unknown knowns, and unknown unknowns). Transformation is not a "one and done" practice; it is a continuous evolution to better future states. The more we learn about leadership, the greater the need is to transform to be more effective. New knowledge has given way to the provisional knowledge that shaped the previous theories.

Skinner showed that interactions with the environment influenced behavior. For instance, if you are in a society where only tall people could become a president or a leader, does that mean you would not be able to be a leader because of your height? Well, that is, in fact, the reasoning behind Skinner's Leadership Theory; an intentional versus inherited approach to leadership was launched.

Enter the Contingency Theory. Fred Fielder, in 1967, posited that when leaders can match their specific personalities and skills to an environment, they will be the most effective. How many times have you heard (or expressed) dissatisfaction when a job or position? At first glance, you may think, Bad employee; however, according to the Contingency Theory, the solution is to match employees with positions that best allow them to effectively use their skills.

The preceding theories have focused on the leader's abilities and behavior. What about followers? James MacGregor Burns, in 1978, introduced Transformational Leadership. The theory further described an intentional relationship between the leaders and followers. Another key difference from previous theories is the inclusion of both positive and negative leadership behavior.

Burns expressed that the leader's character and qualities drive their behavior. This theory supports a fusion of values between the leader and the follower. Burns also makes the distinction between participatory and democratic leadership (ATL) versus being a dictator or a ruler (PTL). While ATLs are idealized, PTLs are idolized. ATLs' leadership can be described as value-based; PTLs, on the other hand, are more emotion-based.

Reflective Discourse

1. How do the social constructs of your generation influence how you lead?
2. In what ways do you create your own unique leadership identity instead of emulating past leaders?
3. How do you measure the usefulness of past leadership traits and those traits that no longer fit with the current times?

CHAPTER 3

Transformational Leadership Model

Leaders are not perfect.

It is imperative to first acknowledge that leaders are not perfect. Continuous improvement is the runway for transformation.

There are four types of Transformational leaders: *Authentic Transformational, Pseudo-Transformational, Transactional,* and *Laissez-Faire.* The Authentic Transformational leader (ATL) is selfless, organizationally focused, and exhibits ethically and morally based behaviors. Is this where you see yourself?

Another type is the Transactional Leader (TL). This leader operates on a contingency model based on rewards and punishments or rewards and withholding of rewards. This type of leadership is often very militaristic, sales-driven, and incentive-driven.

The Laissez-Faire Leader (LFL) personifies the term and is hands-off. They exercise little to no leadership. This type of leadership can be used for high-performing teams or individuals, as they need less governance. Given the needed tools and resources, leaders can trust them to execute the work without supervision.

Finally, the Pseudo-Transformational Leader (PTL) is primarily driven by self-interest. This self-interest is typically induced by ego and fear. That fear is usually twofold: the leaders are fearful and/or drive and instill fear in their followers.

So far, we have reviewed the four types of Transformational leaders. Have you been tracking your leadership style in the model? Have you also identified where other leaders are represented? Let's now discuss the pros and cons of Transformational Leadership behavior:

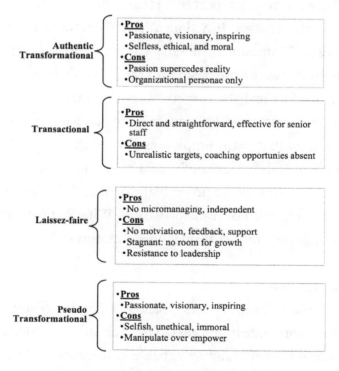

Image 3: Pros and Cons of Transformational Leadership Behavior

Authentic Transformational

ATLs are passionate visionaries with an impressive ability to inspire and communicate. However, the cons are that there needs to be a balance between passion and reality. Passion is great for selling a vision; however, high emotions replicated by followers may have less than desirable effects. Another con of ATL is that their organizational personae is not relatable and may be off-putting to followers seeking a personal connection.

Transactional

Positive aspects of Transactional Leadership include the straightforward performance-based approach to engagement. There is a binary aspect that focuses on contingencies or incentivized activities. If X then Y, sell X amount of product, then receive Y amount of bonus. The straightforwardness of this method leaves little room for gray areas. One con is the attainment of unrealistic targets. Another is that some individuals are not motivated by monetary or material incentives. Studies show that many employees place feeling valued as ranking high on satisfaction. An issue with monetary incentives is that it demonstrates the proverbial carrot and the horse; change is occurring but not transformation. What happens to the individual when money is no longer a motivator?

Laissez-Faire

Laissez-Faire leaders practice a hands-off approach with their employees/followers. The lack of micromanagement is desirable, especially by capable employees. It is the optimal model for high-performing teams and individuals. This model is used in corporate entrepreneurship. Independence, creative freedom, and self-management are exercised, as employees are given the needed tools and resources to perform well. The cons of this model are that since it relies heavily on self-motivation, those who are not self-motivated may fall behind. These employees, as well as new hires, need feedback and direction. Another con is that you can get stagnant, and there's no real room for growth. As a Subject Matter Expert (SME), you are the go-to person and are not considered for promotion or other development opportunities. Finally, employees under Laissez-Faire Leadership may resist hands-on leadership.

Pseudo-Transformational

Are you thinking that there are no pros to Pseudo-Transformational Leadership? There certainly are! PTLs initially display the same behavior as ATLs in motivation, inspiration, and charisma, and they are influential. They certainly know how to talk the talk (not walk the talk). They bring directness and straightforwardness to a vision. Once this leader has secured the trust of their followers, there is a dependency where followers buy into that leader's vision and forego any vetting of information communicated. The leader can now rationalize negative actions, such as saying that the decision is only for the short-term or that the good of the overall population depends on the few sacrifices made now, etc. Before followers realize the seriousness of the issues, they are no longer able to make decisions for themselves. PTLs are often surrounded by "yes people." It cannot be stated enough that both ATL and PTL behavior may look similar at the onset; however, there is a moment when the PTL makes the left turn into behavior with harmful consequences to followers. More to follow on the similarities between ATLs and PTLs.

Transformational Leadership Survey

We asked leaders to perform a 360-degree evaluation of their behavior, including performing a self-assessment. Participants represented the following industries: *medical, energy healthcare, marketing, education, law enforcement, telecommunications, retail, aircraft services, school districts, hospitality, security, social services, media, IT, beauty care, utilities, financials, construction, real estate, government, legal, automotive, entertainment, and religion.* Here are the aggregated responses:

ATLS

Fifty-two percent reported that their stakeholders (followers, peers, customers, subordinates) would describe their behavior as Authentic Transformational.

Fifty-three percent described their own behavior as Authentic Transformational.

Forty-three percent reported that their leader would describe them as being Authentic Transformational.

Fifty-seven percent reported that they would describe their leader's behavior as Authentic Transformational.

Transactional

Nineteen percent reported that their stakeholders (followers, peers, customers, subordinates) would describe their behavior as Transactional.

Fourteen percent described their own behavior as Transactional.

Twenty-one percent reported that their leader would describe them as being Transactional.

Zero percent reported that they would describe their leader's behavior as Transactional.

Laissez-Faire

Six percent reported that their stakeholders (followers, peers, customers, subordinates) would describe their behavior as Laissez-Faire.

Two percent described their own behavior as Laissez-Faire.

Seven percent reported that their leader would describe them as being Laissez-Faire.

Zero percent reported that they would describe their leader's behavior as Laissez-Faire.

Pseudo-Transformational

Two percent reported that their stakeholders (followers, peers, customers, subordinates) would describe their behavior as Pseudo-Transformational.

One percent described their own behavior as Pseudo-Transformational.

Six percent reported that their leader would describe them as being Pseudo-Transformational.

Zero percent reported that they would describe their leader's behavior as Pseudo-Transformational.

So, in a nutshell: Most leaders were aligned with how their stakeholders viewed them as being ATLs; however, there was a noticeable gap between how they described their leader's behavior and how their leaders described them. There may be a communications and proximity issue here. Another note is that 6 percent described their leaders as PTLs; however, their self-description of their own behavior and their stakeholders' description of their behavior was less than 6 percent. Although this percentage is low, it is important to identify factors to curtail PTL behavior sooner than later. Remember that PTL behavior initially resembles ATL behavior; however, left unchecked, it can incrementally become full-blown.

Since transformation occurs over time, it will be interesting to see what further reporting reveals. Mindfulness of behavior, which is what this type of survey triggers, is sometimes a contributor to the desired behavior. Again, pervasive behavior is what needs to be considered.

Image 4: Transformational Leadership Survey

If you would like to participate in this survey, please go to DrPatriciaAnderson.com.

Reflective Discourse

1. Do you believe that leaders' behaviors are above the scrutiny that is given to followers'/employees' behaviors?
2. How do you decide which leadership style to adopt from the Transformational Leadership Model?
3. How do you use the model to transform yourself along with your organization?

CHAPTER 4

Authentic Transformational versus Pseudo-Transformational Leadership

PTL is a zero-sum game.
Decommission PTL and normalize ATL.

An effective leader is someone who influences positive and sustaining behavior in others. ATLs inspire and motivate others to execute the vision. Another aspect of ATL is the ability to function as a role model to future leaders. This type of leader possesses high emotional intelligence or a high Emotional Quotient (EQ) and is an innovative and creative disruptor who solicits the same from their followers, stakeholders, etc.

There are two schools of thought about the relationship between Authentic Transformational Leadership and Pseudo-Transformational Leadership. One theory is that PTL is the direct opposite of ATL. The other portrays both ATL and PTL as occupying the same Möbius strip-like continuum. The movement through this space is influenced by organizational factors such as change.

Based on this premise, leaders can move through the four types of Transformational Leadership (Authentic, Transactional, Laissez-Faire, and Pseudo) as they face crises and disruptions. The uncertainty and fear inherent in chaotic circumstances are triggers. For example, a leader's behavior may be Transactional or even Pseudo-Transformational as they prioritize self-interest and self-preservation during those times.

Julian Barling, in 1985, characterized Transformational leaders as expressing four key behaviors: *idealized influence, inspirational motivation, individualized consideration,* and *intellectual stimulation*. Leaders need to lean into these behaviors, especially during disruption and crisis. Adapting and transforming are key for long-term viability.

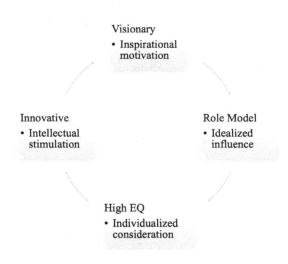

Image 5: Authentic Transformational Leadership Behavior

Inspirational motivation is the leader's ability to communicate a clear vision to their followers. These visionaries are so compelling they motivate followers to achieve mutually beneficial goals.

Idealized influence is the demonstration of behavior that aligns with the organization's values and goals. This transformational driver enhances team members' trust in—and respect for—the leader, motivating them to assimilate with and readily emulate the leader's practices.

Intellectual stimulation is the ability of the leader to engage stakeholders in problem-solving, critical thinking, risk-taking, idea generation, and facing challenges. Failing forward fast is also ascribed.

Finally, *individualized consideration* is the leader's ability to emotionally connect with stakeholders to understand them to better serve them. These leaders are emotionally proficient (high EQ) in their own emotions as well. Coaching and mentoring are important aspects of individualized consideration, as they aid in solidifying the leader-follower relationship.

So what do you think? Idealized influence, inspirational motivation, intellectual stimulation, and individualized consideration sound like great behaviors to emulate...right?

Let's revisit idealized influence and inspirational motivation. Both behaviors are positive; however, if there is an imbalance between the four behaviors, Authentic Transformational Leadership (ATL) can devolve to Pseudo-Transformational Leadership (PTL). Pseudo-Transformational Leadership, also known as Pure Charismatic Leadership, exemplifies leaders who may initially portray Authentic Transformational Leadership behavior but begin to engage in self-serving activities. These leaders utilize their position of power to exploit their followers.

High inspirational motivation usually equates to high emotionalism. Coupled with high idealized influence (idolizing the leader), followers driven by emotions and not vetting out what the leader is saying can find themselves on a destructive path.

ATL and PTL Behavior

Here is a comparison of ATL and PTL behavior. Take note of the commonalities.

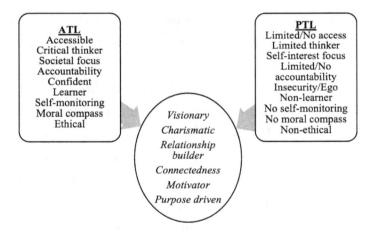

Image 6: ATL versus PTL Behavior

Why did I study and perform research in Transformational Leadership, specifically Pseudo-Transformational Leadership? I wanted to understand and identify triggers that lead to PTL behavior. No one looks at a child with the thought that they could easily become the next "charismatic villain." Yet, some individuals do become Pseudo-Transformational leaders. As a result, I was interested in examining and identifying the gateway to that behavior.

ATLs and PTLs share idealized influence and inspirational motivation, and their foundational behavior may appear the same at the onset. The key is to examine if the transformational end is positive and altruistic or negative and self-serving. Understanding the tipping point in these behaviors will provide better clarity on how to maintain balance.

So ATLs and PTLs are not necessarily opposites; rather, they may occupy a continuum. Bernard Bass, in 2014, observed that it is possible to move from ATL to PTL, as mentioned above. Bass also examined the results of the leadership versus the consequences. We have all witnessed, for example, leaders who doubled the bottom line or ROI. Great on paper, but what are the consequences, and by what means? Are the internal customers (employees) happy? Were any rules or regulations broken? As you can see, a holistic view of leadership is necessary to deem it as truly Authentic Transformational.

Another observation is what happened during the COVID-19 and related crises in 2020. Many leaders pivoted to a seemingly Authentic Transformational Leadership stance; however, as the crises were in the rearview (or not highlighted by the media), they regressed to less Authentic Transformational Leadership behavior. This leads me to make the distinction between intentions and behavior. Behavior sometimes masks intentions and subsequently is one of the differentiators of change and transformation.

Authentic Transformational Behavior

One of the key differences between ATLs and PTLs is the degree to which they institute accountability. ATLs establish and uphold visible and real-time accountability infrastructures and guardrails that support openness and self-reflection. Allowing others to hold you accountable is practiced by leaders who possess authentic confidence. This accountability to the people they work with and serve is a vital difference between ATLs and PTLs.

ATLs walk a line where they cannot exert too much idealized influence or inspirational motivation. Both trigger high emotionalism, and skewed emotions may escalate to undesirable outcomes. Heightened idealized influence and inspirational motivation are present in two spaces: politics and religion. Leaders in these spaces can exert influence on a significant number of people. Consequently, a leader must strive to maintain a balance between idealized influence and inspirational motivation.

The German word *weltanschauung*, pronounced (velt, än, ShouəNG), depicts your worldview, perception, or philosophy on life, including views on marriage, politics, leadership, etc. This worldview exists in everyone and similarly can affect leaders unconsciously by guiding or limiting their actions. This is a problem that ATL fixes by engaging in self-reflective and accountability exercises.

Are you an ATL? See if you resonate (consistently) with these descriptors: energizer, passionate, transparent, accessible, accountable, approachable, clear communicator, positive motivator, critical thinker, genuine, ethical, and moral.

Each of us has aspects of ourselves that are less than perfect. I encourage you to consider three or more of these aspects of ATL to work on consistently. The Japanese term Kaizen specifies continuous improvement because, in transformation, we move toward better future states, ever-evolving but not perfect. However, we cannot use not being perfect as a crutch. Evolving and transforming are what an ATL pursues; otherwise, there is complacency that may trigger PTL behavior.

ATLs are driven to do good for society. They are confident learners who exercise self-monitoring and self-reflection. They align themselves with a moral compass that supports their actions and behavior.

SWOTT

Strengths, Weaknesses, Opportunities, Threats, Trends (SWOTT) is an objective tool used by organizations to analyze products and services or a strategic proposition. Leaders SWOTT themselves by looking objectively at four aspects of their makeup. Strengths and weaknesses are internal and constitute what you bring to the table and what you lack. Remember the knowledge domains? Strengths are known knowns; weaknesses are known unknowns; both are within your control.

Image 7: SWOTT (Strengthes, Weaknesses, Opportunities, Threats, Trends)

Opportunities and threats are external and require you to look beyond your capabilities; they represent unknown knowns and unknown unknowns, respectively. Partnership, collaboration, and learning move a leader through the unknown domains.

Understanding where you are most competent impels an awareness of your leadership practices. Here is where an anonymous survey comes into play. After or while you're SWOTTing yourself, ask other leaders as well as your reports to SWOTT you. Identify and leverage your competencies and identify partnerships, alliances, and other individuals to help you transform your weaknesses into opportunities and strengths. Your diverse organization encompasses a brain trust of experiences and knowledge that provides opportunities to expand capabilities.

Risks are often associated with negativity; however, risks are uncertain future events (positive or negative). An opportunity, therefore, represents a positive risk. Threats are also risks and reside in the domain of the unknown unknowns. Threats at times may encompass events that you may or may not have control over. For instance, many of us have been dramatically affected by the global epidemic (COVID-19). The pandemic was a headwind that disrupted everything about how business was conducted. It made good on that threat and changed (or transformed) how we do business.

External threats may include legal or regulatory standards, protocols, global issues, economic issues, technological advances, and innovations that control what you may promote, produce, or sell. Threats are unknown unknowns. They present opportunities to partner and create alliances. Within the external alliances, there may rise instances in which you must be compliant. This is especially the case when faced with regulatory and legalities. Your competition also poses a threat.

There is always the possibility that a crisis will disrupt your business or organization. However, SWOTTing is not a fast or one-time exercise; it must be performed periodically, especially when there is disruption. It is up to you to put your organization in a position to mitigate negative threats. ATL is the way to accomplish this.

The future also represents the unknown unknowns and sometimes holds uncertainty (risk); it is impossible to have foresight into all its possibilities. How do you prepare for that? Authentic Transformational leaders, through the transformative process, are progressively and adaptively moving toward future better states. In the same fashion, they practice collaboration and intellectual stimulation with their followers and employees to move through the crisis.

SWOTTing helps to highlight competencies and opportunities for improvements. It provides a roadmap to navigate into the knowledge domains. They represent learning opportunities that position leaders to win. Crises present opportunities to revisit the SWOTT. Over time, you should witness weaknesses transforming into opportunities and strengths and threats to opportunities. This is where the final T (Trends) in SWOTT comes into play; you should notice how you are trending—are there fewer weaknesses and more strengths? Are threats migrating to opportunities? Let's take a look at another tool that will ensure that your accountability infrastructure is rock solid.

ATL Accountability Infrastructure

Creeds are the principles and beliefs that guide our actions. They constitute our *weltanschauung*. Creeds allow you to identify and question your views in life. They prescribe your behavior. How do you behave professionally and personally? Do you live and let live? What is your outlook on society? How do you teach?

In the seamless embodiment of the Möbius strip existence, what we let in and out can help form or deform our lives and our interactions with our world. At the core of who we all are personally, philosophically, sociologically, professionally, and pedagogically is a human craving connections bigger than what we believe, stand for, or desire.

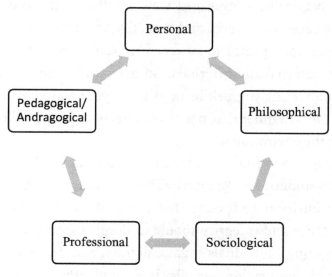

Image 8: Leadership Creeds

We long to create safe places that breed and transcend trust, yielding a collective societal payoff that is concertedly greater than the sum of the parts. In the absence of hard and fast rules that can be applied to any threshold of moral decision-making, the responsibility is shouldered by the hidden or spiritual side of the person, which houses thoughts, feelings, will, intents, and choices.

An aspect of your leadership foundation should include these five creeds: personal, philosophical, sociological, professional, and pedagogical. I call them the 4PS. Your personal creed should include self-reflective discourses. Your philosophical creed should be inclusive of others' viewpoints yet exclusive of unraveling your own without substantiated merit. Since knowledge is provisional, ask yourself and others, "What else has to be true to support my viewpoint?"

Sociologically, a leveraged view of all humans and interactions based on respect and empathy are critical for leaders to adopt. Your professional creed impacts three stakeholder groups: internal and external customers and society. It stipulates conducting yourself responsibly in your actions or lack of actions in a manner that positively affects society, public safety, and the environment.

Being true to your word entails doing what you have promised to undertake. Respect, fairness, and honesty should govern business endeavors that you undertake. Professional competence and integrity should undergird your behavior, as is respecting individuals' rights, dignity, and diversity. Leaders are always teaching, explicitly or implicitly. You are being watched, listened to, and emulated with each interaction you have. Other leaders are also learning from you.

Leaders should embrace the responsibility of providing both meaning and direction to their internal and external stakeholders. Here are my declarations of these five creeds:

1. *Personal*—I believe that I am a self-reflecting being who is wholly capable of making rational choices that drive my existence.
2. *Philosophical*—I believe that my philosophy is grounded in my spiritual faith.
3. *Sociological*—I believe in a sociologically leveraged group of humans regardless of race, gender, economic, religious, or cultural qualifiers.

4. *Professional*—I believe that pursuing a profession is honorable and that customers, employees, and society are the three pillars that strengthen its existence.
5. *Pedagogical/Andragogical*—I believe that teaching is a calling that carries with it divine stipulations to advance knowledge.

Effective internal controls are then the next layer of your foundation. An accountability infrastructure represents individuals who you respect and who value authenticity. Next is a 360-degree evaluation that creates a balanced scorecard where the leaders and followers evaluate each other.

Image 9: Internal Controls

The 360-degree evaluation is a task that will further establish your confidence as a leader. The personal vision is the final aspect of the internal controls. It differentiates between who you are as a leader versus who you are as a person. There is an established corporate vision to support the organization. How does your personal vision support the corporate vision? Ask your internal stakeholders to do the same.

Pseudo-Transformational Behavior

Creeds and internal controls act as transformational guardrails that guide your actions as you advance to increasingly better future states. Your leadership DNA is found in both. The accountability infrastructure is a key differentiator between an ATL and a PTL.

You may be thinking, *I will just do the opposite of a PTL to become an ATL*. Recall that both Authentic Transformational and Pseudo-Transformational Leadership may occupy the same continuum and are not necessarily opposites of each other. Recall also that both ATL and PTL may present the same, initially, in both inspirational motivation and idealized influence. What causes ATL devolvement to PTL behavior? I asked the same question prior to my research.

Pseudo-Transformational leaders usually have limited or no accountability infrastructure. This lack of accountability predicates behavior based on self-interest and furthering one's own agenda as opposed to promoting societal good. PTLs avoid accountability usually due to a lack of confidence. When confronted to take accountability for their actions, PTLs resort to gaslighting and redirecting attention from themselves to others.

PTLs use fear to keep others from questioning their behavior. Ego and fear work in tandem to decrease self-awareness/self-assessment and to create a barrier between a leader and their stakeholders. PTLs are usually fearful because their character has not caught up to their title. PTLs usually thrive in command-and-control organizational structures. There are varying levels of gatekeepers who, in many cases, are interested in their own agenda. They are also eyeing the position of the head PTL.

These gatekeepers are often communication blockers and may reconstruct unflattering feedback to a style that the leader will approve of. This further highlights another key difference between ATLs and PTLs. Unlike ATLs, there is a high degree of competitiveness over collaborative behaviors. On the same note, PTLs are often more manipulative than empowering to their followers. Recall that high levels of idealized influence in followers lead to information from the leader not being vetted.

We asked leaders how supportive or competitive they were with other leaders. Most did not compete (54 percent), 23 percent said it depended on the industry, and 23 percent thought that competition yielded more results.

PTL behavior can also be described as the dark triad of personality traits, which are categorized as Machiavellianism, narcissism, and psychopathy. Machiavellianism applies to individuals who focus on their interests and use manipulation to satisfy them. Similarly, narcissism is characterized by ego and a heightened self-image. Psychopathy is a personality disorder exemplified by egotistical traits. This is also where emotional intelligence comes into play. A high EQ illustrates a leader's proficiency in understanding his or her own emotions and those with whom they engage. The leader uses this understanding to cultivate effective interpersonal relationships.

We asked leaders about upholding behavioral standards for themselves and their internal and external stakeholders. The majority of leaders (87 percent) responded that their behavioral standards should be higher, 9 percent said it should be the same, and 4 percent said that it depended on the situation. Keep in mind that PTLs are also practiced in the Hawthorne effect, where an individual modifies their behavior due to their knowledge that they are being observed. You should now be versed in identifying PTL behavior in both yourself and other leaders. As we have witnessed the rise and fall of leadership, it is clear that stakeholders require transparency and not perfection. Transparency provides a balanced view of weaknesses and can even be regarded as a strength, which in turn creates a bond of trust. PTL is a zero-sum game. Decommission PTL and normalize ATL.

Reflective Discourse

1. Do you subscribe to PTL being the opposite of ATL or that they both exist on a Möbius strip?
2. How do you convert your weaknesses to strengths or opportunities?
3. What accountability infrastructure do you have in place to ensure your ATL status?

CHAPTER 5

Transformational Leaders: Past, Present, Future

Do not conform to this world but be transformed by the renewing of your mind!

As we commence this section, I want to remind you of the transformational mandate: *Do not conform to this world but be transformed by the renewing of your mind!* This also relates to my earlier statement that your mind has to arrive first. Transformation is not a simple mental assent; it is a full embodiment and personification of the metamorphic process. As displayed by the imagery of the butterfly, it evolves from a caterpillar into future states. In the same fashion, you transform from the good to the acceptable and eventually to the perfect.

This reiterates that there is a progression to different stages. Transformation is not binary like change; with transformation, you must instead incrementally progress to future states. Subsequently, it is noted that superior organizational success is boosted by the leader's transformational behavior. This will, in turn, drive employee and follower behavior, motivation, creativity, performance, and productivity. Bear in mind that leaders are not perfect and shift your mind from believing or expecting them to be. However, you can expect a continuous improvement to better and better future states.

To further elaborate on the impact of transformation, let's review some of the key differences, as it relates to change. As stated before, change is focused on the problem, while transformation is focused on the solution. Change is focused on the process, and transformation is focused on people. Changes subscribe to vision; in contrast, vision is prescribed by transformation. This difference highlights the understanding that with transformation, there's no path backward. Another difference is that change is the state of doing while transformation is the state of being. Change is driven by action, and transformation is driven by mindset. Again, your mind has to arrive first. While change is binary, transformation is perpetual. Change is tactical, and transformation is strategic.

Additionally, recall that the transformational theory was the first leadership theory that considered the followers. Previous theories were focused on leaders only and whether they were born that way, were nurtured, or were in the right environment to be effective. The transformational theory was furthered to focus on the followers' needs. This prescribes an intentional relationship between the leader and the follower.

There are four types of Transformational Leadership, some more positive than others. It is ideal to subscribe to Authentic Transformational Leadership (ATL), which models selflessness, is organizationally focused, and is ethically and morally driven. ATLs are positive role models. Consideration is given to the followers/stakeholders as a result of these leaders possessing high EQ and having a connection with employees/followers. The high EQ also means that the leaders are aware of their own emotions and how best to manage them successfully.

In the previous chapter, we discovered the pros and cons of each of the four leadership types. An Authentic Transformational leader can devolve into a Pseudo-Transformational leader during crisis and disruption. Although a PTL can evolve into an ATL, the probability of that is low; the devolvement of an ATL to a PTL is much higher.

There have been countless leaders both from the past and present whose behavior is reflective of the four types of Transformational Leadership. To begin with, some of the more famous PTLs are Adolph Hitler, Jim Jones, and David Koresh. These leaders were more interested in being idolized than idealized.

After gaining the trust of their followers, they used fear to keep them under control. The idolization of these leaders precludes critical thinking and vetting of information from them. Adolph Hitler did not begin his tenure as a PTL; instead, he started talking the talk of an ATL. He galvanized followers by expressing the desire to make the country more economically independent and did not express his ultimate desire. He ultimately used his influence and charisma for ill-fated outcomes, similar to followers of Jim Jones and David Koresh.

If idealized influence and inspirational motivation are too high, there is an imbalance, as exemplified in the cases of Jim

Jones and David Koresh and their unfortunate followers. ATLs such as Doctor Martin Luther King (we conducted a survey where 100 percent of people deemed him an ATL), Mahatma Gandhi, and Mother Teresa represent leaders who inspire versus manipulate. An example of a PTL evolving to an ATL is King Nebuchadnezzar. In contrast to Hitler's devolvement, King Nebuchadnezzar experienced an irrevocable transformation. It is important to note that he had several false starts (change); however, they were based on actions solely and not on a shift in his mindset or belief system.

ATLs are self-reflective, possess high EQ, understand the knowledge domains, and institute safeguards and accountability to assist them in transforming, not simply changing; they are needed now more than ever.

Reflective Discourse

1. Considering leadership catastrophes of the past, how have they influenced you in not repeating those mistakes?
2. Which leader from the past do you emulate most?
3. Which current leader do you emulate most?

CHAPTER 6

Transformational Leadership During Crisis and Disruption

Disruption and crisis are the luminol that exposes fault lines in both leadership and business operations.

Many leaders will remember Q1 of 2020 for different reasons. ATLs were made for this time of uncertainty. The four domains that characterize their behavior were evidenced in their inspirational motivation (being a steadying force that helped to diminish fear and ambiguity), idealized influence (serving as role models to other leaders), individualized consideration (ensuring that clients, employees, and partners felt cared for), and intellectual stimulation (pivoting to alternate means of achieving strategic goals that engaged internal and external stakeholders).

In 2020, the exciting prospect of a new year quickly yielded into an ominous reality. A global pandemic preceded social and political unrest. Disruption and crisis are headwinds that require a shift to navigate successfully. What type of strategies can leaders enact when faced with multiple crises? The most effective approach is to engage transformational tailwinds to counteract the headwinds. They are the driving force that propels you from crisis mode to stability.

Transformational tailwinds comprise strategies and infrastructures to defend against disruption and crisis. This, in turn, will result in the least amount of fallout to internal and external stakeholders. There are three key roles that organizations should put in place that will assist in navigating crisis and disruption: the Transformational Strategist, the Corporate Advisor, and a Transformation Management Office (TMO). The latter provides governance over transformational activities. Having these tools in place allows organizations to be proactive instead of reactive during crises and disruption.

These strategies and roles foster intentional thinking, active listening, and contextually evaluating and bridging mindsets. As a leader, active listening is vital: Listen to not only your leadership team but also to your internal customers, who are chock full of ideas. Listen to your leadership team; however, in certain cases, your team may be too closely aligned to your way of thinking, which leaves other types of inputs unexplored. Remember, you know less than you don't know.

Soliciting and implementing employees' input represents skin in the game for them. Their collaboration is necessary to navigate through a crisis. More on this in the section on Organizational Change Management. These employees can provide you with the innovative insight to spearhead new strategies. Active listening and the ability to bridge mindsets will guarantee that growth and true transformation are taking place within the organization. We will explore this further in the Diversity, Inclusion, Equity, and Accessibility section.

The Transformational Strategist, the Corporate Advisor, and a TMO, offer a prescriptive approach to support agile transformation, executive strategy, and organizational processes. During disruption and crisis, the organizational structure has to be agile enough to move quickly and not be hampered by bureaucracy, red tape, and arcane processes. Larger companies tend to be less agile than smaller companies, which can be flexible and act quickly.

Innovative leaders emerge during crisis and disruption. Why? It is human nature to revisit who we are at the core during these times and, to rediscover our hidden strengths and abilities, recall the unknown knowns. Organizations can stand up corporate entrepreneurship that enables these new leaders to pursue innovative practices. Provide them with the budget and resources to do so, which in turn will offer you the agility to pivot as necessary.

ATLs strategize by using forward-thinking, active listening, and intellectual stimulation, which helps to navigate disruption. Technology has taken a front row in our social infrastructure. Pivoting during the global epidemic meant that we all had to rely heavily on virtual communication and collaboration. New movies went straight to living room premieres, companies realized they did not have to rely on on-site visits to service clients, telecommunicating escalated, Brick And Mortar (BAM) schools and religious organizations pivoted to online, hybrid went fully virtual, and telehealth, in the early adopter stage, quickly matured. Virtual markets sprung up. Physical proximity issues decreased, and leaders wondered, *Why weren't we doing this all along?*

Expanded Product Life Cycle

If we rescope the Product Life Cycle/Diffusion of Innovation model to overlay it with the disruption and crisis life cycle, we can see where we need to practice ATL behavior and where we can introduce new products and services. Products move through a lifecycle that includes an introduction, growth, maturity, decline, and sometimes rebirth. The secondary market can be described as another opportunity for a product to move through the lifecycle again. Let's consider markets as countries. A product that is mature in one country may experience a rebirth in another country.

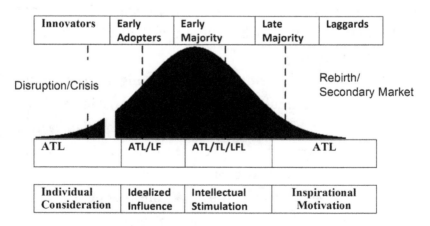

Image 10: Expanded DOI and PLC Model

We can also view crisis and disruption as having a life cycle similar to a product. While the COVID-19 pandemic appeared to be on the decline, we soon experienced multiple aggressive rebirths. The variants of the COVID-19 viruses can also be likened to product enhancements that can generate a secondary market or a rebirth in the current market. The Metaverse represents introduction/growth in a secondary market (the primary being gaming). The pandemic pivot to virtual communications revealed gaps in interaction, which will be filled by the Metaverse's integration of people and things. More on this in the "Metaverse-ity for Leaders" section of the "Leadership Playbook for the Future" chapter.

Crisis and disruption also give birth to new products and services. Many products such as face masks, sanitizers, and wipes quickly saturated the market in 2020. Virtual products and services were also on the upswing, as were products and services to office-fy homes. In contrast, many businesses were inoperable due to their inability to pivot. Restaurants, for example, that previously offered (or were able to pivot to) online ordering and delivery thrived. Those that did not were deficient in the transformational strategies mentioned previously.

The Diffusion of Innovation Theory model depicts innovation and how quickly it is adopted. In light of crisis and disruption, we can use the same concept to either answer the crisis or thrive despite the crisis. Leaders need to be early adopters of strategies to navigate disruption; otherwise, their organizations may not survive.

At the onset of disruption, ATLs should lean into individualized consideration. Go full ATL during this time. Recall how the health care providers were innovators during the crisis and how they exercised individualized consideration. Next, as you move through disruption, focus on idealized influence as stakeholders are looking to you for answers. As the crisis becomes more fully realized, a combination of ATL and LF is optimal. Laissez-Faire (LF) because you have employed intellectual stimulation that guides innovation, collaboration, and buy-in.

By using this comprehensive chart as a guide, you can quickly see how disruption, your products and services, and your leadership behavior coexist, and you can optimize a tenable approach. Disruptions thrust leaders and organizations into the unknowns (known unknowns, unknown knowns, and unknown unknowns). Further, they represent uncertain future events such as opportunities and threats. Transformation, as we previously analyzed, is about moving through the knowledge domains, beginning with the known knowns.

Transformational opportunities abound during disruption. It is vital during a crisis to be hyper-focused on your transformational goals. Leaders are the brand of the organization (inside or outside). Ask yourself, "What does my corporate brand underscore?" This is the time to revisit your creeds and accountability infrastructures. A revisit to your SWOTT is also warranted. Many organizations, in light of COVID-19, zoomed in on two areas: their internal and external customers. Crisis and disruptions present opportunities to relaunch a campaign to (re)educate and (re)assure stakeholders.

During crisis and disruption, leaders also examine their Present Mode of Operations (PMO) to assess its fit to withstand the interference. Examining the PMO usually leads to an improved Future Mode of Operations (FMO) model. The assessment of PMO/FMO usually requires a leader shift. This shift, as mentioned previously, entails moving through the Transformational Leadership continuum (Authentic Transformational, Transactional, Laissez-Faire) and exercising the four Is (inspirational motivation, idealized influence, individualized consideration, intellectual stimulation).

As leaders assess their PMO and desired FMO, they may discover that they need to flatten their organizational structure and remove vertical silos. Flattening the organizational structure has many benefits. Be diligent about flattening the organizational structure, as vertical silos may give place to horizontal silos cropping up. This is usually seen in functional areas, where individuals tend to hoard knowledge. Other types of silos include geographic, cultural, and proximity.

Organizational flattening shortens the decision-making cycle. During disruption and crisis, decision-making is compressed to be responsive. The compressed cycle yields leaner processes and increases knowledge sharing as the company moves through the knowledge domains.

Companies can also launch pre-implementation or pre-sales activities during a crisis. Explore vertical markets for gaps in your product and service offerings. During COVID-19, there was a massive wealth transfer that occurred, intellectual, social, physical, and mental. There was a global, concerted effort to unleash knowledge free of charge to everyone. Capitalizing on these assets put many individuals and organizations in a nonpareil position to move from crisis to flourish.

Here are some key focus areas that provide guideposts to steer leadership activities during crisis and disruption.

ATL Culture

The leadership model that has withstood the test of time is Authentic Transformational Leadership. These leaders are inspiring, motivating, influencing, possess high EQ, are risk-takers, innovative, and collaborative. These behavioral traits are disruption proof; no pivot is required.

Leaders need to manage perception via ethical, incremental, and transparent communications. When we think of incremental, our earlier symbol of the butterfly should come to mind. Transparency is paramount, especially during disruption or crisis.

Leadership styles need to be agile enough to adapt quickly to counteract disruptive forces. In 2020, the answer to social distancing was virtual proximity. Increasing the cadence of leadership communications in multiple formats is essential to connecting to and maintaining the well-being of employees, customers, and other stakeholders. Walking the talk necessitates looking beyond business as usual to a new and better normal that will incorporate dexterity in dealing with the looming state of unknown unknowns. Virtual proximity should include daily check-ins, knowledge sharing that reports on facts only, resource links, conducting surveys, and capturing lessons learned. Virtualize in-person activities, events, and processes—this is not a one-off event; consider virtualization for cultural adaptation.

Knowledge Is Provisional

ATLs know that knowledge is provisional on new knowledge, so transformation is perpetual. Unlike change, which constitutes binary states, transformation continually progresses to sustainable future states given new knowledge. ATLs leverage change as building blocks to bring their organization into incrementally better versions of operating. Forced transformation is the teacher of the leader; galvanizing stakeholders to adapt quickly is the measure of an ATL's abilities.

Threats Are Opportunities

By gauging how their organizations perform during the crisis, leaders can veer lessons learned to address future disruption of business processes; this includes virtualization of those processes. Leaders can conduct surveys as further touchpoints that take the temperatures of their stakeholders' mindsets. These surveys can be aggregated to identify data points that provide insights on effective and ineffective practices during this time. Working remotely provides benefits to both the organization and its stakeholders. Restrictions in travel present opportunities to learn new technology and tools; it also allows time for reflection on previously presented solutions and exploration of alternate solutions. Postponed business decisions such as scaling up or down can be revisited in greater detail.

Small Businesses

Small businesses that do not have the technological prowess or financial leverage of their larger counterparts can exploit free technological tools to communicate and collaborate during crises and disruptions. Technology has become that friend in need. This is the time to consider a niche market, provide other services, or partner with organizations in the horizontal and vertical markets of their product and/or service offerings. Take advantage of virtualized services that are on the upswing.

Mindfulness

Remember the elderly, homeless, the military, prisoners, and workers who are usually not fully represented in stakeholder analysis. Remember the small businesses that depend on the uninterrupted income for their sustainability; purchase gift cards or arrange for delivery. Finally, in times of crisis, capitalize on the united focus and use it to identify new business opportunities, career paths, personal goals, and self-reflective tasks. Dust off those dreams and plans. Crises bring out the philanthropic side of people…be sure that your giving of time and resources represents you accurately. Not an ATL? Now more than ever is the time to pursue Authentic Transformational Leadership. The world awaits.

Reflective Discourse

1. In what ways do you align your business strategies to benefit your internal customers?
2. During crisis and disruption, what role does Transactional Leadership play in right-sizing your organization?
3. Which aspect of the Expanded Product Life Cycle do you find most useful during crisis and disruption?

CHAPTER 7

Stakeholder Engagement

Leaders, read the room: show up as a human being.

First, The Great Resignation is real. So is the war for talent. Employees are no longer tolerant of the status quo, which is focused more on economic ROI instead of the mental and emotional ROI of internal customers. The forced self-focus of the COVID-19 era reoriented priorities for many of us; talent is seeking meaningful engagements in socially responsible organizations. What worked before that time now needs an upgrade or total cessation. Our humanity was put to the test, and we emerged being confident about how to hierarchize our well-being, including our mental and physical welfare.

According to Occam's razor, the simplest explanation is usually the best; at the core of disruption and working and employer/employee relationship is the human being. This approach was never so evident as in the COVID pandemic era when all of the complexities of living and business were reduced to a simple binary choice. Stay alive/healthy. Normalizing simplification is mentally healthy; it allows prioritization.

Studies show a positive correlation between human needs being met (Maslow's hierarchy of needs) and their level of engagement in the workplace. Lean into that model to guide your leadership practice. Leaders should put in place a systematic approach aimed at engaging, exploring, and maximizing potential in every type of employee.

An unhappy workforce includes employees who are not functioning at optimum mental health. They can pose risks to the operations of the organization that range from missed deadlines, absenteeism, accidents, decreased productivity, attrition, and even loss of lives. Some companies may not be as attractive to exceptional talent who place a high value on the organization's focus on their internal customers' well-being. Short-term and long-term ROI will decrease as the internal customers are not equipped to support the external customers.

Employers are being tasked with engaging the whole employee—mentally, physically, emotionally, financially, etc. Mental help support looks like an inclusive multi-dimensional culture that ranges from a diverse executive team to designing workspaces, allowing employees to work from home as needed, and supporting them financially in setting up the home office. Here are some guiding principles for leaders to adopt to improve their work culture:

1. Pivot from the "workplace" (location) mentality to the "workspace" (state of mind) model. When employees design their workspaces, they are more mentally satisfied and perform better.

2. Make work and working more meaningful: engage employees in ways that motivate and stretch them (hire up, reskill, upskill, stretch assignments, etc.).
3. Be prescriptive about employee health by investing in a robust Human Capital Management (HCM) system that provides engagement tools beyond recruitment and promotion activities.
4. Conduct frequent pulse checks of your employees' well-being, especially if life events affect them (personally, locally, nationally, globally, etc.). Provide Employee Assistance Programs (EAP) that value anonymity. Extend benefits to include family members.
5. Leaders and managers, beef up your EQ and polish up your bedside manner. Normalize "I'm not okay" to create safe spaces for employees to not just survive but to thrive!

The best-case scenario for engaging stakeholders is by adopting a hybrid of on-prem and remote work. Increasingly, employers are giving employees the flexibility to choose. In some cases, employers may require a minimum engagement on-prem since some collaboration is more effective in person. Some employees are choosing remote work only, so employers have to widen the talent net to explore the market for more diverse talent who come from the most unexpected places. If the employer requires on-prem employees, they may have to incentivize employees as health concerns and flexibility may be an issue.

The emphasis is on people vis-a-vis The Rise of the Human. People want more control over how they work, engage, and are treated. Societal norms must reflect the "workspace" mentality and support workers in many different spaces. Women are increasingly caring for aging parents and should be supported in those efforts. Men are being more vocal about their mental health challenges and should be championed and provided safe spaces to express themselves.

Further, open and honest (transparent) communications are required from leaders. The receiver of communications filters the message through their weltanschauung (worldview/perception), so the sender has to be sure that the message is not diminished or diluted. Remote communication is different from communicating in person, and there are virtual nuances to consider, including body language and choice of words.

As the talent landscape expands, there needs to be a corresponding exercise in culture mapping. In North America, for example, communicating unfavorable news to employees looks like a sandwich—the bad news in the middle and the outsides contain supportive communication to soften the blow. In other cultures, such as in Europe or Asia or the Middle East, communication is more direct and is bereft of any softening agents. North American leaders who communicate to these other cultures run the risk of the message being misinterpreted.

As previously mentioned, engagement at work is positively correlated to Maslow's hierarchy of needs. Physiological needs, safety needs, and belonging needs have taken precedence over the others. Individuals functioning at the higher level of the model (esteem and self-actualization) have found themselves plummeting to the lower levels, requiring the fulfillment of basic needs. Leaders in HR spaces are now required to provide psychological safety and security to their employees. Engaging your internal stakeholders on that level enables them to properly service your external customers.

The ATL's proficiency in all four transformational behaviors, especially individualized consideration, is paramount to stakeholder engagement. Leaders, read the room: show up as a human being. This is instrumental in communicating your dedication to stakeholder engagement. Self-actualization is the goal, as both leader and follower move through fulfilling basic needs that support their progression to increasingly better future states.

Reflective Discourse

1. Which of the 4Is (inspirational motivation, idealized influence, individualized consideration, intellectual stimulation) do you engage in most often with your internal stakeholders?
2. Which of the 4Is (inspirational motivation, idealized influence, individualized consideration, intellectual stimulation) do you engage in most often with your external stakeholders?
3. How has The Great Resignation impacted your leadership?

CHAPTER 8

Lead, Learn, Level Up!

Leverage knowledge, collaboration, accountability, and learning as powerful transformational tailwinds.

Reminder: "Do not conform to this world but be...transformed by the renewing of your mind." Renewing your mind involves movement through the stages of good, acceptable, and perfect, indicating a progression to better future states. In this chapter, we will elaborate on this progression and analyze knowledge, collaboration, accountability, and learning, as transformational tailwinds to move both the leaders and the organization forward.

Knowledge

How an organization leverages knowledge directly impacts the shared vision. The establishing factor for shared vision is trust, as it promotes ownership and underlies and supports effective knowledge creation, management, and transfer.

Knowledge Creation

A distinction should be made between knowledge and the person who creates it. Organizational knowledge is secerned from knowledge held by an individual and shapes organizational behavior. The distinction is made since the knowledge has to remain within the organization regardless of the presence or absence of the individual or individuals who created it. This objectivity is critical in a leadership position, as knowledge gained from leading has to be packaged objectively so that it benefits the organization as a whole and not just the leader.

In addition, let's uphold a paradigm shift that embraces knowledge as being both a core competence and a strategic pursuit. Knowledge philosophies entail a fusion of creating a culture and establishing methods to support the organization's stakeholders' pursuit and participation in that infrastructure. Executive intervention in tandem with human resource policies and practices is required for knowledge creation and organizational learning.

Knowledge acquisition is the primary focus of organizational knowledge; however, forgetting or unlearning knowledge occupies a sphere in the organization's ability to be competitive or to make allowance for new knowledge. Promoting purposeful forgetting is done by alerting the organization of the succeeding knowledge that will replace its predecessor, the reasons why adoption is positive, and how it will impact the individuals utilizing it.

My team and I instantiated knowledge forgetting with one of my former clients. At the time, we conducted knowledge transfer with their employees on different topics, including health and wellness, business, and technology. We also provided knowledge on personal development. The process of having employees access to the knowledge was tedious, involving coordination in several states and locations. We implemented a new electronic registration and delivery tool, replacing an older tool. The efficiency gains were at least 70 percent, as was the increase in accuracy. The older process was then intentionally forgotten in place of the newly acquired knowledge.

Knowledge Management

Knowledge management must be a strategy that the organization undertakes to fulfill its mission and goals. The human counterpart to knowledge can exhibit resistance in creating, collaborating, or sharing knowledge. They may also possess the inability to make explicit what is inherently tacit. Diverse types of communications warrant specific types of knowledge creation and sharing, so collaboration between humans as well as technology is indicated. Effective unlearning and relearning must occur.

Knowledge management processes involve coding, centralizing the collection of knowledge, structuring knowledge, and communicating that knowledge. Knowledge management and business strategies must be streamlined to add value to the organization. In the best-case scenario, the business strategy should drive the acquisition and management of knowledge. Strategy-driven knowledge management will help to eliminate the disconnect between knowledge and application and avoid a "one size fits all" knowledge management effort. Even in a single organization, varying cultures dictate how knowledge is utilized; a programmer's knowledge of a customer service interface is mostly logic-based, while the user's perspective is functionality-driven.

Knowledge management projects and operations that employ technology usually include the implementation of intranets, data warehouses, decision support tools, and groupware. The premise of technology intervention is that it allows for more codification, storage, and distribution, and the marriage of knowledge management and technology yield and influence better management.

Accidental or purposeful forgetting then are necessary activities that promote the organization's progression to achieve its strategic goals. Knowledge stored in someone's memory can become obstructive and prohibitive. On the other hand, organizations have to, on purpose, "forget" historical practices to facilitate new, improved learning. For example, at an organization, individuals during its early inception may design procedures and policies that were valid for that time but do not support the current environment. Conducting needs analysis help to determine what capabilities are present and how to leverage them, which then unearth more accurate, centralized, and less human-dependent processes to replace manual processes.

Accidental forgetting can occur during this period of transition, making the case against individual knowledge. Organizations can curtail the accidental loss of knowledge by having multiple access points to that knowledge via technology or by training multiple individuals to perform the same functions. Knowledge management ambassadors help to foster interpersonal trust, as it is important to effective knowledge management and identifies a positive correlation between the level of trust and the willingness to share knowledge.

Knowledge Transfer

The transmission of knowledge from one person to another person can be hindered by prior related knowledge, experience, culture, tolerance to change, and other factors that present as perceptive filters. Informal knowledge communications, such as gossip or hearsay, can have damaging effects on the organization's mage. Conflict, power, and politics are both inhibitors and accelerants to knowledge movement in organizations, and their effects are palpable whether their existence is perceived or real. Individuals or groups can resist knowledge sharing in heterogeneous (interorganizational) or homogeneous (intraorganizational) settings. Boundary-specific knowledge presents challenges that are often attributed to a history of interfunctional conflict. Selective knowledge sharing is found to be politically influenced as social capital garners power that can result in hoarding or sharing of organizational knowledge.

Knowledge is transferred effectively, reluctantly, or not at all. Knowledge transfer can be problematic, as sharing knowledge is perceived as being counterproductive to job security. From a business standpoint, effectiveness and efficiency are dual drivers of sustaining foundational underpinnings; however, human rationality that is subject to emotions drives the individuals who make up the organization. A transfer of knowledge is engaged through a shared vision; however, the converse is true; a shared vision impels the transfer of knowledge. The shared vision, however, is usually the predecessor since it asks the pivotal question about knowledge goals, "What do we want to create?" Both semantic and pragmatic boundaries can be overcome by utilizing knowledge facilitating approaches. Cross-functional interactions, boundary spanners, and translators can reduce the negative effect of knowledge blocking. Converting tacit knowledge to explicit knowledge is a priority in knowledge transfer.

Using common knowledge as an entry point or gateway to boundary-specific knowledge creates opportunities to collaborate and converts implicit knowledge at the micro or personal level to explicit knowledge at the macro or organizational level. The foundational aspect of knowledge dictates how knowledge transfer occurs in the organization; this construct is important, as it supports the other aspects of knowledge. Knowledge expectations and goals should be communicated clearly, and stakeholders' involvement in co-creating this foundation is a necessary strategic buy-in for their support of it. The foundation then should support that of a knowledge-sharing establishment whose end goal is collective strengths that uphold the organization's mission and objectives.

The political and symbolic aspects of knowledge sometimes work in tandem to concurrently focus on the stakeholders' and team members' agenda while providing the leadership guidance to inspire and motivate them. Before implementing knowledge transfer that sticks in the organization, understanding how to create a shared vision through problem-solving should be pursued. This exercise underscores knowledge creation and answers the question of what is to be created, and just as important, to what degree, by whom, and how it will be created and sustained.

Informal networks allow for cross-structural knowledge sharing, which then should be linked to human resource practices to deter knowledge loss or gaps. Career advancement, generating sales, and negative perception of executive management are inhibitors to knowledge sharing. An individual bent on career advancement holds knowledge that they believe gives them an advantage. Similarly, a sales-driven organization may pit salespeople against each other to increase volume.

An adversarial relationship with executive management, especially if their decision-making opposes the individual's feelings and emotions, is also a hindrance to sharing knowledge. Being able to share ideas with the organization without fear of retribution has rational implications, which should prompt human resource management to provide the impetus for successful knowledge sharing in their policy structuring. Trust then appears to be the incentive to share knowledge with members on the same team, across teams, and vertically to senior management.

Leaders must possess intellectual humility—awareness of the extent of their ignorance or lack of knowledge. SWOTTing involves examining your strengths, weaknesses, opportunities, and threats. You should then identify any trends in this analysis; for example, weaknesses should be trending to opportunities and strengths. Threats should trend toward seeking opportunities to reinforce organizational infrastructures to withstand future similar threats.

SWOTTing relies on your proactivity in leveraging the lessons learned to optimize your leadership strategy, organizational structure, processes and systems, resources, capabilities, culture, technologies, innovations, and intellectual property. This collection of knowledge represents your core competencies and your strategic advantage.

Recall that strengths and weaknesses are internal, while opportunities and threats are external. Strengths and weaknesses are the areas within your control. For example, one such control is the choice to surround yourself with knowledgeable individuals who allow you and the organization to move through the knowledge domains. Strengths and weaknesses are the known knowns and known unknowns, respectively. Knowledge represents a social currency. Surround yourself with individuals who know more than you do, as Henry Ford exemplified. On his desk was a row of buttons; on the other side of that button were individuals who were experts in their knowledge in specific domains.

Collaboration

Recently, at a year's end, I was with a group of friends who were also leaders in their respective organizations. We were intentional about having a transparent and honest conversation about some hard topics. The type of energy that was released in that corporate interaction was surprising to all of us. We each brought our perspective to the discussion; however, new perspectives and knowledge emerged that we didn't know we knew.

Collaborative engines propel movement through the knowledge domains. There is a positive correlation between collaboration and knowledge. ATLs regularly seek ways to collaborate, drawing on the 4Is that define an ATL: inspirational motivation, idealized influence, individualized consideration, and intellectual stimulation. Intellectual stimulation is the leader's consistent engagement with their internal and external stakeholders in ways that drive problem-solving, critical forward-thinking, and innovation.

Intellectual stimulation may be expressed in the form of corporate entrepreneurship. Leaders can provide innovative spaces and resources to individuals in the organization to fulfill an idea or initiative. Creating innovative and collaborative spaces equips you and your team with the proper framework to resist a survivor's mindset and to remain focused despite crises. Principles and practices have to be established and maintained; shared understanding and responsibilities build a sustaining trust that both supports and transcends collaborative organizational practices. Integrity requires consistency between words, acts, and beliefs to create value in the products and services offered, as well as value in employee engagement.

Ethical relativism thrives in the absence of cultural interactions, so commitment to organizational integrity builds the necessary support that fosters collaboration. Leaders should value results over formality. Formal intervention is necessary, however, not to the suppression of creativity, innovation, and results-oriented behavior. Unwritten principles that tie back to the leadership style are that the leader commits to and owns any initiative that they verbally agree to. This raises the trust factor and accountability between team members and fosters a commitment to the organization's pursuits. More on this in the chapter on Organizational Change Management.

To improve collaboration, focus on principles that are designed to provide a support system for the leader to combat breaches in efficacy. Mitigative support ensures that the leader is protected, mainly against their egos and deficiencies, which promotes deference to the collective wisdom of their leadership community and environment. A locus of guidance that is ethical, spiritual, emotional, and intellectual runs the gamut of collaboration efforts and closes the gaps that threaten the leader's proficiency. The leader in embracing these principles is patently aware of their limitations and avidly seeks complementary and supplementary skillsets from stakeholders and other leaders to emulate or implement as necessary.

Turf protection is a collaborative inhibitor, especially in command-and-control organizational structures or newly minted flattened structures. In this case, the commitment to organizational integrity has not permeated the individual principles. Embracing information democracy can be fully realized by adopting policies to withhold support of information hoarding practices. This is the very instance where "trust" as a verb can be exercised successfully.

When organizations support a competitive culture, there are negative effects on teams; teams are not able to collaborate to work toward long-term goals and objectives and, in turn, will hoard knowledge. These teams operate with formalities and procedures that inhibit the organization from collaborating in effective ways. For example, focusing on short-term gains/goals only may foster the organization's inability to sustain any economic downturns, which then cause employees to mistrust the organizational leaders and affect overall productivity.

Organizations that support a competitive culture usually have a mission statement that drives the culture, which can lead people within the organization to act without integrity. Recall that a PTL operates in competitiveness over collaboration. Non-collaborative cultures within organizations exist not only in the mission statements but in the organization's physical layout. A hierarchical layout is usually found in the command-and-control organization where the executive office floor presides over the maze of cubicles providing physical barriers to a collaborative environment

Non-collaborative language sometimes has its roots in jargon that is only understandable by certain functional teams, such as information technology. In information technology, for example, employees are promoted out of technical positions into management positions, where they sometimes have no interest or training; competence in certain areas does not necessarily translate to overall competence. This happened to me at the beginning of my career. My technological competence put me on the radar to manage the Technology Department. Employees may be good managers of resources but not the "human" kind.

Enabling practices such as desegregating team members and co-location may reduce the command-and-control behavior and instill innovative practices. I have (and I am sure you have too) experienced team members who constantly defer responsibilities to the "next meeting." This behavior eschews responsibilities, which I have termed "pushing words around." Constantly deferring to the next meeting deflates motivation and collaboration and increases frustration. Also, constantly stating that "_____ said" infers that the speaker lacks power and has to "run it up the flagpole" as opposed to sharing and collaborating in real time with colleagues to get input. If we have to constantly say "____ said," then "_____" might as well be there saying it.

Leaders should prepare future leaders to work on collaborative teams that apply innovation, creativity, and cooperation to develop solutions to problems. First, they create a culture committed to continuous improvement: engagement, achievement, and success. Second, they continuously improve leadership practices that align with organizational goals. Collaboration among all stakeholders is essential to obtaining these goals. To ensure collaboration is practiced, they use a network of relationships that transcend organizational hierarchy that limits stakeholders in different functional or geographic regions. Leaders must maximize collaboration and simultaneously minimize organizational politics.

Ideally, high-performance teams needing minimal supervision capitalize on the synergy and innovative climate to work to establish a productive culture in collaborative practices. These practices tear down walls of separation between leadership and followers, functional departments, and organizational, creative assets. Knowledge transfer also occurs as a return on investment in collaboration is achieved as a result of significant investment in strategy and implementation. However, there are challenges to collaboration and instances where despite best intentions, collaboration is not an option.

Challenges to Collaborative Engines

The benefits of collaboration vastly surpass the costs; however, the law of diminishing returns comes into play as the greater the number of resources participating in the collaboration, the fewer benefits may accrue. This occurs when teams possessing similar amounts of knowledge collaborate. It would then stand to reason that inequity in the collaborative teams' knowledge creates a more conducive environment to collaborate to produce greater outcomes.

Collaboration must be specific, strategic, and directed to explicit targets to realize benefits. One hundred plus one hundred does not always equal two hundred. For example, consider a strategic partnership between two power-house organizations with goals to realize double the outcome from their collective inputs. Drivers that produced 100 percent efficiency in their assessment should be doubled. One problematic area could be that the companies are located in different countries, where cultural influence on collaboration sometimes does not easily translate to mutually rewarding results.

Another challenge facing the joint alliance is that under pressure to perform and to report gains to shareholders and executive leadership, the focus can shift to other ventures weakening the partnership and decreasing the chances of the collaboration's success. Analyzing the reasons for collaboration and performing an opportunity cost breakdown will help the organization decide if collaboration is beneficial or even suitable to be undertaken. Opportunity costs calculation considers the opportunities passed up to pursue the desired opportunity. The payoff is the reason to collaborate, so gains in savings, time, revenues, innovation, communication, and reputation, are assessed against the costs. This situation is extremely dicey, especially if the organization passes up on non-collaborative activities to pursue collaboration with its inherent challenges.

Collaborative premium objectively gauges the projected return minus collaboration and opportunity costs. Collaboration costs are multifaceted and can include working across functional and geographic boundaries, which introduce additional challenges that span organizational boundaries, business practices, countries, and cultures. Furthermore, travel, coordination efforts, communication deadlocks, and information sharing can not only contribute to costs and delays but can also simultaneously lower quality, projected results, savings, and sales and undermine and harm relationships between the organization and its internal and external stakeholders.

Ensuring that the team focuses on collective results is challenging enough for one organization to transcend cross-functional boundaries, much less intercontinental teams that operate in myriad ways that can affect the collaboration. Committing to stated results are ways to ensure that the team focuses on the end game, regardless of obstacles; however, this may backfire since vocalizing publicly the intent to win can unnecessarily provoke competitive activities from other organizations or, in some cases, business units within the same organizational culture.

Virtual Collaboration

Phased integration to online collaborative tools sets the stage for virtual collaboration success. Sharing best practices is one of the primary reasons for accessing virtual knowledge. Collaboration births the ability to leverage virtually unlimited intellectual resources. Allowing timely access to information involves the process of reengineering to support a virtual platform that allows the teams' access to knowledge in ways that are meaningful to them. Having the choice of different tools based on responsibilities, accessibility, or even choice and methodology breaks down the collaborative walls and leads to team members embracing the technology. Creating responsibilities with time-based outcomes on a virtual platform will require that individuals utilize that platform to comply with stated deliverables.

Technology's influence on collaboration is evident in electronic meetings, interactive virtual sessions, online resources, virtual conferences, cloud processing and storage, and the Metaverse. Collaboration allows for both knowledge sharing and knowledge creation. Collaboration allows knowledge creation to occupy a space that enables its effectiveness. Organizations that do not allow for physical and virtual communications interchange are deficient in creating new meanings to/for their knowledge and are at risk for improper knowledge conversion. Collaboration helps to remove the ambiguity of tacit knowledge as it moves to shared knowledge that can be objectively assessed.

When Collaboration Is Not an Option

Quantifying collaborative costs (and subsequent gains) is challenging and is progressively elaborated as collaborative projects are underway. Earned value analysis should be utilized throughout the project to assess how project activities positively contribute earnings to the project. The Cost Performance Index (CPI), for example, is used to objectively assesses how much value is earned by the work of a project or endeavor per investment dollar spent. A collaborative effort with a CPI of one point five would indicate that the project is performing well against the invested costs (50 percent more). A CPI of zero point seventy-five, on the other hand, indicates that the collaboration efforts are underperforming (25 percent less) and that the investment in the project is depreciating.

Projects often have stage exits or phase kills, where a determination is made at various milestones to see if the project should continue. All parties involved in collaboration should contribute jointly to continuation or termination decisions. Alternatively, if a proposed collaborative project does not identify key milestones and exit criteria, then collaboration should not be pursued.

Sometimes organizations decide to partner with vendors to provide the needed service, equipment, or materials to their organizations. Engaging in contracts between the buyer (the organization) and the seller (the contractor) should be based on a fair analysis of the required work, the duration, and the cost. These triple constraints should be managed and leveraged to benefit both parties. Different contract types, such as fixed price or incentive-driven performance, should be the basis upon which collaboration is pursued. Premium over penalty should drive the decision to pursue collaboration.

Companies must not overestimate the financial returns of collaboration in their eagerness to realize the gains of collaborative efforts. So, unless a true indication of financial gains is identified, collaboration is not recommended. Collaboration is discouraged in organizations that do not have effective feedback channels and shared knowledge bases. Internal knowledge creation activities are cited for having a positive influence on collaboration, as do individual and collective competencies. These factors that drive collaboration should be benchmarks to assess the reality of collaborative efforts; absent of strong indication of their presence, collaborative pursuits should be avoided.

Situations that warrant not pursuing collaborative cultures include Chrysler's cautionary tale of a $36 billion-dollar acquisition that was later valued at only 1 billion dollars, a mere 2.7 percent of the original value. This situation address miscalculation of collaborative practices of firms that fail to properly analyze the benefits of collaboration. Failure to not assess an organization's strengths against the market and its competitors also leads to failed collaboration efforts. Operating in an internal vacuum without properly gauging the implications of outside influences will lead to collaborative failure.

If turf wars are rampant within organizational units, attempting to partner with internal or external units would only exacerbate the practice and yield negative returns to collaboration. Interestingly, collaboration usually capitalizes on the like-mindedness and the homogeneous culture of the individuals involved; however, collaboration with your competitors is justified if the objective is to solve shared problems.

Companies should, rather than pursue collaboration, instead, be more attuned to which opportunities warrant collaboration. Regularly assessing their strategic health and their ability to capitalize on collaborative opportunities both inside and external to the organization speaks to the new interpretation of collaboration. By consciously practicing collaboration analysis, the organization will be set to capitalize on active collaborative opportunities rather than passive ones.

A collaborative future necessitates a shift in leadership style that moves the mindset from traditional to collaborative practices. One of the challenges is to move from maintaining ownership of knowledge to openly sharing knowledge. In some organizations, misrepresentation and collusion sometimes underscore the issues relating to friction among the staff. Varying sources of information that are either diluted or distilled based on the desired communications outcomes lie squarely at the root of dissension.

Encourage suggestions and ideas from your teams and offer immediate and ongoing feedback. When teams are engaged in suggesting innovative improvements, immediate feedback must be given to reinforce the suggestion or to lead them toward more optimal propositions. This feedback loop fuels the innovative energy that motivates the team members and fosters collaboration, ownership, and accountability, leading to improved performance individually and collectively.

Accountability

Leveraging trust as a competency makes sense strategically and economically. Today's leaders are more likely to respond to company practices and norms if there are economic repercussions. Trust as a competency can be converted to economic returns in a shorter amount of time than it would take to develop trust naturally. There is a distinction between a predictive trust and vulnerability-based trust that is a factor of time and a cultivated relationship. Absent that, trust can occur immediately once the person decides to be vulnerable to the team and the leader and vice versa. Team trust is the focus and not the trust that results from a series of one-on-one relationships.

Repositioning trust from a soft skill occupancy to that of an economic driver addresses factors such as trust dividends or taxes. This creates a competitive advantage in an increasingly distrustful business climate. Leaders must be the trust (noun) that they want to experience. Trust is both a competency (noun) and a soft skill (verb). Stakeholders trust leaders to plan, execute, and be accountable in their respective domains. Efforts to establish trust from a leadership perspective begin with the level or lack of leadership involvement in overseeing activities. Trust is instilled when leaders trust in stakeholders' competence to deliver on agreed-upon objectives.

Principles and practices are established and maintained in circles of trust. These circles represent teams in the workplace but usually extend to the community. The resulting trust (noun) fosters immediate and quantifiable trust dividends that impact present and future intraorganizational and interorganizational undertakings. A mental cost/benefit analysis influences an individual's decision on whether to confront unacceptable behavior and hold a leader accountable. Several factors prevent people from being confrontational, including fear of repercussions, fear of the confrontation yielding non-beneficial returns, and fear of exacerbating the situation. In some cases, the thought of confronting a superior may bring up barriers to buttressing job security or the relationship. The latter example speaks to my research topic, as I strove to assess the characteristics, traits, influences, and behavior that influences Pseudo-Transformational Leadership (PTL). Certainly, not being confronted can falsely lull a leader into thinking that they are doing everything right.

Accountability conversations should be commonplace in organizations. Leaders who have "title-itis" are concerned only with their title and are unconcerned with performing any of the responsibilities that the title requires. Reverting to silence is usually the behavior that most individuals embrace; they default to silence as the only option to confronting the leader. Vocabulary choice, mannerisms, and demeanor offer constructive ways to confront leaders and guide a positive response that promotes problem-solving. These practices, however, must be taught, learned, and practiced, yielding insights and actions that produce accountability. ATLs confront issues immediately to resolve them sooner than later.

Self-perception. Self-awareness. Self-evaluation. This examination of your worldview, as an individual first and then as a leader, must be extended to your internal and external stakeholders. Your creed must be able to answer what you are doing to perpetuate the organization's vision and not solely your personal goals. Similarly, we previously assessed the value of the SWOTT analysis. As a leader, it is critical to be mindful of your weltanschauung, which expresses how you view the world and how you engage within it. Your stakeholders will model their interactions with you based on their perception of your worldview. This may include them framing communications in the context of your beliefs to appease you. They also know how to engage you and how to get you to side with them. Consequently, weltanschauung both frames and limits your worldview.

Regular self-assessment of your worldview implies your examining your creeds (personal, philosophical, sociological, professional, pedagogical/andragogical); they are the aspects of your leadership that you have the most control over. Self-examination involves you asking hard questions regularly. Your accountability infrastructure also strengthens your vigilance in examining your creeds and personal vision, as it relates to the organization.

Learning

Transformational learning is incarcerated under PTL. In light of new experiences, expanded socialization, and advances in learning, we know less than we don't know. The building blocks of a learning organization are a supportive learning environment, concrete learning processes and practices, and leadership that reinforces learning. Leaders should identify processes needing improvements, gaps in learning and application, and conduct an appropriate review of required and implemented processes.

Although an environment embraces differences and maverick ideas, some individuals may still not feel comfortable speaking up. Part of the reasoning is that if you speak up, you own the idea and thus the implementation of it. Psychological safety is instrumental to organizational learning, and it encompasses employees' ability to be open to sharing their thoughts without fear, to fail forward fast, own up to mistakes, or present alternative viewpoints. Learning is not the only way to improve employee performance; in some cases, it may be the wrong choice, as motivation and other factors influence performance. Another reason may be their lack of familiarity and experience with an open and honest work environment

Our society is characterized by continual and rapid changes necessitating the need for an autonomous thinking citizenry engaging in intellectual exploration of mainstream academic, economic, and social issues. The Department of Labor ranks competence in the acquisition, organizing, interpreting, comprehending, and dissemination of information for effective utilization in varied interrelationships as highly sought-after skills for the workforce. The Australian government concurs and cites the utility of technology, mathematical and technological problem-solving, team collaboration, and cultural intelligence as establishing fundamentals for adult learners to achieve proficiency in both short- and long-term social participation and responsibility.

Adult learners are frequently classified as having a hyperfocus on short-term objectives, typifying that of an SME; however, to achieve ongoing effectiveness, fostering long-term competencies are desirable traits in an autonomous learner. In learning how to learn, these processes set the stage for future learning. Leaders who pursue learning do so with the objectives of being privy to information that will help them understand their relative position in the world and how to competently share ideas for desirable effects. Learning leaders are autonomous thinkers engaged in ex-post-factor reflection, and they understand that the gap between the present and the future is bridged by learning.

Additionally, depending on the business environment, learning is binary, and transformational learning is delayed. Recall when businesses had to shut down because of the pandemic. Businesses closed; however, they reopened when it was safe to do so. Although closing was non-negotiable, the transformational infrastructure already in place supported their reopening and doing so in a better future state. The combination of learning acquired from previous and current crises breeds new knowledge that allows organizations to mitigate the effects of the disruption.

Instrumental Learning

Instrumental learning is optimal for achieving short-term objectives since it aims to control and manipulate the environment to obtain satisfactory outcomes. Instrumental learning occurred during the 2020 pandemic. Instrumental learning goals are characterized by problem-solving and cause-and-effect relationships, such as acquiring a job promotion, getting a certification, or learning to cook gourmet dishes. Cause and effect tools such as an Ishikawa diagram or fishbone diagram help leaders diagnose issues and problems. This is predicated on the concept that if the fish head is bad, then the remainder of the fish is also bad. When my mom buys fish, she lifts the gill to examine it; she also looks at the eyes to determine if the fish is fresh.

Deductive reasoning provides intellectual structures that guide the leader in manipulating information and making use of a justified or supported proposition, yielding useful frameworks for philosophical projections. The evolution of instrumental learning progresses from acquiring information to manipulating it in disparate situations.

Leaders can be likened to actors on an intellectual stage, where further reflective character analysis yields a performance that is well reasoned, autonomous, and responsible. The use of metacognition is evident as leaders learn to regulate and control cause and effect relationships to line up with goals and values.

Communicative Learning

The categorical distinction between instrumental and communicative learning is the scope. The tools of communicative learning involve higher mental processes and include the spoken and written word. Leaders perform critical reflection to achieve coherence over relationships rather than manipulation in a hypothetico-deductive task-oriented approach. This is one of its distinctions over instrumental learning. Communicative learners strive for clarification and intersubjectivity and attempt to fit new unexperienced situations into meaningful perspectives that facilitate the interpretation of related patterns.

In cases where there is no fit, new meaning perspectives emerge. Where instrumental learning is dependent on empirical testing, communicative learning relies on consensual validations through norms, and reciprocal expectations, involving at least two subjects. Linguistically explicit rational discourse is necessary since regression analysis is performed to align standards to an outcome, restricting further dialogue until resolution is achieved. Rational discourse faces limitations; political and religious instruments may be utilized as substitutes, serving as educators and, in some cases, imposing on both learner and educator roles.

Comparison of Domains

Communicative learners achieve meaning through language and gestures, as they engage in the designative rather than the prescriptive form of instrumental learning. Insight is gained in communicative interaction, and constructs are identified and explained. The communicative learner's involvement in the hermeneutic cycle of assessing the relationship of the parts to the whole (and vice versa) constructs building blocks of information that are transformed by future insights.

Instrumental learners challenge the validity of truth, comprehensibility, appropriateness, and authenticity, and reassessments may produce corrected epistemic, sociocultural, or psychic distortions. Both domains of learning utilize reassessments of previous learning to facilitate new meaning perspectives.

Application of Domains

Competency-based instruction, training programs, instructional design, and standardized training are examples of instrumental learning. Achieving a Project Management Professional (PMP) certification involves experience in the project management profession, training in the Project Management Body of Knowledge and related curricula, and undertaking an outcome-based assessment to earn the certification. This undertaking reflects the self-achievement culture embraced in the United States.

Transformational psychologists deem self-actualization as a natural bend toward self-mastery and becoming emotionally intelligent and autonomous. Leaders can act both as a promoter or a hindrance to self-actualization, and in the former, it is useful in cultures where marginalization or oppression by power structures exists. Self-actualized individuals contribute positively to society and inspire others to do the same, further establishing an autonomous society.

Comparisons between individual learning and collaborative learning suggest that interpersonal relationships that are cooperative rather than competitive yield better performance, increased motivation, and development of higher levels of thinking; however, a deepened understanding of the collaborative model is needed, especially in virtual leadership. The social interactions that promote social agility between the leader and stakeholders need to be reengineered to fit the online platform, and so does understanding stakeholders' orientation. A high-level approach to stakeholders' orientation may involve learning to know, interact, and understand, learning to reach an achievement, or learning to make an impression on them.

These orientations can be further classified to address the orientation to achieve success (instrumental) or achieve understanding (communicative). Learning-oriented leaders may resist a norm that does not involve an interaction or adequate exploration of materials. On the other hand, achievement-oriented leaders are less interested or participatory in the social aspects of the collaborative environment. Pushbacks occur when leaders are faced with norms that conflict with their meaning perspectives; the leader must be conversant in both domains and further engage in critical discourse to facilitate transformational learning.

Both learning domains coexist, are necessary, and are not mutually exclusive. Where instrumental learning is self-centered and focused on doing, communicative learning centers on understanding. In both cases, transformational learning yields new meaning perspectives that transform the learner and further engage him/her in emancipatory learning that challenges presuppositions and explores alternatives.

We transform by actively engaging in activities that support the learning process while simultaneously limiting the scope of those activities that usurp the process. Learning activates the knowledge domains of known knowns, known unknowns, unknown knowns, and unknown unknowns. There are tools in place to make the unknowns known. All too often, we accept not learning by default since it is easier and incurs less anxiety and stress; however, learning and subsequent transformation entail that justification of distortions must occur, i.e., known knowns.

Let's revisit the 4Is of ATL, specifically, inspirational motivation and idealized influence. Both aspects of ATL involve a mentoring relationship. Additionally, one of ATL's transformational infrastructures includes a pedagogical creed. "I'm looking forward to a mutually beneficial relationship" is how I usually close the welcome message in my virtual learning environments. In stating this upfront, I am involving the learner in a journey that promises to be transformational in the end.

By modeling the "guide by the side" archetype, learners are more open to facets of knowledge than they would to a "sage on the stage" archetype. This collective unconscious gives an impression of knowledge yet to be discovered that has not yet been traversed to the conscious mind. From the stakeholders' perspective, a mentor archetype represents a mental, physical, intellectual, and psychological destination that is yet to be attained, and the ATL possesses the skill set to help them navigate the way to that end. By awakening in them the desire to desire those goals, all share a journey that equips them with tools to be utilized in future endeavors.

The leader/mentor position carries with it intentional teaching that includes remedying distortions. Mentors instigate reflection on the learners' part. Because neither the learner nor the mentor can assess the degree to which the process will succeed or fail, ethical activities should govern the relationship. Transformative learning should be objective enough to foster differing viewpoints but connective enough to nurture growth.

Individual, group, and organizational learning occur as a result of formal training, intervention in work processes, and embedded and emerging learning linked to organizational communications and activities. An organization learns by adopting the intellectual insights of individuals and groups and incorporating them into norms, values, processes, and structures. An organization can also learn when it is affected by learning at the group level. Discontinuous disruption is necessary since knowledge does not flow seamlessly between the levels of reorganization without interposition.

A needs analysis requirement driven by organizational analysis, person analysis, or task analysis identifies which aspect of learning receives implementation priority. After the needs analysis is conducted, a viable approach would be to adopt varying sequences of training, survey data feedback, constructive confrontation, and process observation and feedback

Leadership training and employee development should occur in tandem with the restructuring initiatives identified by the needs analysis, as it will help to align leaders with the newly emerged, self-sufficient organization. For lasting, effective results, a survey-data-feedback mechanism would ensure that leaders are addressing the key issues that are impacting organizational learning and, subsequently, performance.

ATLs can thrive during disruption because of the Knowledge, Collaboration, Accountability, and Learning (KCAL) tailwinds that drive organizational performance. KCAL should also be in place even when there are no crises. The "Lead, Learn, Level Up!" mentality is a progressive and interactive endeavor that counteracts reactive leadership and embraces Transformational Leadership.

Reflective Discourse

1. Knowledge, Collaboration, Accountability, Learning (KCAL) are powerful transformational tailwinds. How does your leadership team practice exemplify KCAL?
2. Collaborative engines are important in transforming weaknesses and threats into opportunities. In your experience, when is collaboration not an option?
3. Which KCAL aspect are you practicing right now, and why?

CHAPTER 9

Transformational Leadership and Organizational Change Management

For OCM strategies to be successful, they must be tethered to Transformational Leadership practices.

I am currently leading Organizational Change Management for several organizations undergoing digital transformation. It's exciting and challenging to gain buy-in from stakeholders at all levels of the organization. Making the business case for the transformation is easier than making the subjective What's In It For Me (WIIFM) case. Once individuals realize they can benefit from what is on the other side of the transition and the opportunities for upskilling and reskilling, they are on board. The OCM aspect requires a prescriptive approach driven by Transformational Leadership so that adoption, usage, and proficiency occur.

Stakeholders view proposed changes through their weltanschauung (beliefs, perceptive filters). Recall that there is a positive correlation between Maslow's hierarchy of needs and the level of engagement. OCM activities usually affect the esteem and self-actualization tiers. Correlating those aspects to the change initiative is important. OCM activities are sometimes an offshoot of disruption and crisis; in that case, the lower tiers of the pyramid have to be addressed first. ATLs are adept at engaging the entire person on all tiers.

Leaders reduce uncertainty about the change by defining what's in scope and what's out of scope. Now is a good place to revisit the "Change versus Transformation" chapter and why Transformational Leadership is critical to change success. Transformation involves the entire landscape of the transition and not just the binary aspect of it.

In OCM, the most common mistake is to focus only on transitioning to the new systems or processes and not on the people. People are the single most important factor that drives successful change adoption. Organizations that fail in delivering their strategic initiatives often find the lack of stakeholder involvement and engagement counterproductive. In the framework of change, moral purpose, understanding change, relationship building, knowledge creation, sharing, and coherence making are critical. OCM incurs practices that are measurable, tangible, structured, and repeatable.

Leaders resolute in the pursuit of change embody it and become the change that they envision. Leaders who champion change also identify other change champions to help them lead the charge. Change should not be forced; rather, it is established via Authentic Transformational Leadership. Fearful, risk-averse stakeholders may resist the change and, in some cases, may even sabotage it. Engaging them early and often establishes their accountability and commitment to the win.

There's less resistance to change if the mind arrives first. Stakeholders will ask, "Why are we doing this?" The concept behind change theory is that we move from the abstract to the "why" and then on to the concrete: This is "how" we're going to change. Keep your Transformational Leadership hat on as you move through change in the organization. Collaborative and participatory involvement leads to adoption.

My experience in leadership supports the fact that the behavior of the leader can seriously impact how the changes are adopted—or not. Certain leaders are not ideal sponsors of change initiatives. I have also learned that timing is critical to change implementation; excessive changes can signal a lack of security to stakeholders and diminish trust in the leadership.

The ideology behind change management has to be rescoped to employ all of the attributes that Transformational Leadership embodies to drive success. As previously stated, change is binary; for example, if we are upgrading to new systems or processes, we move from PMO to FMO. Binary. Since the transformation is ongoing, the belief and mindset about the changes must pervade throughout the transition.

In terms of ATL's strength and efficacies, during times of disruptive changes, they practice leadership elasticity. For example, depending on the severity of the change, Transactional Leadership may be both necessary and vital. On the other hand, the Transformational leader may practice Laissez-Faire

Leadership, which is effective for high-performing teams and individuals; the leader provides resources and allows for their strategic participation in the change. Malleable shifts in leadership allow the project to move forward.

In some cases, senior leadership puts the onus of the change on middle managers and is absent from the endeavor. For change to succeed, senior leaders have to be active, visible, and engaged. Studies show that their presence increases the likelihood of success by nearly threefold. Leaders have to model the change they want to see happen. They have to demonstrate excitement, communicate early and often, and extinguish any uncertainty.

Change inherently carries high uncertainty, which leads to an increased importance of social relationships between leaders and stakeholders. Since the ultimate measure of organizational change is adoption, usage, and proficiency, the social currency of collaboration and participation must be maintained. Operational efficiency and competencies are gained as a result. The resulting shift in mindset and behavior is sustained by transformational tailwinds.

Internal stakeholders usually ask, "What does this mean for my job? Are the computers going to take over? Are you going to automate my job?" So leaders need to be communicating in that social space, alleviating fear and uncertainty. The prospect of change usually instills emotions such as shock, frustration, defiance, and resentment.

The leader has to lean into the 4Is—inspirational motivation, idealized influence, individualized consideration, and intellectual stimulation—to engage stakeholders and garner their participation in the change. Intellectual stimulation seeks their input on how to operationalize the change, while individualized consideration communicates exactly how their responsibilities will look like during and after the implementation. Do you see now how Transformational Leadership is crucial to ensure that the change sticks?

People are what make changes successful, not the technology or the processes. The collective participation of individuals in the initiative brings about organizational change. Show them how participating in it will make them better, more employable, and more promotable. Critical thinking and innovation come into play as you are now automating menial tasks and moving toward solving business-critical tasks.

Organizational change includes project management (focus on processes) and people management (focus on mindsets and behaviors). People management necessitates Transformational Leadership. In extreme cases, the leader may apply Transactional Leadership to monetize change adoption by tying compensation to performance.

Command-and-control organizations usually experience low success in change management since their leaders are usually siloed. Successful change management invokes change agents such as first-line managers and supervisors to evangelize the change. They can identify change resistors (who may be passive or active). Change management allows the creation of new organizational stories.

At the beginning of each change management endeavor I undertake, I conduct anonymous surveys with leadership to ensure they are aligned with the initiatives and with employees to ensure they understand why they are changing. After analyzing the results, I can detect if alignment among the leaders is warranted, if they are communicating the right message to stakeholders, or if there are blockers present. A key question in the survey is to ask all stakeholders how they plan to support the change.

The purpose of the surveys is to establish accountability and alignment and determine if leaders are communicating effective messages. Other data points are identifying lessons learned, prior experience, change readiness, proper prioritization of the change, and level of buy-in. I then meet with the leaders of the organization to share the survey results, after which I meet with the other stakeholders. I engage leaders first because, in some cases, resistance to the change is present at that level. The change may be the initiative of one or more executives and not others, so leadership resistance may be present.

Readiness workshops usually follow; they can be joint (all stakeholders) or separate for each group of stakeholders. There is merit to both approaches; for example, some stakeholders may be reluctant to honestly articulate their concerns if leaders are present. Here is where an organization led by ATLs comes to bear; there is already honest and open communications, so all stakeholders can meet. If resistance is present in leadership, then the workshops should be separate to drive alignment before engaging the other stakeholders.

Change readiness factors include the shift to virtual/hybrid leadership and work, the new "workspace," Zoom fatigue, change fatigue, change versus transformation, and headwinds versus tailwinds. The necessity for speed of adoption usually involves headwinds where a pivot is required. Other types of change may position incremental transformation as the strategy to move to future states. Coaching is sometimes necessary to address change readiness, and if you recall, the individualized consideration aspect of ATL includes coaching or mentoring. Coaching is also instrumental in managing resistance.

Name the change! Giving the change project a name is important in establishing significance. This is another opportunity to solicit participation from affected stakeholders. I once worked with a global organization whose workforce consisted of a large number of volunteers. One of the activities that I performed at the onset was to rebrand volunteers as Vision Implementation Partners (VIPs). This simple shift in optics went a long way in motivating them and showcasing their value to the organization.

Contrary to what is commonly believed, OCM is not simply a soft skill that involves only conducting training. It is measurable, tangible, structured, and repeatable. It is also a method to engage each individual, resulting in collective change for the organization. Change initiatives occupy an ecosystem that requires the construction of several strategies: stakeholder analysis/management, leader/sponsor, communication, resistance, coaching, training or knowledge transfer, and reinforcement or support. There may be other strategies; however, the first four are associated with the behavior of Transformational Leadership and will be addressed here. Failure to address these critical aspects of OCM will derail your initiatives.

Stakeholder Management/Analysis

After anonymous surveys are administered, my next step is to perform a stakeholder analysis. This entails assessing the level of participation of stakeholders, their OCM competency, level of support or resistance, ability to influence other stakeholders as well as an approach to engaging them. Again, ATLs should lean into the 4Is. Inspirational motivation, idealized influence, individualized consideration, and intellectual stimulation are the behavioral blueprint for ATLs.

The 4Is engage stakeholders not just at the onset of the project but during and after. Varying levels of the 4Is are warranted at different phases of the project. Once the stakeholder analysis is complete, a stakeholder management plan is created. Two key aspects of this plan are to identify how supporters can influence resistors of the change. Supporters can then transform resistors into change agents and change evangelists.

Leader/Sponsor Plan

A leader/sponsor plan is used to specify the leaders' active involvement with engaging stakeholders. Leaders usually commission the change and may not be actively involved beyond authorizing the resources. They establish desired ROI. They must also establish a unified value proposition and a call to action to move from PMO to FMO. The leadership style can significantly impact change success. Here is where ATLs shine. They practice inspirational motivation, idealized influence, individualized consideration, and intellectual stimulation to galvanize participation.

Remember the transformational tailwinds? KCAL (Knowledge, Collaboration, Accountability, Learning). No need to pivot here; just scale accordingly, prepare, equip, and support people through the transition.

Attrition may occur as a result of change initiatives. This may be attributed to a history of failed changes, misunderstanding of WIIFM, and change fatigue. Sometimes change is initiated in response to the first T in SWOTT—Threats. Legislation and regulation represent mandatory compliance and adoption by stakeholders. A unified value proposition is necessary for adoption, return on investment, and sustainability.

Performance-based requirements must be in place to measure the adoption to change. Proactive and reactive responses to resistance may include incentivizing the change. Reinforce and recognize change adoption, or else there will be regression to the mean. Here is where leaders may move through the Transformational spectrum to the Transactional model.

Communications Plan

A communication plan outlines strategic participation by the leader. The visionary aspect of the ATLs toolkit is seen here. Adaptive learning occurs during Organizational Change Management. High-risk OCM endeavors demand a corresponding comprehensive degree and quality of communications from leaders. Visible engagement and real-time communication are necessary to build on established trust. Recall the knowledge domains: known knowns, known unknowns, known unknowns, and unknown unknowns. The uncertainty that is inherent in change requires robust communications efforts.

Practice inspirational motivation as you communicate about the "whys" and "hows" of the proposed change. Exercise idealized influence by mirroring and modeling the behavior that correlates with successful change adoption. Show up as a human to empathize with the uncertainty and fear that stakeholders may initially exhibit. Finally, practice intellectual stimulation by involving them in collaboration, innovation, critical thinking, and problem-solving.

Resistance/Alignment Plan

Passive or active resistors can derail your change project. A resistance/alignment plan entails a remediation strategy to counter resistance as necessary. Within the Laissez-Faire leadership style, there is the advantage of empowering change agents and change evangelists as they are both already pro-change. A unified change governance model that includes leadership, project management, and people management is a detractor for resistance.

Equally important to the other strategies is standing up a Change Champion Network (CCN), whose role is vital due to the exponential effort to realize change. Change champions are proactive in identifying and managing the inevitable ambiguity and uncertainty associated with implementing the change. They are also capable of reducing the pressure on the core transition team, and they identify issues on the ground and raise them quickly to the core team. They gather feedback from the communications campaign, identify and manage resistance, and become super users, ultimately assisting in knowledge transfer to other stakeholders.

Another concern with change initiatives is the fact that once the change has been implemented, it is considered final. Without intervention, there is usually a regression to the mean: The change doesn't stick, and previous behaviors are reinstated. Change follow-up and support are key to sustaining change behaviors.

As noted earlier, change is a headwind that may look like force, struggle, or running into opposition versus a tailwind that enables movement through the transition. Leaders must sustain incremental transitions in their organization and use the tailwinds of transformations to drive them.

Reflective Discourse

1. Stakeholders respond better to change when the WIFFM aspect of the change is clearly communicated. What other challenges exist in your experience in onboarding change?
2. For OCM strategies to be successful, organizational leaders must show strong delivery against objectives. How do you accomplish this?
3. The aftershocks of the global pandemic have placed greater demand on OCM activities. In what ways have you had to pivot (change) instead of transforming incrementally?

CHAPTER 10

Walk the Diversity, Equity, Inclusion, Accessibility (DEIA) Talk

Treat every person how you would like to be treated.

The overwhelming majority of leaders (100%) we surveyed indicated that in their hiring practices, they focus on merits only. How do you walk the DEIA talk? Start at home/walk the talk—influence your family and community in how inclusive you are in conversation and practice. Children are truth-sayers, ask your children to evaluate you on inclusive criteria/ask them what to do to improve. As simple as it seems, this is my advice to leaders who are intentional about creating inclusive spaces for human beings.

It has evolved to the point where organizations claiming DEIA compliance have viewed the initiative as merely checking a box and not much more. The intricate mechanism of systematic exclusion remains pervasive because those with the power to alter it do not. We repeatedly witness groundswells aimed at addressing and ameliorating it rise and then fall. The marginalization of certain groups has always been present; however, the perfect storm occurred in 2020 when global disruptions forced us to face ourselves and the many faces of who we are at the core. When we did, we did not like what we saw; we were enraged but later devolved to business as usual. Interventions such as money, power, and consequences should be placed in every aspect of human interactions to promote inclusivity.

In one of the case studies I performed, surveys were administered to the employees to determine if their employers were practicing DEIA. Questions targeted promotion opportunities, mentoring, and career guidance. Respondents noted the lack of inclusion of women in leadership, which was most notably prominent from the optics of the organizational chart, which is viewed both internally and externally. Remediation efforts were put forth by the organization, which then used the evidence-based data to promote several qualified women to leadership. In another survey we conducted, 78 percent of minorities reported that they had to "prove" their professional worth in contrast to others in similar careers.

I was recently interviewed for an article where I offered guidance on designing inclusive workspaces, including shifting from office-centric to human-centric design, which transcends cultural, physical, and social dimensions. Inclusive design is established on the principle that a "design" (of a product, service, workspace, etc.) considers all of the possible human experiences. Inclusive design reorients interactions between people and their workplace to find a correlation where everyone can express their creativity, skills, and capabilities.

Organizations wanting to be effective and efficient must use everything in their repertoire to bring innovation to the market. Leaders have to ask themselves, "Am I using everything in my arsenal?" Not exploiting the full spectrum of human availability and capability leaves "money on the table." Having leadership alignment is not just about agreement on strategic initiatives; it is also about engaging those who think, act, and present differently along with their varied experiences, insights, and contributions. Unless the organization wants to continue to do more of the same, it must continue to do less of the same. Here are some guidelines to ensure you are walking the DEIA talk:

- Activate DEIA (as of 2021, the accessibility aspect of diversity, inclusion, and equity was regulated).
- Model strategic leadership by providing resources, training, and other opportunities to reinforce DEIA. Show up where it counts.
- Ensure your leadership team reflects your internal and external customer base.
- Look at your organizational chart; what are the optics communicating to stakeholders?
- Would your internal customers (employees) rate your leadership as inclusive?
- Allow for stakeholders' 360-degree evaluation of sustained DEIA performance.

- Actuate executive gatekeepers to ensure DEIA. Conduct regular pulse checks to ensure you are on task.
- Institute regular culture mapping exercises to educate stakeholders on barriers to inclusion (economic, class, religion, language, etc.).
- Cancel permissible stereotypes. Inclusivity begins with comfort, safety, respect, and support.

Inclusive Design at Work

Of leaders we surveyed, 63 percent expressed that they were very honest about outdated work cultures. The new office space has been redefined to include both virtual and hybrid. Coffee shops, home offices, and other spaces have reoriented what office space is; inclusive design means thoughtfully shifting from office-centric design to human-centric design. Inclusive design supports employees by transcending cultural, physical, and social dimensions.

Excluded communities (who are camouflaged with exclusive design) are brought back into the design decisions. Inclusive design expands the accessibility aspect of DEIA; all individuals, regardless of differentiators, should be provided the same access to office spaces. Inclusive design is also reflected in attracting, retaining, and promoting talent in the workplace. We asked minorities how their cultural and social background influenced their decision to disclose mental health concerns in a professional setting, and most (86 percent) indicated that it did, while the rest (14 percent) indicated that it did not. Understanding these cultural and social differentiators should help drive the creation of inclusive workspaces.

Before (re)implementing inclusive design, lean into evaluation and collaboration to identify previous design blind spots. Anonymous surveys that ask non-directional questions about current and reimagined design are a good start. Innovation, not replication, is key here. Next, acknowledge that the universal human experience should be represented in the workplace and see color, gender, capabilities, and race to create equity in both opportunity and access. This approach positions the company to think broadly about their employees and that not every employee works in the same manner. When possible, prototype solutions should be tested by employees before a large-scale rollout. Consider building collaborative spaces, but also build spaces where employees can work alone if desired. Proximity bias exists; consider remote and hybrid workers whose voices need to be amplified in the traditional workspace.

Design intervention is more commonplace as the talent landscape broadens to include people from varying backgrounds and experiences. Two of the most common aspects of inclusive design are regulated: wheelchair accessibility in public spaces and safe and private spaces for lactating and nursing mothers. The inclusive design takes into consideration not only what is regulated but what are real barriers to attracting and retaining talent. The employment market has shifted to a buyer's market; prospective talent has a bigger voice in not only what their working environment should be like but is also instrumental in influencing organizations in general to put more inclusive design in place.

Recently, I visited the offices of OshKosh B'Gosh (Carter's) on an architectural tour, and two aspects of their inclusive design stood out. All of the offices had glass doors that did not lock, allowing visibility and accessibility for all employees. Also, their managers and leaders who traditionally occupy top floors were placed on middle floors, equidistant from their reports on the upper and lower levels. In many organizations, assigned seating has given way to ubiquitous seating. They do not have private offices; instead, all employees have access to all offices; they book an office on a first-come, first-served basis when they want to work in the office.

Benefits of inclusive design include deterring social, physical, gender, and cultural exclusion. An increase in mental wellness is represented when the static workplace begins to morph into a more dynamic workspace. Socially responsible organizations that practice inclusive design are more desirable to diverse, prospective talent. Inclusive design also creates spaces for workers to rethink other unconscious biases.

In the aftermath of compounded crises, employees are increasingly looking to their employers for psychological safety. An environment that is welcoming and inclusive equips employees to perform better, increases retention and productivity, drives innovation and collaboration, and maximizes workers' performance, both individually and collectively.

Leaders who want a truly diverse workplace practice an inclusive recruitment system that supports all applicants. Accessibility in the workplace begins with inclusive spaces in the recruitment process. I am extremely optimistic about the capacity of the human spirit, especially in times of crisis and disruption. We rise to levels of compassion and inclusion that outpace any exclusion. We have to ask ourselves the question,

"Do we want to resolve this issue?" If we do, we become aware of our role in perpetuating the issue and are intentional about resolving it. If we don't want to, we have to determine what it takes to spur us to want to treat every person how we would like to be treated.

Reflective Discourse

1. How have your leadership practices provided the nexus for meeting DEIA goals?
2. How has your organization used inclusive work design to fill the gap left by The Great Resignation?
3. How can you prevent future shock as innovations, including technological ones, initiate in the workplace?

CHAPTER 11

Women in Leadership

Be yourself; everyone else is taken.

Fortune 500 companies with women positioned on their boards yield a stronger Return on Equity (ROE) than those with fewer women. These companies consistently maintain at least a 26 percent performance lead over their competitors in the same market. Of the Fortune 100 companies, eight CEOs are women, and there are no women of color. Since women in the US influence more than 83 percent of buying decisions, it makes sense that there should be a relative distribution of women leaders in those organizations.

Women in leadership make economic sense. Conceptually, this is valid; however, there exists a gap between conceptualization and the realization that women lead only 8.1 percent of Fortune 500 companies and hold only 19.7 percent of corporate board seats. Women-led companies have a more balanced board, 33.5 percent females versus 19.4 percent when run by males. An examination into the causes and effects that are limiting or reducing the number of women in leadership positions is warranted.

Internal and External Barriers

Substantial barriers to women leading are both implicit and explicit. These obstacles are present in academia in general and in the science, technology, engineering, and math fields. For instance, researchers cite "male-dominated networks, intimidation, and harassment" as detractors to women pursuing leadership positions. Developing women leaders, on the other hand, is a step in the right direction. Educating women on leadership practices and challenges and providing viable support will help to ameliorate some of the challenges that are prohibitive to their interest and pursuit of leadership positions.

Recruitment efforts for women are not as robust as the efforts to attain and retain their male counterparts. Additionally, the perception of female leaders by both males and females overall is that women are less competent, and in male-dominated leadership cultures, fewer women at the top indicate less support for those aspiring to those positions. We asked women in a recent survey if they were given the same opportunities for a raise or promotion and development as their male counterparts. Nineteen percent stated yes, while 81 percent stated no.

Sexual harassment is also a deterring factor. Perception and reality both serve to dissuade women; they play out a less than desirable scenario mentally and then decide not to pursue these positions. An uphill battle is what they expect, and some choose to go with the flow rather than muddy the waters. Women (56 percent) reported in a recent survey we conducted that they would be hesitant to report harassment for fear of retaliation. Men, on the other hand, may view a woman's presence in leadership as a threat, and employers view women, because of childbirth and child-rearing, as being less productive and costlier to the company.

Non-inclusive architectural, emotional, and mental design in "workplaces" does not consider the collective contributions of diverse mindsets. Women want to be observed for their capabilities, especially in fields that have been historically associated with men. Shifting mindsets goes beyond inclusive design, which may backfire (either conceptually or actually) for these women. Inclusive design has to, therefore, be seamless and unobtrusive. Additionally, there is non-inclusive succession planning where leaders in the C-suite usually look for more of the same and do not exploit what diversity (knowledge, experience, innovation, insight) brings to the table.

We surveyed women in the workplace, and 81 percent reported that they were not given the same opportunities for raises, promotions, or development as their male counterparts. Despite research evidence to the contrary, men still hold most leadership positions. In the areas of decision-making, sociologists cite women as being conditioned to be more empathetic, consistent, and sensitive to others' perspectives in decision-making. Why, then, do men hold most of the leadership positions? Cultural standards, gender socialization, as well as perception play vital roles in how women are treated in the workplace and subsequently frame their ascendancy through the leadership ranks. Since the primary responsibility of the household usually falls on the women, men, by default, can focus more on their careers, promotional opportunities, and career development.

Gender schema theory originates in the home and can transcend to the workplace, affecting women in limiting their perspectives about gender roles and subsequently defaulting leadership roles to the male to fulfill. Some women may feel that taking on the role of a CEO means they may have to project male characteristics rather than simply being themselves. We asked women leaders if they adopted a stronger personality when interacting with their male counterparts; 50 percent said no, while 25 percent responded that it depended on their role, and the remaining 25 percent did it to avoid intimidation. It does make a difference that men hold the lion's share of the leadership positions since research consistently identifies desirable leadership traits as more prevalent in women than in men. In that case, the more qualified person should lead regardless of gender.

Benefits of Women Leadership

Benefits of women's leadership abound, especially in the areas of economics, politics, government, healthcare, education, arts, athletics, and religion. Since women possess strong problem-solving skills, they are better communicators and negotiators. Conflict resolution is a top trait for leaders; women in these positions are more adept at facilitating beneficial outcomes that are well thought out and advantageous to the organization.

Science, Technology, Engineering, Mathematics (STEM) careers and specifically technological careers have historically been underrepresented by females, most notably in leadership positions. As a female leader in a technology space, there is still underrepresentation, especially for women, and in particular, women of color. To be disruptive in these spaces, you have to possess the acumen for both technology and leadership. Educating male counterparts is a necessity; the more credible you are, the more confident you are, and the more disruptive you can be. Fortunately, the world is currently disruption tolerant.

Women in leadership positions motivate and inspire other women as well as young girls. They also reeducate males on the potential that women possess and project their usefulness to the workforce. A strong system of women-to-women mentorship would benefit women everywhere. Since the media is largely responsible for the perception of women's roles and their usefulness, more women at the helm would present a more balanced view of all types of women functioning in various roles.

Women in leadership positions possess the agency to yield "more transformational and contingent reward behaviors and fewer management-by-exception and Laissez-Faire behaviors." Additionally, women considering promotion to CEO are well-advised to employ inspirational motivation for their male followers and individualized consideration for the females. Women possessing a blend of both types of leadership motivational skills are more likely to ascend to the ranks of top leadership in a company.

As better decision-makers, women are naturally effective in leadership positions. Female leaders also possess participative, charismatic, value-based, humane-oriented, and team-oriented skills that are viewed as ideal by followers. This model of leadership traits contradicts one that is solely based on goal-oriented outcomes, which is more associated with male leaders.

Relationship building forms the basis from which women lead, and Authentic Transformational Leadership operates from the standpoint of the leader caring about the follower's well-being. Women would then be more effective as Authentic Transformational leaders than men, and their presence in leadership roles in that vein is viewed as less threatening by males who are more adept at other types of leadership. Women's role in leadership is important enough not only to other women but to society at large, and it warrants further research, application, legislation, education, and support.

I was recently interviewed by an end-to-end recruiting HR company about what it takes to attract, retain, and promote qualified women in the workspace. Here is an excerpt of my advice to them.

Stop doing the following:
- Stop normalizing male-specific characteristics as the only acceptable professional behavior.
- Stop instilling stereotypical work tasks on women.
- Stop imposing the belief that pregnancy or marriage is detrimental to professional leadership capacity in contrast to views toward males with similar responsibilities.
- Stop pitting women against women....allow spaces for all women to thrive.
- Once women have "arrived," stop inflicting imposter syndrome on them.

Keep doing the following:
- Keep creating spaces for women to feel accepted, supported, and respected since women tend to have more off-the-job responsibilities.
- Keep creating on-site childcare.
- Keep and extend maternity benefits.
- Keep operationalizing the Diversity, Equity, Inclusion, Accessibility (DEIA) agenda.
- Keep conducting regular performance reviews and pulse points.

Start doing the following:
- Start asking women for guidance in creating requirements for career development and advancement.
- Start creating a more positive view of familial responsibilities.
- Start parental leave before delivery.
- Start creating more inclusive healthcare benefits that are cognizant of the issues that face women.
- Start creating a better gender balance to encourage women to be more expressive and participative.

Inclusive Workplace/Workspace Design for Women

Studies show that women are less likely to return to the traditional office than men are. Making a female-friendly inclusive design is not only better for women but also for all. Inclusive design can have a cascading effect and have intersectional influences on other groups of individuals with respect to race, gender, and age, who have been personally and socially impacted by exclusive design. Females are often the primary caregivers of both younger and older individuals and are functioning in multiple roles, so amplifying their voices in ways that support them is key. In addition to DEIA practices that support women, the following are some key female-friendly design element considerations for the workplace:

- More windows, light, glass doors (offices), plants
- Natural woods and stones in architecture
- Allow customization of individual workspaces
- Daycare on-site enclosed in glass, with cameras
    - Capable women (and men) who have young children can observe their children from their desks or from nearby
    - More time is spent working versus deciding on off-site daycare, pick up, and drop off
- Personal items in bathrooms
- Mobile desks (sit/stand)
- Happy days (massage, facial, meditation, etc.)
- Name office assets (ex: conference rooms) after discoveries/inventions/breakthroughs by women
- Proximity to restrooms and multiple restrooms
- Ambient environment (adjustable lighting, heating, etc.)
- Quiet zones
- Seasonal Affective Disorder (SAD) lighting; SAD affects more women than men

Female-friendly inclusive design, however, may unwittingly put women in the unwanted spotlight. In terms of leadership, companies should consider not only the effects of female-friendly design on the target group but also the impact on the ones that are not targeted to not shift into the exclusive design.

Supporting Female Disruptors

"Be yourself; everyone else is taken." Although mentors are helpful, it is important to emulate and not duplicate them. In my first management position (right after college), I did not understand how to manage, so I mirrored what I saw other managers do. I remember connecting to one of my reports who was noticeably upset by the style I expressed. I immediately knew not to practice that style of management.

Female disruptors are risk-takers who drive innovation. Disruptions are always good; mistakes can be parlayed into opportunities. Being a disruptor sometimes means breaking away from the pack and doing things differently. Quiet disruption should not be overlooked; neither is disrupting the disruption. Negative disruption, however, needs to be disrupted and quickly.

I received some great advice from a male leader during my tenure in the Armed Forces. I was up for a promotion and sought his guidance. I am sure he said many great things, but I remember him saying to wear a skirt. I never forgot that as I witnessed women trying to fit in traditionally male spaces by mimicking them in clothing and other aspects. Of course, I do wear pants in and out of male spaces; however, the takeaway for me was that femininity is empowering, and forsaking that power to adopt a pseudo-male persona to be accepted is not only tragic to the woman doing so but to the other women who they are paving the path for.

The formal education delivery industry has been disrupted in very positive ways. Learner demand has driven suppliers to be diverse in scope, offering, pricing, and structure. Further, formal education has been redefined and is more agile and responsive to market needs. Women's needs are at the forefront of this. With the advent of the Metaverse, we will witness another disruption in education delivery as prototyping, simulation, and immersive learning takes front and center before traditional education.

Social media has provided the platform to disrupt industry standards about women's beauty standards, which like the Metaverse, puts the power in the hands of the majority and not just a few key players. These new beauty standards have created inclusive communities and extended the definition of beauty. However, this movement has seemingly regressed to the norm and has now created a standard where there is a prototypical projection of what beauty is. This is especially harmful to young girls who, instead of (or sometimes, despite) strong role models, see social media as defining crucial aspects of their lives.

"He's just not that into you!" I remember how relieved I felt after hearing one of the male characters on a popular movie offer unsolicited advice to a group of women who were (pseudo) psychoanalyzing the reason why one of them was ghosted. That advice has helped me tremendously in dealing with people. It is important that, as women, we get the male's perspective about their counterparts and understand what they prioritize while doing our best to prioritize ourselves as well.

DR. PATRICIA ANDERSON

Reflective Discourse

1. How can women leaders create opportunities and resources to help other women pursue leadership roles?
2. How can women embrace their femininity and be effective leaders as well?
3. Looking ahead, where do you see women leaders playing the most significant role?

CHAPTER 12

Leadership Playbook for the Future

*Move from Transactional Leadership
to Authentic Transformational Leadership.*

The future will be interesting. Technological advances will influence how we work and live. It is an exciting time to see what options we have for improving our quality of life in the Fourth Industrial Revolution (4IR) and World Wide Web 3.0 (WWW3). The seamless integration of Artificial Intelligence (AI), IoT, genetic engineering, quantum computing, robotics, etc., presents many opportunities for learning and interacting differently and more effectively.

Alongside the 4IR/WWW3 is The Rise of the Human movement. These themes may seem diametrically opposed; however, there are opportunities to occupy the same space. Commensurate with technological pursuits, stakeholders are pushing the Leadership as a Service (LaaS) model. They are requiring leaders to exhibit intentional behavior rooted in honesty, transparency, and ethics. Ultimately, the human experience (internal and external stakeholders) will provide the single source of truth that drives the application of technology to organizational leadership activities.

In the future, normalized disruption will drive the need to move through the knowledge domains (known knowns, known unknowns, unknown knowns, unknown unknowns) more strategically. We know less than we don't know. This will necessitate the adoption of evergreen leadership. Future-proofed leadership looks like Authentic Transformational Leadership.

In my research and experience, it is the only sustainable leadership style that is pandemic, crisis, and disruption-proof. It is a form of deep leadership that engages stakeholders on multiple levels, including mentally, emotionally, and intellectually. ATLs walk the talk and are learning leaders. ATLs also realize that knowledge is provisional, and they are adaptable, open to input, and accountable.

The Future of Work

We are currently experiencing a buyers' market; employees have the power. Employers must shift to employees' demand for more meaningful experiences at work. The talent landscape has changed from the status quo, and employees are determining how they want to work. Talent mapping is indicated as organizations strive to be the right fit for prospective talent.

The workplace has been redefined as the workspace (from a place to a state). When asked how they coped with pivoting from familial to work responsibilities in this space, 65 percent of leaders had a schedule in place, while 31 percent prioritized familial obligations. Employers (and employees) have to adjust to this ubiquitous "workspace," and augmented reality will play a part in how teams collaborate at work. The convergence of people and things—IoT—will revolutionize how we work, learn, and collaborate. It also has implications on the talent lifecycle (attraction, retention, growth).

Here are some notes from the future:

- *Transparent, ethical, accessible leaders.* Drop the organizational personae and the suit and engage with your stakeholders at the human level.
- *Inclusive talent landscape*—explore all opportunities for diverse talent, hire up, upskill, and reskill. Explore and reduce geographic and other imposed boundaries.
- *Redefine the workspace.* Pivot from a (physical) place to a state (of mind). Assess where/when/how talent is more productive and adjust accordingly. This is an iterative process, as they may elect to work from both at home and on-prem, so be flexible.
- *Move from Transactional to Authentic Transformational Leadership.* The Transactional approach to work has been "produce and get paid." Employees are looking for different types of engagement. Lean into Authentic Transformational Leadership (inspirational motivation, idealized influence, individualized consideration, and intellectual stimulation). In short, inspire, motivate, model, stretch your EQ muscle, and promote critical thinking.

- *The Internet of Things.* The convergence available in WWW3 presents yet another digital disruption. Consider how this will impact the talent lifecycle and get ahead of the disruption by adopting incremental strategies.
- *The gig economy* will continue to thrive as employees seek both multiple streams of income and meaningful engagement. Commercial spaces are increasing their technological assets, so there are connection points for computers, tablets, etc. Such ubiquity requires flexibility in how people work.

Social engines such as advocacy, boycotting, and voting are instrumental in transforming the work culture. Let's be clear; we want transformation instead of change (which is binary). The internal customers of the workforce are pumping out products and delivering services to the external customers. An alignment of both types of key strategic stakeholders will influence decision-makers to move the needle toward a better culture.

Here are a few tips on how leaders can support their employees better:

- Drop the corporate personae; employees want to connect to the real you.
- Incentivize work from home; pivot savings from on-site engagement to support the home/work environment.
- Provide at-home technical support.
- Employees' mental health is a critical success factor for high engagement at work. Prioritize this above all else.

In light of The Great Resignation, company leaders are exploring the best approach to spin up flexible working conditions, including a hybrid workplace. Here are some considerations to help prioritize employees' mental and physical health upon their return to the workplace:

- *Use a reservation system.* An efficient first come/first served system ensures that employees maximize their on-prem time and offers predictive analytics to help companies plan for future collaboration. This also helps organizations reduce their carbon footprint.
- *Conduct a survey.* Understand what motivates employees to return to work. More specifically, ask why they would return to work. Understanding the WIIFM motivator will inform the workplace/workspace/design approach. Thoughtfully shift from office-centric design to human-centric design.
- *Prototype solutions.* Studies show that stakeholders that are involved in decision-making are more likely to adopt the proposed archetype. Use employee feedback to test the new work environment. Phase in the return-to-work solution by offering hybrid work as an entry point.
- *Rebrand mission/vision/values.* Employees will sign on to the organization's goals if they understand the vision. In some cases, a new or improved vision that highlights social responsibility is required.
- *Practice ATL.* Authentic Transformational leaders (ATLs) are innovative, collaborative, and adaptable. Their keen

insight into individualized consideration and intellectual stimulation enables them to engage resistant employees and influence them to embrace the transformation to on-prem work.
- *Incentivize.* Offer gas cards, expense credit cards, free parking, etc. These costs are offset by the cost savings of employees working remotely. Upskill/reskill/coach employees. The buy-in is that on-prem employees will possess a specific set of skills not acquired by working remotely.

We surveyed leaders to ask how they were handling The Great Resignation. The responses were varied: 38 percent were focusing on retaining their top talent, and 38 percent were conducting qualitative exit interviews. "Leavers weren't happy anyway," reported 19 percent of them, while 6 percent of leaders stated that they needed help in the endeavor.

Mental Well-Being

Leaders that we surveyed (63 percent) said that they were honest with their mental health concerns and actively created safe zones; 25 percent had a community of support, while 13 percent stated that others could not relate to their concerns. We also asked leaders about what measures they use to ensure their employees' well-being. The majority of leaders (86 percent) responded that they had built close connections with employees to enable them to open up about their well-being; the rest (14 percent) viewed sick days as a measurement of mental well-being.

Employees (including leaders) not functioning at optimum mental health pose risks to the operations of the organization. Your organization may not be as attractive to exceptional talent who are increasingly interested in the organization's focus on their internal customers' well-being. Short-term and long-term ROI will decrease when the internal customers are not mentally equipped to support the external customers.

During the pandemic and subsequent disruptions, there was an exposure to the inadequacies of organizations in supporting their employees' mental well-being. The exposure to these inadequacies was a good checkpoint for everyone. Employers are responsible for the overall health of their employees while at work. Employees are increasingly expressing concerns in the interview process as they represent crucial decision points. Employers can use effective practices as a selling point to prospective employees; however, they have to ensure that they are maintaining those standards and not just riding the wave from the pandemic era. The pandemic pivot is temporary and not sustaining. Real transformation has to occur.

Think sustainability; there most certainly will be another disruption; perhaps the next one will be "going dark," i.e., no Internet access. The most recent disruptions exposed gaps in operational efficiencies, denoting an optimal time to revisit the organization's mission/vision. Staying mindful of your stakeholders is especially crucial during disruptive times because of the intricate transition from the current state to future states. This transformation requires consistent stakeholder engagement to sustain an awareness of their mental and emotional disposition.

Remote Leadership

Employees are increasingly more prescriptive about the work they perform, and employers are adapting to meet their demands. The 4IR will provide opportunities to close those gaps as more jobs are being created. Employers should use other metrics to measure the gaps; for example, "jobs" may define traditional structures (nine to five, W-2, etc.) and exclude other structures such as the gig structure.

Many employees struggle with working remotely as working on-prem has been the status quo; they miss the social aspects of being on-prem and are challenged in establishing virtual connections. Other employees are used to being "managed." Self-management also poses challenges to them in terms of meeting deadlines, prioritization, and communicating virtually. Immersion in the home/work environment prescribes a wider lens on multiple priorities in that workspace. Childcare, elderly care, and intrusions, in addition to work responsibilities, occupy the same space. Employees subsequently have to modify their home/workspaces to be efficient and productive.

Employers also face challenges in transforming from managing physically to managing remotely. PTLs accustomed to leading in siloed organizational structures will find this transformation challenging. Here is where Transactional and Laissez-Faire Leadership can be applied. Recall that ATLs engage stakeholders in problem-solving, critical thinking, innovation, and collaboration. These activities are not limited to physical spaces solely. The trust and autonomy that you place in your stakeholders will bear out virtually as well.

Here are some aspects of virtual leadership to consider:

- Instead of visually confirming work is being done, trust that remote employees are being productive. Studies show that they are.
- Validate your trust by using metrics that track deliverables and outcomes.
- Engagement will be an issue, as will the talent landscape, which has expanded to be more diverse. Hire up; talent may not check all of the responsibilities boxes, but they possess the capacity to learn and adapt.
- Employees are increasingly looking to the HR Department to assist them with mental health, financial health, physical health, direction, and support. Your Human Capital Management assets have to scale up to support those needs. If you are a small to medium-sized business, consider economic solutions such as fractional HR services.
- Incrementally adopt a remote strategy. Start with volunteers of non-critical business requirements and processes, then scale your operation to be led virtually.
- Adopt a 360-degree evaluation of leaders by employees so that both groups of stakeholders share responsibilities for a successful outcome.

Organizations that missed the first wave of digital disruption are now being forced to come on board. They now view digital transformation as a necessary strategic pursuit. Some companies are prioritizing their Human Capital Management

(HCM) transformation to enable their internal customers to support their external customers fully.

Future-proofing your leadership begins with Authentic Transformational Leadership practices. Organizations headed by ATLs experience continuous growth and transition. Recall that one of the differentiators between change and transformation is that change looks to the past and the present, while transformation looks toward the future and all of its possibilities. ATL is focused on long-term benefits and progressively moves toward exponentially better future states and outcomes.

Human Capital Management

Transformational leader Richard Branson is a status quo disrupter. Businesses in the early nineties, at the cusp of unleashing the power of technology, were justifiably hyper-focused on external customer service. Branson surmised then that an organization's employees, not their customers, came first. He reasoned that employees were drivers of customer success, and helping employees to help customers made business sense.

Today's world of unleashed technological prowess appears to be positively correlated with increased attrition, knowledge leak/transfer, under-skilled and overworked employees, and escalating onboarding time and costs, all threatening to undermine the gains companies made by putting customers first. A recent Employee Engagement Report has described "the end of employee loyalty." Correspondingly, one hundred percent of leaders we surveyed said they do focus on their internal customers. Given the zeitgeist of The Great Resignation and The Great Awakening, is it time to revisit Branson's rationale?

The Unleash World Conference is the standard for HR and recruitment leaders and is the platform where questions meet capabilities. The platform targeted Authentic Transformational leaders who were intentional in pursuing an internal customer service strategy. From my purview, exhibitors positioned smarter tools as the conduit by which talent recruitment, retention, and management would transpire. Presenters described the value propositions of engaged employees, speed to value talent development, strategic collaboration, and unleashed creativity and innovation.

The word "unleash" implies an awakening, a release of something that has been withheld, suppressed, or underutilized. Further, what emerges is agile, focused, and needed. It may not be a coincidence that the City of Light hosted this event; illuminating and illuminated thought leaders shared their views of what they believe will unleash the restrained potential of a business workforce that leverages the power of human capital in ways that add value to the business's internal and external environments.

My objective in attending this conference was to learn how these technologies would help to foster a people-powered future. Vendors showcased performance management systems that effortlessly mine and filter data via digital dashboards. These dashboards empowered non-technical, decision-making users to quickly master insightful diagnostic-driven analytical capabilities. Preconfigured dashboards displayed key metrics from deep analytics to foster agile leadership practices. This type of predictive analytics can shorten the time to market for not only goods and services but also employee onboarding and development.

Other products were aimed at optimizing talent recruitment, onboarding, and regulated learning. Employee wellness (health, financial, assistance) and talent engagement coexisted in integrated software platforms. These tools provide the transparent framework from which performance-fueled conversations, engagement, and learning evolve. HR technology alone does not drive the people's experience; culture plays a role, as does the environment.

I attended an interactive panel discussion where leaders debated employee experience versus employee engagement. Panelists agreed that the relationship between HR and other software systems in the organization would be the driving force that defined the employee experience. Some leaders touted machine language and artificial intelligence as spearheading the future of HCM software. Self-learning bots can integrate with the system's communications network to deliver real-time solutions to employees. These microservices allow users to connect with their organization, customers, and teams, ensure policy conformance, transform arcane processes, reduce churn, and increase the time for decision-making.

The Unleash World Conference is a space that exhibits the groundwork for the innovative and collaborative future that Authentic Transformational HR leaders envision. According to Forbes.com, we are only beginning to capitalize on the full capabilities of cloud infrastructure. The future is cloudy for Transformational leaders seeking to unleash the capabilities of their employees. By harnessing the scalability and flexibility of the cloud and other emergent technologies, organizations can participate in the larger context of the cloud revolution.

The future is also sustainably focused and collaborative. Human capital investment calls for a unified strategy between technology and Transformational leaders. The call to action for a people-powered future entails a transformation of organizational culture, communications, and processes and is what Richard Branson envisioned in the nineties. Moving at the speed of business needs more than technology; it demands Authentic Transformational leaders.

Organizational Storytelling

One hundred percent of leaders we surveyed stated that they had elevated their organizational storytelling. Authentic Transformational leaders are innovative storytellers. They know that leadership tools emerge from organizational history. The prospective for a successful organizational future requires positioning employee satisfaction alongside the company's key focus—their customers. Leaders should enable employees to do business through carefully engineered intuitive tools that untether them from tasks that are less purposeful to focus on solving key business issues.

Deepened stakeholder engagement means better organizational stories. Adopting the dual objectives of optimizing customer and employee experience is not only tenable, but it is also critical to KPI-driven organizational growth. ATLs are learning leaders who identify a need for change, craft the mechanisms to effect said change, and motivate and galvanize their workforce to simultaneously not only change processes and systems and themselves. Failing systems require that HR's traditional role with employees expand to occupy a psychological space in the organization.

This role expansion is a consequence of transpiring events outside of the organization that affects employees. Individuals are requiring psychological safety from HR leaders and a redirection to attend to the whole person—not only what they do but who they are. The focus should shift from not only profit drivers of their organizations but also to workers, suppliers, and the community. Repurposing and refreshing commitment to these individuals will, in turn, restore their commitment to the organization.

ATLs exercise their emotional quotient when they provide individualized consideration to their talent, which, in turn, affects how they relate to the organization's internal and external environments. ATLs are also collaborative. They focus on their core competencies and collaborate with organizations that also focus on their core competencies; this effectively drives transformative cultures.

ATLs are compelling visionaries whose expert storytelling breeds collaboration. Employees, customers, and competitors all engage in digital storytelling, which, when analyzed by digital listening dashboards, informs the organization of the "word on the streets." The propagation of data to knowledge to real-time actionable initiatives helps organizations to become more responsive.

ATLs are culturally astute. Cultural relativity explains fluctuations in employees' perception of and behavior in the organization. Areas of opportunities occur where messages between diverse cultures are lost in translation. Culture maps promote the use of cultural scales depicting dimensions such as communications, conflict, and feedback. A culture map identifies areas of similarities where communication is more effective.

Streamlined communications bolster work effort and results. The complexity of a global workplace necessitates a deep dive into understanding the contextual interaction of various countries and cultures. Culture mapping positions global leaders to exploit proximity-based synergies while strengthening cross-cultural collaboration and removing geographically imposed boundaries.

ATLs possess an environmentally responsible worldview. Leaders can disrupt the digital disruption by providing opportunities for employees to connect with a world that may not be digitally accessible. Environmental stewardship starts with education. Understanding the supply chain of common goods and services enables employee consumers to make sustainable choices. The message is clear; organizational leaders hold the responsibility of providing opportunities for their employees to engage with the external environment in meaningful ways.

Solidifying the organization's story requires a critical assessment that begins by identifying past contributors to the story and by assessing the current perception—usually pain points. The resultant areas of focus may require a business model adjustment. Telling the organization's whole story involves every stakeholder, especially talent.

Digital Transformation

My first job out of college was working with country clubs and their virtual markets by supporting their digital transformation. At a particular country club, there was an elderly woman who cried tears when told that her work would be automated. After patiently working with her to reinforce that her sustained value and contributions (WIIFM) to the club would not cease and exploring the ease with which she would be able to work, she was won over. First came the smiles, then she became the strongest advocate for the transformation.

Some leaders focus on the technology side of digital transformation and leave out the more significant aspect—the people side. Collective individual transformation is what drives organizational transformation. The success of the transformation is contingent on the adoption and usage of the technology.

I am currently enabling company leaders to perform agile digital transformation by employing ATL-specific principles that promote collaboration and buy-in, lower resistance, and result in higher levels of stakeholder adoption, engagement, and utility, which in turn increases ROI. The combination of ATL behavior and digital-driven insights is disruptive in that it appears to be mutually exclusive; however, each is powered by the other.

I am excited to work in this space as the extensive research I have performed on Transformational Leadership comes to bear in the successful implementation of these projects. There is a learning curve for both leaders and stakeholders, and the opportunity to grow is interminable. Especially in digital transformation, the most challenging aspect of the undertaking is not the technology; rather, it is the mindsets of individuals who will be the most impacted by the transformation.

Digital transformation is both a disruptor and a growth fuel. Digital transformation should be positioned as continual improvement and not a one-off activity. ATLs actively engage their internal customers in collaboration, critical thinking, and innovation, all designed to keep moving the needle forward. Digital transformation is a good fit for companies experiencing slow growth or no growth, those who want to enable technology-driven solutions, and those who want opportunities to collaborate digitally, just to name a few.

I worked with a global organization to transform its BAM operations online. The transformation would make their products and services available to a larger, previously underserved market, which in turn would drive revenue and ROI. The transformation enabled twenty-four-seven operations, which allowed for self-service and freed up internal customers from repetitive and mundane tasks to engage in more meaningful activities. There was a significant negative correlation between costs and revenue, which allowed the organizations to offer more services. The transformation was successful and imperative to recently imposed social distancing, which would be problematic in the BAM environment.

Deploying an OCM strategy is imperative for successful digital transformation and adoption. Additionally, the change management methodology should be tethered to the project's implementation cycle for maximum effect. Leaders should focus on the people side of the transformation by employing ATL core practices:

- *Inspirational motivation.* Tell a compelling story about what the transformation means to each individual first and the organization as a whole. Many leaders are in crisis mode, which requires them to prescribe a sustaining vision to support their stakeholders.
- *Idealized influence.* Leaders who model adoption behavior are engaged, visible, and active before, during, and after the transformation. This behavior sends key messages to stakeholders, especially resistors. Walk the talk.
- *Individualized consideration.* Communicate WIIFM buy-in to affected stakeholders. This is instrumental to adoption.
- *Intellectual stimulation.* Engage stakeholders early and often in the transformation endeavor. Get their buy-in. Allow them to make decisions. Engaged stakeholders are less likely to be resistant to transformation.
- *Be a learning leader.* You know less than you don't know.
- In a recent survey, 75 percent of respondents indicated that digital transformation had improved their leadership in and outside of the workplace.

Supply Chains of the Future

Disruptions are not only necessary,
but they are also organizational health indicators.

The cascading impact of the supply chain breakdown witnessed in the past few years not only shattered Just In Time

(JIT) practices but also catapulted leaders into an involuntary boot camp to refocus their efforts from optimizing costs to (re)constructing and (re)imagining supply chains that are impervious to choke points. Researching backup chains are the strategy for 50 percent of the leaders we surveyed, while 50 percent stated that they were building new collaborations.

Disruptors to the supply chains included the lockdown of manufacturing and transporting raw and finished goods. Other disruptive forces, including The Great Resignation, The Rise of The Human, and The Great Rethink, quickly ensued. Stakeholders (employees, clients, customers) proceeded to evaluate organizations on social issues that included performance, compensation, safety, and social responsibility.

Some stakeholders moved on from the organizations, resulting in a lack of personnel to move goods from shipping ports to warehouses. The resulting labor shortage unearthed another weak link in the chain. Subsequently, a simultaneous interruption in the supply and demand of goods and services, as well as decreased labor, further elevated the disruption.

Here are focus areas for leaders wanting to mitigate the effects of disruption:

- Optimize supply chain with AI, robotics, digital twins, machine learning, drones, driverless vehicles, 3D printing, etc.
- Smooth out demand to make demand levels more predictable.

- Consider insourcing to shorten the supply chain and re-shore and localize suppliers.
- Make supply chains disruption agnostic, exploit digital tools that represent an optimal mix of human and machine capabilities to prevail over current and future disruptions.

Leaders must be prescriptive and reactive during this time. The breakdown of supply chains witnessed during the pandemic provides transformational opportunities for organizations. The complexities of supply chains dictate a transformative effort to collaborate with other leaders, governments, banks, investors, Third-Party Logistics (3PLs), health and regulatory agencies, suppliers (distribution and transfer), and their respective suppliers.

This delicate ecosystem must be reinforced with tools that integrate humans and technology in ways that are adaptive and corrective. The playbook for ATLs upholds transformational opportunities rather than short-term pivots to countermeasure disruption. The results are lean, efficient, optimized, sustainable, and agile supply chains. Here's how:

- Disrupt the disruption, unchain the linear supply chain, and use dynamic alignment that yields a circular and potent supply chain.
- Leverage Business Intelligence (BI) and other analytics to identify opportunities to drive efficient operations.
- Maintain supply chain transparency—be clear and communicative about pricing models, inflation, exchange rates, etc.

- Establish and maintain cash liquidity to be able to pivot as needed.
- Reshape a business strategy that withstands disruption.
- Establish anticipatory and forensic supply chains to identify risks using scenarios.
- Practice ambidextrous leadership.
- Learn from pandemic-related demand for perishable goods:
  - The shift to home offices decreased demand for social products/services.
  - The resulting run on certain products and services created short-term supply/demand issues.
  - Reduce the risk of multiple suppliers—review over-engineered products (employ Occam's razor—simple is better). Scale accordingly.
  - Assess external factors/threats—regulations, economic, unknown unknowns.
  - Use blockchain and IoT technology to authenticate, trace, and provide transparency of transactions.
  - Institute plans B, C, D; supplier diversity decreases risk and balances cost and reliability.

Disruption has taught us that leaders must optimize their supply chain strategy. The COVID-19 pandemic put the digital disruption on fast-forward. It compressed decision-making and positioned ATLs as the enablers of successful transition from disruption to transformation. ATLs knew that they knew less than they didn't know; COVID-19 leaders operated with a foreseeable and limited scope of disruption to their supply chains.

Supply chain resilience is steered by both a prescriptive and a reactive approach that works in tandem (known knowns and unknown unknowns). Leaders must drive digital transformation that aligns executive strategy with supply chain capabilities. Optimize supply chain strategy by adopting the following:

- Leverage digital supply chains as a company capability and a competitive advantage.
- Practice individualized consideration and intellectual stimulation with employees and suppliers to drive innovation.
- Consistently assess supplier performance.
- Optimize digital leadership.
- Provide supply chain executives with an empowering C-suite seat at the table.
- Employ HCM tools; employee stickiness decreased during the crisis. Upskill, reskill, and train. Use disruption as an opportunity to diversify and close skills gaps.
- Leverage ATL with OCM to galvanize supply chain response to disruption.

Disruptions are not only necessary, but they are also organizational health indicators. Although the order of magnitude is disruption-dependent, it remains that the organization's scalability and agility are at risk. The reality is that capable Authentic Transformational leaders transcend disruptions; ATLs are innovative, collaborative, empowering, adaptable, and learners. They have had over a year and a half of understanding a global disruption. They are not only positioned to thrive during disruptions, but they are also built for it.

Metaverse-ity for Leaders

Virtual Reality (VR), Augmented Reality (AR), digital twins, Artificial Intelligence (AI), virtual skins, avatars, holograms, Web3.0/3DWeb, IoT, cryptocurrency, Non-Fungible Tokens (NFTs), blockchain technology, digital singularity, virtual fashion, and digital real estate (Decentraland) comprise the language of businesses operating in the Metaverse. The time and space continuum is enhanced in this world of collaboration, affecting how we live, learn, and work. If you're like me, working on multiple monitors (six at last count), digitizing the desktop means you have access to digital monitors without cluttering your desk. Unpacking the "things" of the Internet of Things is on the minds of innovative leaders as they address what the full expression of a Metaverse existence entails.

The Metaverse is here and represents increasingly blurred lines between the physical and virtual worlds. Leadership oversight on strategizing how to bring their products and services from outside in is required, as both positive and negative risks abound. Products and services will have to be converted to experiences and lifestyles and redesigned in 3D format. New jobs are being created around creating, building, and securing assets in the Metaverse. How should leaders prepare for the next phase? The evergreen aspects of Authentic Transformational Leadership are articulated in this endeavor as digital leadership becomes de rigueur.

Recently, the physical world has become extremely worrisome. A global pandemic, social injustice, political unrest, wars, mental wellness, The Rise of the Human, and The Great Resignation coupled with the Great C-suite Purge, are all progenitors of The Great Escape. The Metaverse represents the inflection point for untethered human interaction with their environment and the opportunity to create virtual worlds from the ground up. On one hand, the Metaverse seems like it will diminish the human experience; on the other hand, it is an extension of our capabilities; there will be more tools in our tool kit. One thing is certain: transformation is imperative.

Behaviors and practices that we want to stop, start, and keep doing in the physical world should be positioned as building blocks in virtual worlds. Existing barriers to entry into the physical world can be nonexistent in the Metaverse. By being inclusive about the technology that builds the Metaverse, we can at least have a diverse hand in what it should look and feel like. Inclusive design should be foundational. Can the Metaverse drive true equity and inclusion?

The stage is set for a seminal collaboration and an unprecedented opportunity to not recreate failures, exclusions, and inadequacies in a space where the runway is as limitless as the contributions from a diverse human race. Although the Metaverse is in flight, early adopters are gearing up for another digital disruption and poised to exploit proximity-based synergies. Decentralization is one of the objectives of the Metaverse; instead of content being prescribed by only a few digital mega players, this digital evolution entails equitable ownership of the virtual worlds. The open architecture of its design makes the Metaverse an active rather than a reactive pursuit.

Opportunities

The COVID-19 pandemic forced us to go inside, literally and figuratively. (Paradoxically, just when it was safe to go outside, it appears that the Metaverse is ushering us back inside.) What emerged from the pandemic was the need to identify a place to collaborate should we ever face another disruption that prevents human physical interaction. However, as we pivoted to a virtual workplace, it was clear that it was lacking some of the human elements that foster deeper connections.

The Metaverse represents a great escape from life (work, school, etc.). It overlays digital information on our physical worlds and is a space where we can put our best foot forward to a more ideal version of ourselves, which in turn can impact how we feel in real life. The fusion of both physical and virtual worlds leads to the realization that whoever and whatever we are in the real world can be intensified in the Metaverse. Customizing our identity will be commonplace partly because of the social pressures of acceptable appearances. However, we may start competing with our digital twins or conflating our real selves with our digital selves in a zero-sum game. Seeking a balance between virtual and real-world interaction is essential. Lessons learned from the physical world should form the basis of what not to bring to the interoperability of the Metaverse.

Photorealistic experiences that cancel the physical distance between individuals are the drivers for virtual interactions. In this barrierless community, there is a depth of communication that is lacking in virtual communication as it is today. Instead of a screen, you can go behind the screen and live out your communications fully, as opposed to just sharing pictures and other content. This immersive deep learning experience allows you to live and collaborate in shared spaces.

Although rapid-scale development in the Metaverse is not advised, leaders resisting the next evolution of the Metaverse are fighting the wrong battle. With The Great Resignation underway along with other disruptions, leaders are seeking ways to optimize their workplace. Human design thinking is an aspect of ATLs' individualized consideration that prioritizes human needs above all else. Effective business transformation begins with redefining a workplace into a workspace. An immersive experience extends to virtual boardrooms, conferences, and meeting spaces, transcending physical boundaries such as traveling, weather conditions, geographic barriers, and time zones. Physical interactions can become more limited as economic and wartime activities define and limit how products and services are delivered; immersive virtual communications will be heightened as a result.

Here is an opportunity to revisit the change versus transformation model. The foray into the Metaverse should not be a pivot or a change but rather a scaled, intentional, and organized approach that considers what is known and how it will add value to what is already valuable. Before gold rushing into the Metaverse, leaders should consider what facets of humanity will be impacted and how to transform aspects of the organization that will be positively enhanced with this level of immersion. A refactoring, rescoping, and/or a reset of strategic goals and pursuits may also be indicated.

Considerations

Our physical homes are an escape from the outside world; however, the virtual worlds offer no such respite. From cyberbullying, on the extreme side, to targeted, personalized content and advertising, these stressors affect humans in ways that may manifest long after their exposure to virtual experiences.

Historically, the virtual worlds have negatively impacted people, especially the youth. There has been an inverse relationship between screen time and their ability and desire to have meaningful social interactions in real life. Immersive exposure to the exponentially expanding digital landscape means that they are exposed to much more adverse risks than they would outside of this domain. Just as parents, caregivers, and responsible parties limit virtual content to young children, who are not mature enough to discern harmful content, so must leaders employ human moderation and countermeasures to understand how the Metaverse will impact employees and followers in the long run.

Preparing for the Metaverse looks like full engagement in HCM practices, especially mental wellness. For example, despite the need for human interaction, your internal customers may find it easier to interact and confide in certain issues in an anonymous VR or AR space. Correspondingly, this is an opportunity to attract more diverse talent and remove language barriers. In capitalizing on the full talent landscape, consider the use of different compensation models such as cryptocurrency or the use of NFTs for intellectual property.

An unfathomable divided consciousness (physical and virtual) is certain and will introduce new stressors. Humans, although escaping into the virtual worlds, will have challenges in managing their physical world as well. Your brain has to maintain two sets of consciousness, which is a strain on your mental capacities. At first, immersion is binary, either all in the virtual world or all in the physical world. Further immersion in the virtual worlds may render you unaware of your physical surroundings and ability to function in both. Remember reports of individuals so immersed in VR that they step into traffic, crash into trees, disregard traffic signals, etc.

For every negative impact of a virtual world, there should be a corresponding virtual or physical remediation. For example, use smart devices to engage in digital phenotyping that tracks behaviors that are indicators of anxiety and/or depression. These markers include sleep duration and movement, for example. Leaders should leverage these low-hanging fruit to help employees and followers assess and manage mental and physical wellness before subjecting them to increased virtual immersion.

Leaders and followers alike have an unparalleled possibility to shape a world that focuses on the benefits to human beings and the responsibilities that this entails. The current indictment on leaders' behaviors requires Authentic Transformational Leadership, which advocates mutual accountability between leader and follower. Environmental, Social, and Governance (ESG) criteria ensure that factors other than financial ones are considered in strategic endeavors. Accordingly, the physiological ROI of stakeholders should be prioritized alongside economic ROI to shareholders. Other components of adoption include costs and regulations, data privacy, security, content, and hacking. Deep fake manipulation, for example, is of warranted concern. This technology obscures the line between real and fake content, which renders one indistinguishable from the other. The dark web will become even darker with the elements that are available with the Metaverse.

Leveraging Lessons Learned

I am reminded of technology's impact on the dot-com boom and subsequent bust. During the early nineties, many companies duplicated existing business models from early adopters to launch their online presence instead of designing and cultivating their own. As a result, the dot-com bust served as an educational experience for leaders. Furniture stores, for example, needed an on-ground presence for customers to touch and feel and subsequently make their purchases online.

Other contributors to the bust included limited knowledge of social and cultural differences; for example, one size of Spanish does not fit all. Although the operability of the Internet was significantly improved with the introduction of Graphical User Interface (GUI) browsers, companies needed to implement their own business models to capitalize on the then-latest technology. Leaders should lean into their mission, vision, and core competencies before engaging with the Metaverse and develop compelling use cases for adoption; perceived value should precede investment. This approach, like the ATL tailwinds, has to be solid to take on the magnitude that is the Metaverse.

Recall how the unplanned global pandemic and crisis necessitated a digital disruption and shift to virtualization? In this case, the disruption is expected, purposeful, scalable, and calculated. ATLs should lean into the four pillars of their behavior: inspirational motivation, idealized influence, individualized consideration, and intellectual stimulation. This evolution into the future must be collaborative to be truly transformational.

Summary

The Metaverse is a status quo disruptor in ways that are value accelerators and value extenders. The future is both cloudy and green; digital fashion and virtual collaboration will reduce carbon footprint. The product life cycle extended via the Metaverse may experience a longer growth and maturity phase. On the other hand, the immersive aspects of the Metaverse can shorten the product life cycle. Countercultural behavior such as intentional physical interactions must accompany the immersion into Metaverse activities to maintain the human connection that is the basis of who we really are.

The Metaverse is in the innovators/early adopters phase of the product life cycle. ATLs can leverage learning, innovation, collaboration, and accountability to complement, not supplement, physical human interactions. These powerful transformational drivers will yield more responsive solutions. The Metaverse can help remove bias from gender, race, ethnicity, physical abilities, age, etc., especially in talent acquisition. Human interaction and emotional intelligence (ATLs excel at this) will play a major role in whatever the Metaverse becomes. Humans with social phobias may be more at home in a Metaverse interaction; still, there still needs to exist a one-to-one correlation between solving human issues with human solutions.

We asked leaders about collaboration and connecting via the Metaverse and most responded that it will be actually easier (75 percent). The rest (25 percent) responded that they were still vetting it out. Early adopters of the Metaverse have so far invested hundreds of billions of dollars in its infrastructure. Some of these investors who historically prescribed virtual content see the value of the consumer-driven model of collaborative content creation.

Failing forward and fast is not only necessary, but it is also a vital aspect of transformational activities. Leadership capability will be a focal point; we are currently experiencing multiple crises and disruptions, and the Metaverse may present a disruption that does not yet warrant full attention. Or does it?

The intellectual stimulation tenet of Authentic Transformational Leadership thrusts leaders at the forefront of the evolution of the Metaverse, and idea generation via collaboration and innovation is as pivotal as digital literacy and design thinking. This aspect of leadership is what ensures the organization, its purpose, products, and services, are evergreen. The Metaverse represents an untethering of the human imagination from physical boundaries to a full expression of user-generated data. From a SWOTT perspective, the Metaverse presents both opportunities and threats. The ROI in the Metaverse is largely unknown; however, for that very reason, the possibilities are endless. One thing is certain, a revisit to the knowledge domains is necessary; regarding the Metaverse, we certainly know less than we don't know.

SPECIAL FOCUS

Christian Leaders and the Metaverse

Meta-sheep and the Metaverse

The Metaverse promises omnipotence, omniscience, and omnipresence: all-powerful, all-knowing, and ubiquitous digital sheep.

Nothing epitomizes *You Know Less Than You Don't Know* as the Metaverse does. The future is cloudy; physical interactions will move to digital spaces inclusive or exclusive of spirituality. Unlike other leaders, Christian leaders are charged with watching over the souls of the sheep. How do they do so in both the physical and virtual worlds? Shows like *Upload* promise to extend your soul by creating an afterlife where you can interact with the physical world. The Metaverse is following suit.

For many, the Metaverse represents a modern-day virtual Tower of Babel, where the convergence of people and things represent a one-world, uni-language force that is powerful in inception and application. For others, it represents a component of the eschatological conditions of humankind. For others still, it looks a lot like humans placing themselves in the role of their Creator, especially in three key facets that the Metaverse allows for, *omnipotence, omniscience,* and *omnipresence*: all-powerful, all-knowing, and ubiquitous—digital sheep. How do leaders reconcile spirituality in these virtual worlds that eschew space/time/capabilities and barriers?

Versed in the Verse

The Metaverse is here; what does that mean for Christian leaders? It is imperative that you stake your claim in the Metaverse and decide what content and tools you will provide to engage, educate, guide, and be responsive. This is an opportunity to be on the right side of history. More than ever, people will need the choice of a spiritual landing place that offers spiritual health and rest to make sense of what is happening in and out of the Metaverse. Think about how you want to show up in the Metaverse and do so sooner than later.

Christian leaders and institutions must become early adopters of the Metaverse to offer choices to their followers. Late adoption is not an option, as a society already immersed on the Internet has cultivated an appetite for more interactivity in virtual worlds. Followers will certainly have more choices in mirror worlds where they can experience real-world events virtually. A corresponding countercultural presence must pervade to strike the needed balance between creating our worlds and our worlds creating us. Leaders must capitalize on social engineering such as confirmation biases; people believe what they want to believe. Hire up and skill up on digital technology; remember it is the user of the tool rather than the tool itself that brings about transformational outcomes.

The GOAT of ATL

The scripture on people *"running to and fro"* and knowledge increasing in the earth is evident. This running to and fro is an indicator of people looking for answers outside of themselves. Revisit and strengthen your core values and beliefs, as they are the springboard from which engagement with the Metaverse will occur. Remember *weltanschauung*...the framing and limiting aspects of your worldview will be at stake here. Known knowns are critical...knowing what you know is essential in making ethical choices. Just as the changing of the guard should be unobtrusive to core operations, so must entry into the Metaverse not be disruptive to core beliefs.

Christian leaders have an unprecedented opportunity to evangelize, convert physical meeting places into digital spaces, and skill up in the virtual worlds. Christian leaders should lead with love and forgiveness, as exemplified by the GOAT of Authentic Transformational Leadership, Jesus Christ. Through grace, Christians possess a supplementary system that transcends the knowledge domains...known knowns, known unknowns, unknown knowns, and unknown unknowns. The Metaverse represents the "creation groaning" in expectation of transformation. It is time for the sons and daughters of God to be revealed for all to see. Those who know their God shall do exploits.

Reflective Discourse

1. What aspects of remote leadership do you find the most challenging?
2. What activities are you engaging yourself and your stakeholders in to ensure mental wellness?
3. What aspects of your organization are vetted and Metaverse-ready?

Hello, ATLs!

I am grateful that you decided to embark on this transformational journey and that you found this leadership playbook helpful. I need your help "to transform the world one leader at a time"; there will be more pandemics, crises, and disruptions, so stay true to the evergreen ATL precepts and bring other leaders along by flexing your inspirational motivation and idealized influence. Continue to collaborate with stakeholders using intellectual stimulation and individualized consideration to expand your knowledge and drive innovation.

Read, share, lead discussion groups, and have reflective discourses on the topics presented.

Please let me know what impacted your transformation the most.

DrP@ATL.Team

DrPatriciaAnderson.com

APPENDIX A

Conversations at the Top

In this section, leaders share their unique perspectives on leadership during and after crisis and disruption, their takeaways, lessons learned, and how they safeguard against future disruptions.

DR. PATRICIA ANDERSON

Howard Anderson | Chief Information Officer

I sat down with Howard to discuss his leadership before, during, and after the COVID-19 and ensuing crises of 2020/2021. Topics include strategic growth, digital disruption, manufacturing the COVID-19 vaccine, virtual leadership, expanding the talent landscape, mental wellness, and The Great Resignation. Here is an excerpt from our interview.

Let's go back to a couple of years before COVID—BC—and after COVID—AC. In terms of your experience, what was it like for you as a leader? Talk us through it. Your experience right before and then during the crisis. What did you put in place? What questions were you asked?

So I work for a biotech company, and we have a niche product in a set of services that we offer. Our focus was moving the company from an initially half-a-billion-dollar company to a billion-dollar company, and we're looking at doing that through the development of a portfolio of products that we offer in that niche space of public health threats. There's a lot of work in terms of vaccines and therapeutics and devices that would help people during a public crisis.

In addition to that, we're very government-focused because, typically, governments are the ones who are very interested in doing that on a broad scale. It's not an $80 billion or a $100 billion market, so that allows us to take a big stake. So BC, my role as a leader was building up the information technology capability to support the company; we were very low on the maturity scale in terms of an IT organization supporting a biotech firm.

My job was to begin building the discipline and structure that's necessary to allow us to scale and be flexible and agile in the future. For me, come coming from Big Pharma, you did massive, big things. One of the reasons why this opportunity attracted me was that it was the "build from scratch" type of opportunity. You never get to do that in a big company; you can incrementally improve but not have a major impact like that. So I was having a pretty good time.

In the past, during several five-year strategy periods, we've doubled from 250 to half a billion dollars, and then we're looking to do $1 billion to $2 billion in 2020 and beyond. From a leadership perspective, what was required is helping people to see that the future is different from where we are today and what got us to the success to go from 250 to half a billion and then to $1 billion is not going to get us to a $2 billion company or a $5 billion company and beyond.

So, from a leadership perspective, it's putting the mirror in front of us and saying, "This is who we really are, and thank you for getting us to where we got to." Obviously, there are a lot of folks that have gotten their jobs with a very specific set of requirements and job descriptions, and they are saying, "Hey, this is what I signed up for. This is what I do every day. I want to continue doing that every day even though the business is changing."

When I look toward the future, both the skill sets and where we need to focus to ensure the success of the future were different. In the back of my mind, I knew just based on experience that we were not going to be able to get there completely organically because folks are not going to be able to get up to speed in terms of their skill set as fast as necessary. That said, I did want to provide an opportunity for people to grow, so you have to balance the challenge of the needing to make progress and bringing people along and so that that's really getting their heads in a different space than it was before.

Digital disruption experienced growth before COVID and was accelerated exponentially during and after. How did your role affect that aspect of the organization?

One of the big drivers that I brought to the table was to look at information technology differently than they had in the past. IT as a function, in many companies, was solely the technology piece. The relationship that we typically have with those who we serve, both within the company and outside the company, was more of an order taker model where we go, and we sit down with them, and they say, "Hey, I'd like to do XYZ," and we'd say "Okay, that's fine; we'll go back, and we'll work with you, and we'll get it implemented."

That is a model; it's not a bad model necessarily. It's a model that IT has lived in for most of its time because when folks see the IT folks coming in, it's about tech. The shift that I was looking to drive was around the focus of IT being a value driver for the company and that IT is a means to an end. It's not the end itself; the end is always moving the company forward. We have people [in IT] that understand the business, and we can partner with you in such a way to better understand the outcomes you're trying to achieve and then properly apply information technology processes and the right culture to achieve the outcome. That is a massive shift from people who have been focused on just technology implementation.

The biggest challenge and driver of success in organizational change is to transform mindsets and beliefs to embrace the future state. Talk to us about the transformational aspects of this initiative.

This move, this transformation, from an IT perspective, was transitioning from an order taker to a business partner. That's a mindset change first. We're not going in being order takers. That means we're not just sitting there until you tell us what to do. We'll go and do it, and we'll bring it back. That is important for an organization for services and products to be delivered on time, on budget, and with a high degree of quality. That's a foundational thing that we should do, but there's more value that we can deliver. So first, we need to get IT's head in the right space that we're not just there as technology purveyors. And then the how we do that now comes into digitally enabling the enterprise to be more of an insights-driven organization, really using the information as the lifeblood to drive.

We then came up with three pillars that would be the engine as to how we would live into that business partner role and drive the company. The mindset change was harder than doing digital initiatives. We had to install a new structure to make that happen. It wasn't just going to happen by just getting people to understand what a business partner was versus an order taker; we had to make some major changes.

So you're pursuing a growth strategy, shifting the mindset of what IT means to the organization. So BC, you're on a good path, yes?

We were on track and actually did deliver a billion before 2020; we delivered in 2019. Our growth plan was working really well to the point where we were going to achieve in four years what we had planned to achieve in five years. So in 2019, the company restructured its five-year strategy for 2020 to 2024. So 20 percent faster than we had originally intended.

The first quarter of the year, we were doing a lot of work in that space, and then we realized obviously that there was this massive pandemic that was getting ready to start, and I'm sure like every other company in March, we declared that everybody is going to stay home and then in parallel with that we started conversations with the government about preparedness for this. This is what we're there for: this pandemic that was in front of us and how we could play a part in that. It was major. This is the opportunity that we have to live into the mission of the company.

The other products that we had been driving have been life-saving against public health threats: anthrax, smallpox, etc. Narcan is another one of our products that is saving lives every day on the street. With every vaccine and every treatment and therapeutic we send out, we actually measure the number of lives that we save with results. And so, as we look at this particular pandemic that was obviously killing people all over the world and vaccines hadn't been developed yet, the goal was to manufacture hundreds of millions of vaccines for the US first and then the world. Our mission is to save 1 billion lives and improve those lives.

I'm sure you had no idea of the role that you were about to play, which was going to re-prioritize everything else that the company had put in place in terms of strategic plans. So moving to a hybrid workplace is now a priority?

We didn't have an infrastructure that enabled the entire company to work from home and not miss a beat. Even with this major step up, we still need to have people on-site during the pandemic because folks need to actually do the manufacturing of the vaccines in our business. The role that we played in Operation Warp Speed was to take a vaccine that typically took two to three years of development down to six to nine months of development. And that doesn't mean we're skipping steps. What that means is that the manufacturing, the hardware, the services, and the supplies all had to come into place very quickly.

The government began to help us to mobilize, to get priority access to these major manufacturing devices to get established in our sites. We now had the opportunity to demonstrate the value of the virtual meeting versus the in-place meeting: stepping up to enable the company to operate seamlessly and engage with our customers seamlessly.

This pandemic was an opportunity for us to shift the organization to a different model than I mentioned before. We had just announced the arrangement that we had with the government to be part of Operation Warp Speed and what we were accountable to do in the years 2020 and 2021, which was to ramp up quickly and begin manufacturing this vaccine. It was a little scary; just because it's a great opportunity, there are also a lot of risks associated with it.

So amid the COVID-19 pandemic, another crisis erupted. Where did that land in terms of your strategic pursuits?

We have regular leadership meetings to align the major functional owners along with our R&D folks and our sales folks, so everybody at the top of the organization gets together pretty regularly. I was part of a leadership meeting associated with this. This is happening during the George Floyd situation. Businesses are on fire, and people are marching and want our people to help to mobilize. How do we consider that?

We transitioned from talking about this massive opportunity we have in front of us to talking about how people were feeling, and it wasn't about "here's the answer to the solution; this is what's going to solve it." It was more about expressing where we were, and so we went around the room, and those who felt comfortable spoke up about how they were feeling. It was a really interesting flip and transition to that conversation in light of this pandemic that was going on. I am sure, in that meeting, there were people with many different perspectives on this whole George Floyd situation and all the things that followed. I'm not trying to say we had one united perspective; I think it was more of having a dialogue and having a conversation about what it was.

A conversation about America broke out in our mobilization of pandemic resources, and it was really good. There were maybe three [black people] on the call, but I felt obligated and had a desire to speak up to provide one black man's perspective on what is going on in this context, at least to shed light on what others might think about how we're feeling and probably surprise folks with some of that.

So, not only the pandemic, but we're also dealing with multiple things, and how do we continue to be sensitive and provide spaces for people during this time, knowing that that, yes, you have your work life and your personal life? It's silly to believe that things that are happening in your personal life may or may not impact the things that are happening in your professional life. So what was critical there is that we need to come to deal with both of those things, and it spawned other things that we did during the year to begin giving people space and opportunity to talk about where they are while we are doing this work.

So you're here; you're on the brink; you've got the government supporting you because now you're going to be walking out the vision and mission. However, you have to navigate the dynamics of working remotely and virtual leadership. Take us to where you start to manufacture the vaccines.

We are ramping up to manufacture tens of millions and hundreds of millions of vaccines; that was the work in 2020. How do we enable customers and the government, who would typically tour and provide us insights into how to manufacture their product? In a pandemic environment, we can't have everybody just come and look. IT has to first find and tee up virtual ways to enable them to see their process flow on the manufacturing floor and in the laboratories as well. And so it was about quick thinking of how we can do things differently than we've done before because we've never had the driver to have to do that.

The second was sharing information in a very secure way; there was a major concern that the information that we are sharing could, from a cyber perspective, be captured in different ways. We want to make sure we are securely sharing that information; we have the recipe for making critical vaccines, and during that time, there was a lot of concern.

Then there's the virtual company. One of the things that we had established was to stand up a collaboration tool to have meetings and to share information, and so we sped that up and accelerated and implemented one within a month. Another focus point was on onboarding new employees. Today there are some employees that I have not met in person! How do we make the process of onboarding people and do that in such a way that enables them to be productive on day one? Our then onboarding process was a physical one, where they come to our corporate headquarters, and there's a whole set of meetings associated with that. It was a multiple-day process, and now how do we virtualize that?

While we are growing, we needed to onboard almost 500 people in a short period because of the growth that's happening in the manufacturing space; so we had to step up to enable that. You're hiring people and had to onboard them on site. We were big on on-site; we wanted everyone to be on-site but now have to pivot and do it virtually. It did also present an opportunity in the midst of all of this. Just before that, in the first quarter of 2020, folks were asking about remote working, and that was just not an option for us. By the time we got to the middle of the year, that was the primary option.

Frankly, we saw it as a potential drawback because it was based on the model that we were using before. We're in 2022 now, so we're just coming up on two years of our being virtual as the primary way of working. Then we began to realize that we were getting folks that are in states where we didn't have a presence, and they were high-quality employees. This is about talent, and it's a war on talent. You saw people moving from San Francisco and New York and all these high-rent places. This is our opportunity to engage that talent that we would have never before. Someone in California would not move to the East Coast.

We realized that we can still have a lot of value, enabling them to operate, and yes, we can get our objectives done virtually as we could never before. Some people felt, "I can't see him. I'm concerned whether they're working or not." It is a need to operate differently, and you know there are many things that we did to drive that. But here's the question. Did we miss any of our objectives? Did we exceed most of our objectives?

The answer was yes and yes. If people want to have face-to-face, is it an absolute requirement? No, it's not a requirement. At best, it's a hybrid type of a situation; a significant amount of folks are just living into it, so that's been a fundamental change for us as well.

There's an aspect of ATL, which is intellectual stimulation, which is what calls upon the experiences and the innovation and the ideas of the collective and not just a few to move the company forward. During the COVID-19 pandemic, everybody galvanized—the government and everyone involved in terms of the vaccine got it down to months instead of years. So, since we were able to get so much done and so in a short amount of time, why haven't we done this before?

I would say that historically, the crisis has been the driver of innovation when there's no other choice but to think differently. The challenge for us to your point is how do you spark that and catalyze that thinking while there's not a crisis? There are things that do happen, but the biggest achievements that we have had have been in a major crisis.

Currently, there's a huge focus on mental health. There is concern about everyone's mental wellness, including those at the helm. A few weeks ago, a CEO stepped in front of a moving train. What are our thoughts about mental wellness in the workspace and beyond?

I'm more acutely aware of mental health as a challenge. Society has been less aware of this and those who are experiencing it or have family members or friends who are experiencing it. Pandemic or not, you are much more aware of it, but I think the pandemic just made it more acute in terms of where folks' heads are.

I have friends who have children with mental health issues, and they have been sponsors and drivers because they were experiencing it. They tell me all about how society does not look at this in the right way, and folks are not getting treated and the implications of this. So there's that extreme where folks are needing medication with their mental challenges. This anxiety challenge and depression challenge that folks are having are real. We're certainly seeing that in our employees and needing to give people space.

We have some medical programs that we're enabling that are newer than before, where folks can call in and talk to a therapist. That said, in terms of how leaders are doing in that space, I felt the pressure. There's high pressure in terms of delivery of your job because it's very important to continue to keep the organization running, so I absolutely, positively experienced this essence of anxiety and my role in that, and it weighs heavy. It weighs heavy.

I'm not going to say I'm the best at handling these things, but I think, for me, my faith is what allows me to be able to feel like I can deal with this in a way that is not overly detrimental. I get concerned and anxious and maybe depressed about where things are, but I'm able to get myself out of that as I live into my faith. If I didn't have that, I don't think I would be there to be able to deal with walking in on April 1st, 2020, from this growth company to all the challenges associated with the crisis up until now and then maintaining positive progress toward our goal and keeping people motivated.

So there's a balance that you have to take on as a leader. You need to help people understand where we're headed. Show people where we need to go. That's what a leader does and with that, to get people's heads in the right place, also being genuine and even a little vulnerable as well. I think it's something that from a leadership perspective, whether we want to admit it or not, I think we all want to say, "Oh no, I'm resilient; I'll be able to handle it. I can do it." All those things are felt and are real, and I think we just don't show it as well. And for me, I think other leaders handle it better than others, and for me, it's my faith that helps me through.

So The Great Resignation is another crisis that leaders are facing. What has been your experience?

Some people left the company at the higher levels of the organization; either they didn't believe in the vision or didn't believe that we can get through the vision, or they didn't sign up for this. Leaders are telling me, "Hey, Howard, you brought us on for XYZ. Is that going to happen now?" Some of that happened.

There are the highs and lows of the story that I just told in terms of where we've been. In 2020, it was very easy to attract anyone as they saw our mission and that we were part of the solution. And then 2021 comes, and continuing to keep people motivated in this environment as well as dealing with trying to respond to the challenges that we had, from a manufacturing perspective, puts a lot of pressure on us.

People are just asking a lot of questions: "With all the challenges that we have, are we going to be able to get over this." "It doesn't seem like we're going to get there. We have to keep them motivated and not motivated by telling them some fairy tale about the challenges that we had, having to live into those saying, yes, there was an issue, yes, we have some challenges, yes, our stock is going to be impacted by this. But there is a way out. It's not something that's going to be happening in a month. It's going to happen, probably in another year, and trying to get people's heads wrapped around that. I feel very invested in being genuine and transparent at the same time and to be human.

Dr. Leola H. Orr | Retired Principal

Dr. Orr is experienced in leading a university and shares her thoughts about exemplifying effective leadership. She addresses the aspect of intellectual humility and the book's title: "You Know Less Than You Don't Know."

Becoming Leaders of Leaders

In the new culture of shared decision-making, strong leaders recognize the need to continuously improve the leadership ability of those they must work with. In the belief that leadership is learned and can be nurtured, they take responsibility for arranging training that is focused on three areas:

- interpersonal skills
    - o team and group skills
    - o conflict identification and resolution skills
    - o oral and written communication skills
    - o persuasion skills
    - o diplomacy skills
- conceptual skills
    - o the ability to conceive and implement new ideas essential to change
- technical skills
    - o the ability to use electronic tools to access, accumulate, and manipulate information from local, state, national, and international databases

Individuals in the role of leading leaders have several responsibilities:
- Recognize, reward, and support the work of the new leaders.
- Coach the leaders on the values, mission, and goals of the organization.
- Provide the leaders with the necessary resources, such as released time, money, staff support, facilities, and equipment.
- Give the leaders tools to review and reflect on their work.
- Provide the leaders with the opportunities to continuously sharpen their knowledge in learning, teaching, and leadership, as well as skills for working with others.

A good leader has to have a purpose that is larger than he/she is and the balanced personality and skills to put that purpose into action.

> "I alone cannot change the world, but I can cast a stone across the water to create many ripples."
> —Mother Teresa

Dionne Vernon | SHRM, PHR-CP, MBA

Dionne is a career strategist coach and leader of people, and she shares her perspective on effective leadership.

I think it is so important now, more than ever before, for all leaders of people to **LEAD**.

Lean in closer to employees; don't lead from a distance!
Engage! **E**mpathize!
Ask questions; don't assume everything is okay.
Develop and empower your employees.

I hear so many stories about managers who lead from a distance and are disengaged from their teams. I am very sensitive to the indelible impact this can and has had on employees. The career trauma one experiences can be very crippling to one's performance and ability to move forward. Never has there been a time where engaging with employees has been more important. The stakes are too high for employers and employees alike. Employees are humans! I would like to see us shift from using the term "employee engagement" to "human engagement."

During the first year of the pandemic, I became very demotivated and could not understand why. Thanks to Adam Grant's article on languishing, I was enlightened. I vulnerably and transparently shared how demotivated I felt with my team while in our virtual collaboration squares. I also shared how the article provided well-needed insight! Suddenly, the flood gate opened; my team immediately expressed that they felt the very same!

    We engaged as humans, and my team thanked me profusely for being so open, as it made them realize they didn't have to mask their emotions; they could speak freely. We now spend a vast majority of our team meetings engaging as humans; the work-related topics proceed that. While it's important to have engagement strategies and programs, it's more important that we **LEAD** and be kind, empathetic, and compassionate humans.

Dr. Mathew Christian | Autism Dad and Agent of Social Change

Dr. Christian commiserates on the similarities between leadership and parental responsibilities.

If leaders learn just one thing from The Great Resignation, it needs to be this: The leadership ability of middle management requires more attention and investment. If you're not prepared to do what you've asked your team to do, you're not leading.

Leadership is like parenting. You're going to make tough, even unpopular, management decisions, experience the fullness of all your emotions, and probably make mistakes. But remember, at the end of the day, the reward is seeing your team manifest that emotional investment to live fulfilled lives and add value to the organization throughout its stages of growth. Leaders are not perfect, nor should that be an expectation.

APPENDIX B

Leadership Case Study

Pseudo-Transformational Leadership mimics Transformational Leadership but is inauthentic, particularly in moral and ethical behavior. The complexities of Pseudo-Transformational Leadership warrant a study to first identify its presence in leaders, then describe the behavior perceived by subordinates, and lastly, identify its drivers. Pseudo-Transformational Leadership studies rank low among the other types of leadership, necessitating a process to observe the behavior in real-time. The Transformational Leadership model framed this case study using one-on-one structured interviews with twenty-two participants in the North American division of a global entity who ranked their leaders as exhibiting one of the four transformational behavioral types. The purpose of the intrinsic case study was to illustrate within a large global organization subordinates' perceptions of their leaders' behaviors as being Authentic Transformational or Pseudo-Transformational based on self-interest. The participant sample represented the organization's demographics in age, country of citizenship, ethnicity, male-to-female ratio, and remote versus non-remote. An analysis of the results indicated the following Transformational Leadership behavior and their corresponding percentages were perceived: Authentic Transformational, 45 percent; Transactional and Laissez-Faire, 29 percent and 14 percent, respectively; and Pseudo-Transformational, 12 percent. Of the participants who observed Pseudo-Transformational behavior, 76 percent reported self-interest as a driver. Findings may drive positive changes in the organization by identifying the presence of leadership behaviors and the influencers. Non-profits, for-profits, and governmental organizations can benefit from understanding how Transformational Leadership behavior is perceived. Learning leaders can see how their behaviors affect their employees, customers, products, and processes.

Keywords: Transformational Leadership, Laissez-Faire Leadership, Transactional Leadership, Pseudo-Transformational Leadership, self-interest.

CHAPTER 1

Introduction

Superior organizational success is boosted by positive leadership behavior; leaders' behaviors drive employee motivation, creativity, performance, and productivity (Engelen, Gupta, Strenger, and Brettel 2015; Obeidat, Zyod, and Gharaibeh 2015). Conversely, turnover, attrition, absenteeism, and mental and physical health issues can be attributed to negative leadership behavior (Barling, Akers, and Beiko 2018; Hentrich et al. 2017; Triana, Richard, and Yücel 2017). Subordinates' perceptions of leaders' behaviors, regardless of whether or not they are positive or negative, drive their level of effectiveness, engagement, and commitment to the organization (S. B. Choi, Kim, and Kang 2017; Einarsen, Aasland, and Skogstad 2016; Jaiswal and Dhar 2015; Schmitt, Den Hartog, and Belschak 2016). Evaluation of subordinates' perceptions of leadership behaviors can inform organizational strategy, decision-making, collaborative pursuits, investment in social capital, hiring practices, and employee development (Para-González, Jiménez-Jiménez, and Martínez-Lorente 2018). According to Hancock and Algozzine (2016), describing how subordinates perceive the behaviors of their leaders can be accomplished using structured planning, data collection, careful analysis, and unbiased interpretation and reporting of findings.

In this case study, I explored subordinates' perceptions of their leaders' behaviors. The background and conceptual framework of the study, statement of the problem, the purpose of the case study, and the research question used to guide the study are presented in this chapter. Next, the rationale, relevance, and significance of the study, followed by definitions of terms used, are identified. Finally, this chapter concludes with a detailed explanation of the assumptions used in the study and a summary.

Background and Conceptual Framework

Pseudo-Transformational Leadership, also known as personalized charisma, Pseudo-Charismatic Leadership, Inauthentic Transformational Leadership, and Unethical Charismatic Leadership, is the antithesis of the moral and ethical behavior ascribed to Authentic Transformational Leadership (Pandey, Davis, and Pandey 2016). Pseudo-Transformational leaders, unlike their Authentic Transformational counterparts, utilize their authoritarian influence to further their gains (Cohen 2016). Authentic Transformational Leadership qualities, when distorted to overblown charisma, were cited most often as directly affecting a leader's engagement in behavior perceived by subordinates as being Pseudo-Transformational (Hughes and Harris 2017). Both types of Transformational leaders are forerunners for the change process as these individuals identify a need for change, craft the mechanisms to effect said change, and motivate and galvanize followers to concurrently change, not only processes and systems but themselves (Northouse 2016).

Positive and negative leadership behaviors have been researched by theorists seeking to understand what makes leaders effective. The great man theory (Carlyle 1888) emerged as the standard for capable leadership. Carlyle purported that leaders, because of innate abilities, were great men. Critics of this model advanced alternate theories to support efficacious leaders who were nurtured versus possessing natural abilities as advocated by Carlyle. The introduction of the trait theory in part supported the great man theory and its endorsement of natural-born leaders; however, Allport (1937) claimed leaders are not necessarily born that way, as Carlyle maintained. Instead, Allport stated that individuals should be analyzed and tested for the presence of leadership traits.

Leadership theorists acknowledged the need to study not only the traits of leaders but also their behaviors and impact. Behavioral theory, as advocated by Skinner (1945), showed that interactions with the environment influenced behavior, and thus, behavior was learned, not inherited. Since that time, other leadership theories have emerged, including contingency theory and transformational theory. Contingency theory, according to Peters, Hartke, and Pohlmann (1985), is the leaders' ability to match their specific skills to an environment where they will be the most effective. The preceding theories have focused on the leader's character and behavior. Transformational theory (Burns 1978) evolved with a focus on followers' needs. The theory further described an intentional relationship between the leaders and followers. The transformational theory includes different types of Transformational Leadership behavior, both positive behavior and negative behavior.

Positive Leadership Behavior

Malmendier and Tate (2015) noted that an example of positive leadership behavior was Chrysler's chief executive officer, Lee Iacocca, describing Iacocca as personifying and displaying Authentic Transformational Leadership. Malmendier and Tate asserted this type of leader is morally and ethically driven and strikes a balance between task-oriented (directive) and people-oriented (participative) leadership. Bolman and Deal (2017) described the competing priorities of directive versus participative leadership as the litmus test of Authentic Transformational Leadership. Iacocca's Authentic Transformational Leadership style and approach were instrumental in identifying the people-oriented issues that impacted the operations at Chrysler Corporation. The company's problems hampered organizational performance, halted revenues, and placed Chrysler in seemingly irrevocable failure (Harish 2015).

As CEO, Iacocca was able to strategically shift the paradigm of Chrysler Corporation, affecting both the company's performance and its perception by employees and the public. Iacocca's previous tenure at Ford Corporation, although not organizationally transformational, served as a platform for him to focus on his transformation as a leader. As a learning leader, Iacocca was able to leverage his knowledge to improve the organizational performance at Chrysler Corporation (Rosenbach 2018). One of Iacocca's strategies in transforming the Chrysler

Corporation was his belief and implementation of a participative and collaborative leadership style. He then systematically incited the organization toward mutually beneficial goals. At the onset of his tenure, he removed ineffective executives who suppressed the creativity of subordinates, and he allowed unrecognized talent to rise and influence organizational activities (Malmendier and Tate 2015). These changes transcended subordinate satisfaction to include customer satisfaction in the company's goods and services.

Negative Leadership Behavior

Conversely, Henry (2016) reported an example of negative leadership in the well-publicized Jonestown Massacre. Henry described Jim Jones as initially behaving like that of an Authentic Transformational leader; his stand on equality and socialism influenced his followers' perceptions, beliefs, and subsequent actions, as his behavior appeared to be morally and ethically based. Northouse (2016) noted this seemingly moral stand is a descriptor of the Pseudo-Transformational leader. During the Civil Rights era, Jones emerged as a role model, standing up for and articulating perceived shared moral values with his followers. Henry contended Jones was viewed by his followers as being competent and able to voice their concerns. Henry explained Jones was a leader to mostly ethnic followers, expressing the desire for someone to champion their cause, and thus he quickly convinced them to move to California and subsequently, to their detriment, to Guyana.

Pseudo-Transformational leaders are more effective when their ideologies have moral overtones (Northouse 2016). Armed with this knowledge, Transformational leaders can leverage the moral objectives of subordinates and either wield this power to produce good or evil outcomes. One of the negative outcomes of Pseudo-Transformational Leadership is moral cynicism (Yasir and Mohamad 2016). This cynicism extends beyond the leader's organization to society at large. Leadership can have a significant impact not just on the organization but on its external environment (Yasir and Mohamad 2016).

Subordinates must be willing to be led for an Authentic Transformational leader or Pseudo-Transformational leader to be effective (Miller 2015). Charismatically communicating vision and mission are touted by both types of leaders; however, Burns (1978) noted that Authentic Transformational leaders draw subordinates to an organizational mission, whereas Pseudo-Transformational leaders draw subordinates to themselves. Authentic Transformational leaders represent the organization's interests, while Pseudo-Transformational leaders represent their interests (Miller 2015). Iacocca was effective in communicating Chrysler Corporation's vision to the subordinates and the general public, while Jones was successful in utilizing his persona to solicit personal commitment and obedience from his subordinates (Henry 2016).

Impact of Transformational Leadership on Subordinates

Burns (1978) and House (1971) noted the importance of assessing the immediate effects of Transformational Leadership on subordinates. Einarsen et al. (2016) called into question the lack of empirical studies on Pseudo-Transformational Leadership; studies on Pseudo-Transformational Leadership usually are conducted well after the behavior occurs, reporting on leaders such as Adolf Hitler, Jim Jones, and David Koresh. Further, the information provided was generalized, describing the character of leaders rather than the leaders' influence on subordinates' perceptions (Avolio and Bass 2004; Henry 2016).

Conceptual Framework

The conceptual framework for this study followed the model of Ravitch and Riggan (2016), using actual case studies to establish the rationale for using a case study research design. Ravitch and Riggan described a conceptual framework as being both broad and specific, an analytic component by which research is designed, justified, informed, and guided. Another purpose for a conceptual framework entailed the components that comprise the structure, such as personal interests and goals, identity and positionality, literature review, topical research, and theoretical frameworks. A conceptual framework encompasses both the reason and rigor that underscores conducting valid research.

The integrative conceptual framework process advocated by Ravitch and Riggan (2016) offered both the flexibility and support necessary to review and make changes and provide focus as necessary. I realized the importance of revisiting the conceptual framework as I moved through the case study processes, checking for essential alignment to conceptualize and support the research. The ability to adjust the methodology as necessary at each stage offered valuable insight in producing measurable milestones that supported the research process.

Theorists responsible for furthering Transformational Leadership concepts served as the bedrock from which the research study was supported. The conceptual lens of Burns's (1978) transformational theory, Bass's (1985) theory on Transformational Leadership, and Barling's (2014) theory on the effect of Transformational Leadership on employee commitment directed the literature review and research methodology. According to the theorists, Transformational Leadership is comprised of both Authentic Transformational Leadership and Pseudo-Transformational Leadership (see figure 1). The conceptual framework provided by Burns (1978), Bass (1985), and Barling (2014) will underscore the basis for the study on subordinates' perceptions of their leaders' behaviors.

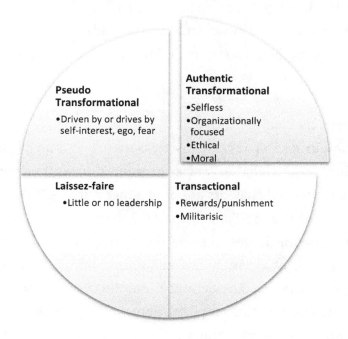

Figure 1: *Transformational Leadership Model*

Statement of the Problem

The leadership model of the organization at the focus of this study was self-described as transformational, and at the time of the study, the organization was engaged in multiple concurrent changes. Over the past five years, the changes included leadership and subordinate turnover. No formal, proactive root cause evaluation had been conducted to address the attrition trend, resulting in ambiguity surrounding the impact of leadership behavior on subordinates. The organization's leaders did not possess objective knowledge of how they were perceived by subordinates. Subordinates' reluctance to report on their leaders' behaviors for fear of retaliation introduced knowledge gaps in the organization. The problem is subordinates in a large global company are not allowed to convey their opinions anonymously or confidentially and cannot share their perception of their leaders' behaviors and how these behaviors affect them.

Purpose of the Study

The purpose of the intrinsic case study was to illustrate within a large global organization subordinates' perceptions of their leaders' behaviors as being either Authentic Transformational or Pseudo-Transformational based on self-interest. Allowing subordinates to share their perceptions was important because of attrition and communications affecting the work environment. The organization's executive leaders were interested in exploring employee perception and in identifying if there were gaps in communicating and implementing the organization's strategy. Additionally, the leaders wanted to identify viable talking points, which would equip them to directly address the subordinates' perceptions. Also, executive leaders were interested in proactively crafting Authentic Transformational behavior and were seeking tools that were intentional, goal-oriented, and measurable. The organization's executive leaders anticipated the results from the case study could serve as inputs into initiatives that would impact the subordinates' levels of commitment and propel both leaders and subordinates to mutually rewarding outcomes.

Research Question

The research question for this study was:

How do subordinates describe their perception of whether leaders' behaviors are Authentic Transformational or Pseudo-Transformational based on self-interest?

Rationale, Relevance, and Significance of the Study

Rationale, according to Creswell (2016), is the need to research a specific issue. Additionally, Ravitch and Carl (2015) advocated the rationale of a study should relate to the existing literature about the topic, either confirming, refuting, or extending it; this relationship, they stated, can identify gaps in either research findings or methodologies. Subsequently, leadership models should evolve to represent the current leadership demands and not rely on previously held assumptions, actions, and behaviors.

Creswell (2013) recommended using a case study to observe occurrences over time and then report on those findings. An intrinsic case study was best suited for this study because it was used to depict an occurrence that was underway (Yin 2003). Other case study types were evaluated; however, the environment of change at the study site represented a phenomenon that was observable and aligned with the methodology of an intrinsic case study.

Stake (1995) advocated designing the intrinsic case study based on specific issues that could be bounded to facilitate a deeper comprehension of the case. The specificity of subordinates' perception of leaders' behavior fits within the intrinsic case study structure based on specific issues that could be bounded to facilitate a deeper comprehension of the organization's scenario. Additionally, Yin (1994) advocated using an intrinsic case study to examine contemporary issues and understand the root causes of those events. Prior research aimed at identifying triggers to Pseudo-Transformational Leadership included personality traits, moral aptitude and identity, and situational leadership (Politis and Politis 2016; Salehzadeh, Shahin, Kazemi, and Barzoki 2015; Skubinn and Herzog 2016). Studies on situational leadership included the leader's adoption of Pseudo-Transformational Leadership to facilitate change management (Law-Penrose, Wilson, and Taylor 2016; Lee, Wang, and Piccolo 2018; Pater 2015). Leaders straying from the initial moral foundation personified by Authentic Transformational Leadership may exhibit Pseudo-Transformational behavior, so providing an opportunity for subordinates to describe this behavior in their own words was important (Collins and Jackson 2015).

Relevant research may guide organizations to pursue sustainable success. Relevancy is supported by practical and real-life applications (Johnson and Christensen 2019). The responsibility for driving collaborative performance rests on progressive and innovative leaders (Creswell 2016). These leaders possess a composite of leading and learning nuanced in meaningful ways that incite subordinate connectedness, breed consensus-building, and foster knowledge sharing. Understanding leaders' impact on subordinates can yield performance- and incentive-driven initiatives, which establishes accountability (Ghoshal 2005). Human possibility triggered by thought transformation is how leaders become effective and accountable (Burns 2003). Psychological and monetary expenses can be decreased by increased understanding of the effects of subordinates emulating their leaders (Ghoshal 2005; Tourish 2013).

Through relevant research, the organization's human resources and business units can develop real-time feedback loops that assess their leaders' behaviors. Strategic solutions such as team building, mentoring, and coaching opportunities can build quality relationships across the organization and drive retention (Barling 2014; Bass and Avolio 1994). Relevant research can also identify feedback loops that cultivate an environment of continuous improvement that is collaborative and not exploitative. An unbiased view of how leaders can curtail destructive leadership behavior may provide the organization with a roadmap for change. Responsive leadership empowers subordinates (Burns 2004). As a result, new and existing organizations can proactively implement positive leadership cultures that invest in the strategic value of their human capital.

Relevant research can help organizations bring the perception of leadership behavior to the forefront and heighten contextual awareness of how their behavior impacts others (Avolio and Gardner 2005). The occurrence of Pseudo-Transformational Leadership behavior may be difficult for employees to assess, especially if the organization supports a traditional hierarchical structure that silos its leaders from the subordinates (Bass and Steidlmeier 1999; Dashborough and Ashkanasy 2002; Price 2003). Avolio and Gardner (2005) distinguished between leaders' images and their actions as a way for subordinates to assess Pseudo-Transformational Leadership behavior.

Significance is the ability of a study to affect policymaking, influence practice, or generate further research (Burkholder, Cox, Crawford, and Hitchcock 2019). Seeking the voice of the subordinates communicates collaborative messaging and investment in their well-being. Value is placed on their perceptions; subordinates are allowed to express their ideas freely without fear of retaliation. Areas of significance include noting the similarities shared between authentic and Pseudo-Transformational behavior and shifting the optics from the leaders to the perception of subordinates.

Significant research has focused primarily on the character and traits that influence the Transformational leader's behavior (Patterson, Grenny, McMillan, Switzler, and Maxwell 2013; Reiley and Jacobs 2016). Other research has focused on the outcomes resulting from leaders' behavior (Cikaliuk, Erakovic, Jackson, Noonan, and Watson 2015; Cohen 2016). Extending the leadership scorecard to include other factors such as subordinate perception is one way to fully explain and understand the practice or lack of Transformational Leadership. Barling, Clegg, and Cooper (2008) called for additional research to better understand subordinates' perceptions of their leaders' behaviors. Burns (2004) agreed, stating more studies have focused on leaders rather than on followers, and the interchange between them is important to the leadership body of research.

Scholarly recognition of leadership is needed to establish its importance alongside other disciplines (Burns 2004). Seldom is adequate testing of theories performed in the social sciences; the exception is in Transformational Leadership (Bass and Avolio 1994). Maintaining the momentum of Transformational Leadership studies will extend existing knowledge to frame leadership more accurately while also filling the gap that exists with the imbalance of studies relating to Authentic Transformational Leadership versus Pseudo-Transformational Leadership. This balance is important since both types of leadership share similarities. Holmes (2015) maintained that the behavior of both types of leaders sometimes masquerades as charismatic personality types, which may make it difficult to assess which leadership practice is in place.

Definition of Terms

This list of relevant terms is designed to help the reader understand and interpret them in the context of Authentic Transformational and Pseudo-Transformational Leadership.

Authentic Transformational Leadership. Leaders whose inspiration stimulates both subordinates and them to achieve together what they individually could not. These leaders empower subordinates by aligning objectives and goals that impact the leader, subordinates, and the organization (Burns 1978).

Dark triad personality traits. Personality traits are characterized by Machiavellianism, narcissism, and psychopathy. Machiavellianism applies to individuals who focus on their interests and use manipulation to satisfy them. Narcissism is characterized by ego and a heightened self-image. Psychopathy is a personality disorder exemplified by egotistical traits (Paulhus and Williams 2002).

Emotional intelligence. A leader's proficiency in understanding his or her own emotions and those with whom they engage. They use this understanding to cultivate effective interpersonal relationships (Salovey and Mayer 1990).

Entrepreneurial leadership. Leadership in large corporations is based on adapting the agile capabilities of small and medium-sized businesses in responding to and exploiting opportunities (Engelen et al. 2015).

Followers, also known as employees, subordinates, report. Anyone who is overseen by a leader, manager, or supervisor (Burns 1978).

Going native. The researchers' knowledge of the research community skews their ability to remain objective (Creswell 2013).

Hawthorne effect. Participants modify their behavior because of their awareness of being studied (Landsberger 1967).

Intrapreneurship. The application of entrepreneurial principles in large complex organizations. The term entrepreneurship in this structure is usually relegated to leadership, while intrapreneurship relates to the employees they influence (Valsania, Moriano, and Molero 2016).

Laissez-Faire Leadership, also known as Delegative Leadership. Little or no leadership participation. The leadership is mostly exhibited with high-performance teams that lead under little supervision (Lewin 1944).

Leader, also known as manager or supervisor. An individual who oversees and influences the activities of subordinates can dictate the activities performed (Loewenstein 2017).

Leadership shadow. The hidden side of leaders unconsciously affects their actions (de Haan 2016).

Machiavellianism. The practice of manipulating others for one's benefit and self-interests (Jakobwitz and Egan 2006).

People-oriented leadership, also known as participative leadership. A leadership style that is focused on individuals. This is the opposite of task-oriented leadership, where the focus is on task completion (Bass 2008).

Positivist approach. A research approach that relies on scientific evidence to describe a phenomenon (Klein and Myers 1999).

Product life cycle. Products often go through five stages: introduction, growth, maturity, saturation, and decline. Technology products, such as cell phones and computers, are examples of products that go through the five stages (Vernon 1992).

Pseudo-Transformational Leadership, also known as Pure Charismatic Leadership. Leaders who may initially portray Authentic Transformational Leadership qualities but quickly devolve into self-serving activities. These leaders utilize their position of power to exploit their followers (Burns 1978).

Psychopathy. A personality disorder that is characterized by manipulation and a lack of remorse for one's actions (Viding, McCrory, and Seara-Cardoso 2014).

Situational leadership. Flexible leadership shifts from the task-oriented style of leadership to the people-oriented leadership style based on the subordinates' readiness or ability (Thompson and Glasø 2015).

Task-oriented leadership, also known as directive leadership. A leadership style that is focused on task completion (Bass 2008).

Transactional Leadership. Leadership based on contingencies. Followers, employees, or subordinates are rewarded or punished for not meeting stated or assumed objectives. In some cases, the punishment constitutes a withholding of rewards (Bass 1985).

Weltanschauung. An individual's philosophy or worldview on certain topics such as leadership, marriage, politics, etc. This worldview guides their actions (Mezirow 1994).

Assumptions

Assumptions frame a researcher's worldview and approach to inquiry (Levitt et al. 2018). An assumption I made within this study was that the research might be limited by participants' reluctance to report their leaders' behaviors for fear of retaliation. I expected that some participants might not respond because of these fears, and further, if they did respond, they might not be as forthcoming with their answers. Another assumption was that the North American organization was experiencing changes, which may affect the employees' perception of the leadership, who may temporarily adopt a Pseudo-Transformational Leadership style in the interim and resume Authentic Transformational behavior once changes were implemented (Law-Penrose et al. 2016; Lee et al. 2018).

Participants' self-awareness can inform their replies, which is known as the Hawthorne effect (Landsberger 1967). The Hawthorne effect implies that participants' responses may not be as forthcoming because of this self-awareness. Furthermore, self-assessment by the participants who were also leaders was another assumption; self-assessment by these leaders might not accurately reflect how these leaders are being perceived.

Summary

In chapter 1, I introduced the Transformational Leadership model and the relationship between Authentic Transformational Leadership, Pseudo-Transformational Leadership, and its effects on subordinates. The conceptual framework connecting both types of leadership styles and the behavioral mechanism that influences subordinate perception was based on three theories: Burns's (1978) transformational theory, Bass's (1985) theory on Transformational Leadership, and Barling's (2014) theory on the effect of Transformational Leadership on employee commitment. The problem is subordinates in a large global company are not allowed to anonymously convey their opinions, nor are they given a formal process to share their perception of their leaders' behaviors and how these behaviors affected them. The purpose of the intrinsic case study was to illustrate within a large global organization subordinates' perceptions of their leaders' behaviors as being Authentic Transformational or Pseudo-Transformational based on self-interest. The following research question guided the study: How do subordinates describe their perception of whether their leaders' behaviors are Authentic Transformational or Pseudo-

Transformational based on self-interest? The rationale for the study is to determine the causes of leadership behavior. The study is relevant in contributing to organizational strategies. The significance of the study extends the knowledge of leadership behavior to include subordinates' perceptions of that behavior. Within chapter 2, I will present a literature review of studies relating to understanding how subordinates perceive the behavior of their leaders.

CHAPTER 2

Literature Review

A review of literature establishes the research study in the existing body of work on the research problem. The problem is subordinates in a large global company are not allowed to anonymously convey their opinions, nor are they given a formal process to share their perception of their leaders' behaviors and how these behaviors affected them. The literature review includes a review of the search strategy utilized to find empirical literature focused on three theorists, Burns (1978), Bass (1985), and Barling (2014), who were responsible for promoting Transformational Leadership. The chapter further includes a review and synthesis of information on the future of Transformational Leadership, followed by a critique of literature related to leadership styles and subordinates' perceptions of those styles. A summary of chapter 2 segues into an introduction of chapter 3.

Literature Search Strategy

According to Machi and McEvoy (2016), a literature search strategy is important in planning how the information will be used in building the research argument. The search strategy was constrained by the conceptual framework, which provided direction, focus, and qualitative insight to target related research to support the study topic (Ravitch and Riggan 2016). The search criteria were limited to current Transformational Leadership research performed within the last five years.

The search of the literature was focused on peer-reviewed, primary studies published since 2014. I used the Concordia University library to search peer-reviewed, scholarly articles through the following databases: ABI/INFORM Trade and Industry, Gale, SAGE Journals, ProQuest, Taylor and Francis, and Google Scholar. The search culminated in findings from various research tools such as interviews, observations, case studies, focus groups, and questionnaires. Search terms I employed included *Authentic Transformational Leadership, dark side leadership, dark triad leadership, ego, ethical leadership, exploitive leader, follower, influence, Laissez-Faire Leadership, leader behavior, manager, narcissism, narcissistic, organizational change, power, Pseudo-Transformational Leadership, relationship, self-interest, self-regulation, servant leader, subordinates, supervisor, Transactional Leadership, Transformational Leadership, tyrannical, unethical behavior,* and *vision*.

A foundation from which both styles of Transformational Leadership could be compared emerged after I reviewed the literature. Of the two leadership models (Authentic Transformational Leadership and Pseudo-Transformational Leadership), the Pseudo-Transformational Leadership search resulted in the least amount of research and resulting information. Further refinement of the search strategy offered alternative characterization for Transformational Leadership to include subordinate perception of leadership.

The search strategy resulted in a pattern of binary categorization on what constitutes Authentic Transformational Leadership or Pseudo-Transformational Leadership. According to the literature, binary categorizations included transformational or Pseudo-Transformational Leadership as depicting qualities that were either innate or taught, character or behaviorally ascribed, or described from the vantage point of the actions of leaders versus the leadership effects on subordinates. The effects of leadership behavior on subordinates were evident; however, very little literature was available that focused on the perceptions of subordinates on the leader's Transformational or Pseudo-Transformational behavior (Cikaliuk, Erakovic, Jackson, Noonan, and Watson 2015; Copeland 2016; Cuadrado, García-Ael, and Molero 2015; Dartey-Baah 2015; Einolander 2015; Jensen 2018; Khalili 2017; Meuser et al. 2016; Otchere-Ankrah, Tenakwah, and Tenakwah 2016; Özbağ 2016; Sharma and Pearsall 2016; Wall, Bellamy, Evans, and Hopkins 2017; Wolfe and Dilworth 2015).

Judge and Piccolo (2004) found Authentic Transformational Leadership and Pseudo-Transformational Leadership are strongly correlated to two other types of Transformational Leadership: Transactional (Bass 1985) and Laissez-Faire (Lewin 1944). Judge and Piccolo discovered that some correlations were stronger in the business sector as opposed to other sectors such as the military or education. Judge and Piccolo's findings apply to this study because the study site used in this research was a business.

A full range model of Transformational Leadership included all four Transformational Leadership types: Authentic Transformational, Pseudo-Transformational, Transactional, and Laissez-Faire Leadership (Bass and Avolio 1994). To further understand authentic and Pseudo-Transformational Leadership behavior, I expanded the search to include the terms: Transactional Leadership and Laissez-Faire Leadership. The second search yielded several articles relevant to both types of leadership in various settings, including education, religion, business, and athletics (Barth and Benoliel 2019; Eklund, Barry, and Grunberg 2017; Klenke 2017; Ola 2017; Pitts 2017; Sayadi 2016; Silva 2016; Tetteh-Opai and Omoregie 2015).

Conceptual Framework

Three theorists presented leadership perspectives from an organizational standpoint and the effect on the subordinates. Burns's (1978), Bass's (1985), and Barling's (2014) respective views on Transformational Leadership and Pseudo-Transformational Leadership are related to the current study on how subordinates perceive their leaders' behaviors. By utilizing Barling's model of examining the quality of leadership, important findings indicated which type of Transformational Leadership was present. Burns, Bass, and Barling agreed on the moral and ethical foundations of an Authentic Transformational leader and the absence of moral and ethical foundations in the Pseudo-Transformational leader. The theorists also concurred on the leader's effect on subordinate performance and satisfaction and that high-quality leadership characterizes Authentic Transformational Leadership. The three theorists' approaches differ, however, in measuring either the leader's moral fabric or the outcomes of their decision-making on subordinates and the organization.

James McGregor Burns (1978), in proposing the Transformational Leadership Theory (TLT), positioned leadership as being both descriptive and prescriptive; Transformational Leadership describes a behavior, and it also prescribes how the leaders should adopt that behavior. Burns stated that Transformational Leadership calls for a structural transition that points to the leader's character and qualities as drivers for the subsequent empowerment of the subordinates. Burns (2003) also defined the Transformational Leadership style as being participatory and democratic as a way to foster the increasing effectiveness of subordinates and their purposes and boost propensity for becoming leaders themselves.

Furthermore, Burns (2004) made the distinction between the moral use of power by a leader versus that of a ruler. The former is depicted by leaders who are Authentic Transformational, while the latter is characterized by those who are Pseudo-Transformational. Mutual transformational goals are characteristic of the Authentic Transformational leader (Burns 2004). In opposition, goals masked as pursuing collective gains are merely the pursuit of personal gratification by the Pseudo-Transformational leader.

Burns (1978) expressed reservations about the significance of emotions in Transformational Leadership by citing historical evidence to support the emotional context of pure charismatic or Pseudo-Transformational Leadership. Burns's stance supported a change from an emotion-driven leadership model, which describes Pseudo-Transformational behavior, to one that is values-based, supporting Authentic Transformational Leadership. The transition, Burns (1978) maintained, can inform cognitive outcomes in both leaders and subordinates.

Emotion-driven Pseudo-Transformational Leadership predicates demagoguery, and subordinates blindly cooperate with the leaders' views and subsequent actions, often to their disservice (Burns 1984). The integral leader-subordinate relationship that supports a healthy and beneficial exchange is lacking in Pseudo-Transformational Leadership. This type of leadership is often typified by the unquestioning loyalty of subordinates. The mutual empowerment demonstrated by Authentic Transformational Leadership, Burns (1984) asserted, is necessary, as both leaders and subordinates play roles that contribute to each other's betterment.

Burns (1978) described the transformational process as usually headed by a visionary charisma who is either a liberating and empowering leader or an enslaving one. Burns (1984) qualified and quantified the effects of Transformational Leadership on subordinates. He verified the quantifying effects of leaders' actions in satisfying subordinates' needs. Additionally, Burns (1985) maintained Authentic Transformational leaders pursue fulfilling qualifiable psychological needs, whereas Pseudo-Transformational leaders do not.

Burns's (1978) Transformational Leadership theory draws from principles that are based on ethically-sound decision-making, which in turn addresses psychological needs and defines subordinates' behavior. Burns also observed that the leader's positive response to challenges exemplifies Authentic Transformational Leadership, which, he concluded, separates the leaders from the rulers. Empowering values, Burns contended, are what drive both leaders and subordinates into achieving intentional change. The lack of these values in leaders is normative to Pseudo-Transformational Leadership, according to Burns.

Integral to Authentic Transformational Leadership are transforming values; therefore, when these values are missing, leadership is ineffective and Pseudo-Transformational (Burns 1978). Transformational leaders are precursors for the change process as they motivate and stimulate others to concurrently change, not only processes and systems but themselves. These leaders impart passion that is all at once infective, refreshing, and stimulating. Transformational leaders foster a joint identity that induces subordinates' fidelity, sometimes to a fault. Burns stated that gains in Authentic Transformational Leadership are reflected in higher moral and ethical activities in both leaders and subordinates. Also present is a broadening and subsequent elevation of perspectives as individual and collective actualization follows.

The Transformational Leadership theory upheld by Burns (1978) is the basis from which subsequent models of Transformational Leadership evolved, including the antithesis of Authentic Transformational Leadership—Pseudo-Transformational Leadership. A solid understanding of the premise of Authentic Transformational Leadership leads to clearer insight into recognizing Pseudo-Transformational Leadership. Both types of leadership realign values in subordinates, which inform their perception of the leader. Burns (1978) observed a variation between ideological (Authentic Transformational) versus idolized (Pseudo-Transformational) leaders and the fusion of values of both leaders and subordinates that brings about change. Burns's position on transformation versus change, the difference between a leader (Authentic Transformational) and a ruler (Pseudo-Transformational), and emotional versus value-based leadership are distinguishing aspects of Authentic Transformational Leadership versus Pseudo-Transformational Leadership.

Further refinement of Transformational Leadership was performed by Bernard M. Bass, who ascribed the characteristics to be used to measure Transformational Leadership behavior. Bass (1985) further described a dichotomy where varying levels of each characteristic can contribute to either Authentic Transformational Leadership or Pseudo-Transformational Leadership. Bass (1983) termed idealized influence as governing the connection between the subordinate and the leader. This leader is often charismatic. Inspirational motivation is the leader's cogent communication of the organization's vision so that subordinates own it and are vested in its fruition (Bass 1985). The ability to engage subordinates in problem-solving, critical thinking, risk-taking, idea generation, and facing challenges, comprise the intellectual stimulation component of Bass's model. Lastly, individualized consideration speaks to the leader's ability to emotionally connect with subordinates to understand them to better serve them. High emotional intelligence describes this leader's interaction with subordinates. According to Bass, coaching and mentoring are important aspects of individualized consideration, aiding in solidifying the leader-subordinate relationship.

These leadership characteristics measure the effectiveness of a leader based on the degree to which the leader exploits them individually or collectively: idealized influence, inspirational motivation, intellectual stimulation, and individualized consideration (Bass 1994). For example, Bass stated leaders could exploit idealized influence and inspirational motivation to capitalize on the subordinates' perceptions and thus further their gains. Bass contended that the lack of ethical and moral values is the distinguishing factor between Authentic Transformational leaders and Pseudo-Transformational leaders. Bass's introduction of the term *Pseudo-Transformational Leadership* was based on this premise. Bass further contrasted the leader's exhibition of positive behavior, which is used to mask their real participation in narcissistic intentions.

Bass (1985) theorized that the opposite of Authentic Transformational Leadership is Pseudo-Transformational Leadership. He made the distinction between leaders' intentions and their behaviors, which are often contradictory in the case of Pseudo-Transformational leaders. Bass strengthened his argument by stating that individuals' ethics, morals, and philosophy, rather than their behavior, were indicators of Authentic Transformational Leadership. From that premise, the Pseudo-Transformational Leadership model gained its differentiation from the Authentic Transformational Leadership model and deviated from positive leadership theory.

Pseudo-Transformational leaders create artificial crises where a dependency on the leader is needed. These artificial scenarios perpetuate subordinate compliance to ameliorate the predicament to pursue short-term gains (Bass 1985). Long-term goals, values, and subordinate development are characteristics of Authentic Transformational Leadership, with authentic influence bringing authentic transformation among subordinates. Bass (1985) noted the connection between leaders and subordinates as serving to raise the levels of morality and performance in both, while the lack of connectivity breeds Pseudo-Transformational behavior.

The model that Bass (1985) prescribed as a measurement of idealized influence, inspirational motivation, intellectual stimulation, and individualized consideration has important ramifications on indicators of the level of self-interest inherent in the leader's behavior. Bass expanded Burns's (1978) Transformational Leadership model to include leadership behavior and not only the leaders' characteristics. The subordinates' well-being is instrumental in gauging the effectiveness of the leader, which advances leadership application and influence. Bass (1998) also determined a leader should motivate subordinates to look beyond their self-interest. Bass made the distinction by differentiating between Authentic Transformational Leadership and Pseudo-Transformational Leadership, using behavioral metrics to indicate if the leader's actions were organizationally biased or self-serving.

Burns (1978) presented a cause-and-effect dichotomy that points to leadership character as a driver for ethical decision-making. However, Bass (1985) noted that one of the characteristics of a Pseudo-Transformational leader is being adept at masking behavior that appears to be morally directed. Bass proposed that the leaders' actions and not their character are true indicators of their motives. Both Burns (1978) and Bass (1998) addressed the emotional context that underscores the Pseudo-Transformational Leadership model, exhibited in the articulation of high idealized influence and hero worship (Bass 1985; Burns 1978). Bass (1985) initially described Transformational theory as being amoral, hence inclusive of Pseudo-Transformational Leadership, but later amended the theory after his conversations with Burns (1978).

Julian Barling (2014) theorized that understanding the antecedents and the causes of Pseudo-Transformational behaviors in leaders is more effective long-term, as these components are more instrumental in understanding and preventing the behavior than merely focusing on the consequences. Barling identified three similarities that Authentic Transformational and Pseudo-Transformational leaders share: (a) impacting the way that subordinates think about themselves, (b) their relationship with their leaders, and (c) their work.

Empowerment of subordinates yields both individual and collective benefits (Barling, Clegg, and Cooper 2008). Transformational Leadership practices enable subordinates to look beyond their self-interest toward collective gains (Barling, Fullagar, and Kelloway 1992). These positive manifestations are attributed to Authentic Transformational Leadership. Outcomes of Pseudo-Transformational Leadership include absenteeism, turnovers, physical and emotional health issues, and most recently, the trickle-down effect has impacted individuals beyond the work environment to include their homes. Barling, Fullagar, and Kelloway (1992) described three leadership styles occupying a continuum. Transformational Leadership occupies a continuum, oscillating from morality centered to egoism and narcissism centered: Transformational Leadership, Laissez-Faire Leadership, and Pseudo-Transformational Leadership.

Pure charismatic leadership is usually depicted by the results of Pseudo-Transformational Leadership and not the quality; the quality of leadership should be the defining nature of leadership rather than the consequences of that style (Barling 2014). Further leadership styles, such as Transactional and Laissez-Faire Leadership, can also be termed destructive based on their influence on subordinates. Pseudo-Transformational leaders engage in self-serving behavior that affects their subordinates. In some cases, this behavior goes through cycles rather than being constant in the organization. The short periods of abuse followed by longer periods of normal behavior falsely lull subordinates into a sense of hope that the abusive Pseudo-Transformational Leadership cycle is over. Trustworthiness, as seen by the subordinates, is the currency by which Authentic Transformational Leadership transpires (Barling 2014).

A rise in Pseudo-Transformational behavior by leaders is credited to their respective leaders exhibiting the same behavior toward them, thus, extending the trickle-down effects toward subordinates (Barling 2014). Subordinates engage in Pseudo-Transformational behavior toward other subordinates and even toward family members. Notably, the behavior was usually targeted toward individuals who appeared weak or unable to defend themselves; for example, subordinates who performed poorly were usually targeted. Accordingly, Barling maintained root cause analysis that identified the antecedents and causes should be the focus rather than only the consequences. Self-control is ranked high by Barling as a mechanism the leader can use to not repeat antecedent abuse to their subordinates.

Barling (2014) corroborated Bass's (1985) model of measuring leaders' effectiveness on subordinates. Both Barling and

Bass concurred idealized influence is more influential than high inspirational motivation, further dictating the necessity for self-regulation by leaders. Pseudo-Transformational Leadership is the unethical facet of Transformational Leadership, according to Barling. This behavior is depicted by a specific combination of Transformational Leadership descriptors, low idealized influence, and high inspirational motivation and is mostly exhibited in leaders who submit to their own egotistical and self-interested values. These leaders advance their self-serving agendas by dominating and controlling their subordinates. In focusing on self-interest, Pseudo-Transformational leaders are more intent on becoming personal idols than on the collective ideals that might benefit their subordinates.

Conceptual Framework Summary

Three leadership theories have been presented to explain both Authentic Transformational Leadership and Pseudo-Transformational Leadership. Burns's (1978) characterization of the Authentic Transformational Leadership model included charisma, intellectual stimulation, individualized consideration, and communication. Bass (2008) later expanded the Transformational Leadership model to include a more effective and widely practiced archetype composed of idealized influence or charismatic leadership, intellectual stimulation, inspirational motivation, and individualized consideration. Avolio and Bass (2004) called for a balance in the application of the model's elements, stating, for example, that an imbalance in inspirational motivation can influence unethical behavior in both leaders and subordinates.

Burns's (1978) theory purported that morality-based character and subsequent moral decision-making define the Transformational leader. Lack of morality precedes leadership decisions that adversely affect subordinates and their perception of the leader's intent and motives. Alternatively, Barling (2014) pointed to the quality or causes of leadership rather than to the consequences or effects. Comparing the leaders' character and values (Burns 1978), the results and consequences of their behavior (Bass 1985), and the quality of their leadership (Barling 2014) provides a deeper understanding of Transformational Leadership.

Review of the Literature and Methodological Issues

The term Transformational Leadership indicated both types of leadership styles: Authentic Transformational Leadership and Pseudo-Transformational Leadership. Their classification was used to address each separately. The research findings comprised both the process and behavior of negative leadership—Pseudo-Transformational Leadership—and how to recognize and derail the conduct that disrupts the positive leadership model—Authentic Transformational Leadership. The following themes were noted in the literature and are reviewed in this section: (a) origins of effective leadership, (b) leadership behavior triggers, (c) economic effect of Pseudo-transformational Leadership, (d) mechanisms for identifying transformational behavior, (e) Transformational behavior versus transformational character, (f) leadership challenges and emerging trends, (g) effective and ineffective leadership effects and practices, and (h) the future of Transformational Leadership.

Origins of Effective Leadership

The great man theory of effective leadership promoted decidedly masculine qualifiers (Carlyle 1888). This theory appeared to be commensurate with Pseudo-Transformational Leadership behavior and style, where leaders are portrayed as males and heroes who are unquestionably followed. A further distinction between a great man (leader) and a good man (behavior) supported the examination of the great man theory, as its practice could lead to the conscious or unconscious perpetuity of Pseudo-Transformational Leadership in organizations.

Leadership Behavior Triggers

The behavior versus the character of both Authentic Transformational and Pseudo-Transformational Leadership styles was evidenced as some researchers focused on the role that attentional resources play in limiting self-regulation (Collins and Jackson 2015; Kim, Choi, and Vandenberghe 2017). Several authors cited that an increase or decrease in self-regulation correspondingly could result in a positive or negative correlation with either Authentic Transformational Leadership or Pseudo-Transformational Leadership (Delegach, Kark, Katz-Navon, and Van Dijk 2017; Hetland, Hetland, Bakker, and Demerouti 2018; Kark, Van Dijk, and Vashdi 2018).

Self-regulation is an Authentic Transformational Leadership practice that may result in destructive or Pseudo-Transformational Leadership if not employed by the leader. Several researchers advocated a positive correlation between low stress and low negative emotional expressions resulting in more constructive self-regulation (Arnten, Jansson, Olsen, and Archer

2017; Collins and Jackson 2015; Liborius 2017). Other researchers showed how high-stress situations influence high negative emotional expressions that, in turn, suppress self-regulation tendencies, leading to Pseudo-Transformational behavior (Lepine, Zhang, Crawford, and Rich 2016).

Economic Effects of Pseudo-Transformational Leadership

A second theme prevalent in the literature was economic effects. From the business standpoint, several researchers focused on the economic ramifications of destructive leadership or Pseudo-Transformational Leadership (Garretsen, Stoker, and Weber 2016; Zehnder, Herz, and Bonardi 2017). The authors positioned the inequity between the company's rate of return and economic growth as factors that contribute to economic repression. This predicament ultimately impacted leaders' responsiveness in embodying Pseudo-Transformational behavior to pursue economic rather than moral endeavors. Other researchers cited subordinate engagement, job satisfaction, and burnout as indicators of distinct levels of dysfunction in leaders and drivers of Pseudo-Transformational behavior (Barrick, Thurgood, Smith, and Courtright, 2015; Bonner, Greenbaum, and Mayer 2016).

Mechanisms to Identifying Transformational Behavior

Additionally, research studies on Pseudo-Transformational Leadership recommended establishing effective mechanisms for identifying overt and covert behavior in the hiring of leaders as a means to proactively curtail the prevalence of future dysfunctionality (Caillier 2018; Fowler, Posthuma, and Tsai

2016). Authentic Transformational Leadership is leveraged on the constructs of purpose, motivation, trust, and respect, while Pseudo-Transformational leaders level these traits toward adverse ends. Trends were revealed in the transition from Authentic Transformational Leadership to Pseudo-Transformational Leadership (Law-Penrose et al. 2016). Some authors ascertained that leaders initially established the positive traits but leveraged them detrimentally to abuse their positions (Henry 2016; Lin, Huang, Chen, and Huang 2018).

Transformational Behavior versus Transformational Character

Another theme observed in the literature was the identification of leaders' behavioral tendencies, as opposed to their character traits. Bedi, Alpaslan, and Green (2016) sought to explore the constructs fully to locate the boundaries where errant behavior occurs. The focus then entailed only the explicit behavior of leaders rather than the implicit influence they have on subordinates. In both Authentic Transformational leaders and Pseudo-Transformational leaders, charisma and motivation are shared, which may represent two sides of the same coin; the extent to which the leaders leverage their effect on subordinates represents the good or bad side of the coin. This dichotomy supports Bass's (1985) model regarding how varying degrees of idealized influence, intellectual stimulation, inspirational motivation, and individualized consideration can inform either Authentic or Pseudo-Transformational Leadership.

Leadership Challenges and Emerging Trends

Further themes identified included leadership challenges, emerging trends, and studies that contrasted several leadership styles and their effectiveness. Analysis of subordinate commitment, satisfaction, and performance, as linked to leadership style, was evaluated as a benchmark to measure leader effectiveness (Ahmad, Abdul-Rahman, and Soon 2015; Atmojo 2015). For this intrinsic case study, literature studies were limited to the business environment to fairly assess comparative work environments. Specifically addressing this environment will lead to and expand the amount of literature available for business leadership styles and effects. A close examination of workplace conflict between supervisors and subordinates offered insight into leadership quality and relationship building.

Effective and Ineffective Leadership Practices

Grasping leadership challenges and trends requires appropriating perspectives from both leaders and subordinates on effective and ineffective leadership practices. Hughes and Harris (2017) portrayed Pseudo-Transformational Leadership (ineffective) as evolving from Authentic Transformational Leadership (effective), so a comparison of both styles of leadership is warranted. This comparison is important since, foundationally, the two styles share common traits that are further negatively exploited to influence Pseudo-Transformational Leadership behavior.

Authentic Transformational Leadership. Historically, Authentic Transformational Leadership has emerged as an answer to publicized immoral and unethical behavior by leaders (Yasir and Mohammad 2016). Authentic Transformational leaders not only model ethical and moral behavior but also communicate it to subordinates, who then replicate that behavior

(W. Zhu, Zheng, Riggio, and Zhang 2015). This modeling-communicating-modeling continuum stems from consistency between the leader's beliefs and their behavior. The consensual or tacit agreement leads to a mutual pursuit driven by joint Authentic Transformational activities. W. Zhu et al. (2015) made a distinction between a moral person and a moral leader. They argued that the moral person possesses moral attributes, while the leader personifies and acts out on those beliefs.

W. Zhu et al. (2015) also claimed that the Authentic Transformational leader intentionally influences the decision-making of the subordinate by demonstrating ethical principles, values, and standards. Effective interpersonal communication, they asserted, is another facet of the Authentic Transformational Leadership style; by remaining in constant communication with subordinates, the Authentic Transformational leader's behavior is reinforced in subordinates. This level and quality of communications bolster trust in leaders and reinforce and measure the effectiveness of the communications (W. Zhu et al. 2015).

Other research on Transformational Leadership contrasts Authentic Transformational Leadership, which is deeply rooted in practices that are ethically and morally bound, with the self-serving dispositions that Pseudo-Transformational Leadership employs. Dark triad personality traits, characterized by narcissism, Machiavellianism, and psychopathy, are ascribed to leaders whose behavior is driven by a focus on short-term returns rather than the big picture (Birkás and Csathó 2015; Cohen 2016). On the contrary, the Authentic Transformational leader is focused on a broader view that benefits the entire organization, rather than just themselves.

Authentic Transformational leaders affect the behavior of their subordinates (Alavi and Gill 2017). This influence transcends beliefs, instills hope and optimism, and subsequently impacts individual and collective performance in the organization. By affecting the perception of subordinates, leaders can introduce change that is accepted by subordinates, culminating in their participation in change-driven activities.

Pseudo-Transformational Leadership. Several authors noted a distinction between a character-driven Pseudo-Transformational leader and a leader who temporarily adopts Pseudo-Transformational behavior. These authors affirmed that a consistent focus on short-term returns describes the Pseudo-Transformational leader; however, an Authentic Transformational leader may adopt this behavior for the short term, especially to facilitate strategic organizational change. According to these authors, leaders then resume Authentic Transformational behavior once the change has been successfully implemented (Alavi and Gill 2017; Anand, Vidyarthi, and Park 2018; Babalola, Stouten, and Euwema 2016; Balogun, Bartunek, and Do 2015; Buch, Martinsen, and Kuvaas 2015; Chen, He, and Weng 2018; Hughes and Harris 2017; Pater 2015).

Staats (2016) described situational leadership as entailing a focus on disparate situations and employing the right type of leadership response to yield positive outcomes. Per Staats, leaders who adopt situational leadership can influence subordinate perception, belief systems, and subordinates' subsequent behaviors. Graham, Ziegert, and Capitano (2015) explained that a situational leadership style is typically ascribed to the Authentic Transformational leader; however, this style can also describe the Pseudo-Transformational leader. Further, task-oriented leadership can also describe Pseudo-Transformational leaders who focus on the task at hand rather than the impact on subordinates (Blair, Helland, and Walton 2017).

Pseudo-Transformational Leadership behavior, despite traditionally being undesirable, is increasingly gaining both popularity and visibility. This behavior is driven in part by readily available content such as social media and streaming devices, which furthers a focus that is heavily bent toward self-centeredness (Nübold, Bader, Bozin, Depala, Eidast, Johannessen, and Prinz 2017). Pseudo-transformational narcissistic behavior is driven by power and control (Boje, Rosile, Saylors, and Saylors 2015; Ford and Harding 2018). However, subordinates are more perceptive of these practices than are the leaders themselves (Lin, Huang, Chen, and Huang 2017; Peck and Hogue 2018).

Well-intentioned Authentic Transformational leaders who are intent on pursuing pro-organizational goals can unwittingly exhibit Pseudo-Transformational behavior. This behavior occurs if the organizational goals are not ethically and morally aligned (Belschak, Den Hartog, and Kalshoven 2015; Effelsberg and Solga 2015; Graham et al. 2015). The authors observed that self-awareness stemming from high emotional intelligence is valuable and necessary in Authentic Transformational Leadership. Strong correlations exist between self-awareness and leadership efficacy, which in turn drives subordinate perception, engagement, and corresponding behavior (Matthew and Gupta 2015).

Effects of Authentic Transformational and Pseudo-Transformational Leadership. Authentic Transformational Leadership describes a leadership style that is engaged in enacting long-term positive changes in an organization (Creswell 2016). These changes include subordinate development, which is subsequently tied to organizational outcomes (Thompson and Glasø 2015). Organizational image is usually tied to leadership image, so the internal and external perception of the organization is usually focused on the leader's behavior (Malmendier and Tate 2015). Public personas can be cultivated to affect public perception (Malmendier and Tate 2015). In this sense, leadership behaviors are predictors of organizational outcomes and success. Since Transformational Leadership includes both Authentic Transformational and Pseudo-Transformational leaders, the outcomes stemming from their actions can be either positive or negative.

The derivative impact of Pseudo-Transformational Leadership can influence organizational pursuits. If one considers this correlation, it is important to examine trends in leadership. Buch et al. (2015) expressed the importance of examining this relationship since they deduced that Pseudo-Transformational Leadership was another facet of Authentic Transformational Leadership. Future trends in leadership that will be impacted by Pseudo-Transformational Leadership include (a) organizational success, (b) change leadership, (c) entrepreneurial-oriented leadership, (d) intrapreneurship, and (e) organizational restructuring.

Organizational success. Cote (2017) cited that a leadership approach is instrumental in instilling and, in some cases, remediating ineffective practices. Impactful drivers of organizational success include how subordinates perceive a leader's effectiveness. This perception is often linked to the leader's motivation, performance, and efficiency (Damij, Levnajić, Rejec Skrt, and Suklan 2015). An organization's critical analysis of leadership qualities that promote success creates workplaces that are proactive in assessing both leaders' and subordinates' work behaviors (DuBois, Koch, Hanlon, Nyatuga, and Kerr 2015; Gaddis and Foster 2015).

Collins and Jackson (2015) proposed a self-regulatory model for leaders to enhance their propensity toward Authentic Transformational Leadership. The model also differentiates between the characteristics that define constructive (Authentic Transformational) and destructive (Pseudo-Transformational) leadership styles. Assessing the distinction between Authentic Transformational Leadership and Pseudo-Transformational Leadership can prescribe how a company recruits, retains, and supports its leaders and, ultimately, the performance of the organization.

Leaders and subordinates can co-create agreed-upon objectives so accountability generates future actions. Individuals who participate in this practice are self-aware since actions should align with predetermined outcomes (Bucklin, Alvero, Dickinson, Austin, and Jackson 2000). Collins and Jackson (2015) introduced a brain-based attentional mechanism to explain how self-regulation is activated and argued that destructive leadership embodies both contextual and dispositional factors: leaders amid pressure to decide usually make rash decisions based on inaccurate or insufficient information.

The lack of this preemptive mechanism was shown to directly correlate the role of Pseudo-Transformational Leadership to both the mental and physical states of subordinates (Bergethon and Davis 2018). Placing leadership in the broadest possible context takes into consideration the interdependencies and impact of decisions (Kossek, Petty, Bodner, Perrigino, Hammer, Yragui, and Michel 2018). Local, national, and international communities are impacted, and notably, the conflicting definitions and responsibilities of leadership roles can be problematic, which, in essence, can promote bad behavior in leaders (Kranabetter and Niessen 2017; Ogbonnaya, Daniels, Connolly, van Veldhoven, and Nielsen 2016).

Authentic Transformational Leadership stipulates self-regulation and, therefore, the need to identify destructive behavior patterns that sometimes exhibit themselves as charismatic personality types (Collins and Jackson 2015; Holmes 2015). Research in leadership's best practices, as well as identification of deterrents to positive behavior, is necessary to further gains in productivity and efficiency. As the leadership paradigm continues to shift, so must engagement in research follow to provide informed, innovative, and proactive guidance.

The Future of Transformational Leadership

The dynamics of Transformational Leadership necessitate growth and further application of the principles that are foundational to the leadership style. Eight leadership trends are currently being exploited to support the growth, challenges, and competition that organizations poised for future success face. Trends in future leadership include pursuing effective change management, entrepreneurial leadership, intrapreneurship, restructuring organizational hierarchy, agile leadership, thought leadership, and knowledge management as strategic advantages. The following leadership trends will be examined further: (a) change management, (b) organizational entrepreneurship, (c) organizational intrapreneurship, and (d) restructuring organizational hierarchy.

Change management. Transformational leaders have embraced change management. In the past, facilitating organizational reformation was a core activity advocated by leadership theory (Wang, Demerouti, and Le Blanc 2017; Zhao, Seibert, Taylor, Lee, and Lam 2016). The problem-solving Transformational leader is sought after to help the organization gain operational efficiencies because of and during organizational change. Change leadership is critical in shifting cultural precepts and implementing new strategies (Pater 2015). Research results can guide the Transformational leader's actions in sustaining meaningful change. Effective change leaders possess a composite of both intellectual and ethical foundational qualities that drive organizational conversion. Transformative learning requires deconstruction and reconstruction; sometimes, to go forward, one must retreat to where weltanschauung gained its inception (Mezirow 1994). Transformational learning engaged in self-reflective practices based on previously established foundations is critical to leadership efficacy. Another facet of the transformative theory involves collaborative decision-making.

Critical inquiry and innovation-driven leadership promote better relationships in the organization. Anticipatory leadership practices for the future point to research that will guide leadership development (Ardichvili, Natt och Dag, and Manderscheid 2016). Strategic leadership challenges are growing commensurate with the complexity of the global environment (Sowcik, Andenoro, McNutt, and Murphy 2015). Adaptive change that decreases ineffective Pseudo-Transformational behavior and retains Authentic Transformational behavior is necessary. Innovative research is required to align leadership practices that move the organization into a future that leverages human capacity.

The leadership-subordinate narrative is one of collective problem-solving that builds on an existing relationship where the subordinate's perception of the leader's trustworthiness is the currency of organizational effectiveness. Attracting and retaining loyal and productive subordinates can be problematic if Pseudo-Transformational Leadership is perceived. In the Ohio State Studies, Stogdill, as cited by Northouse (2016), established the difference between leadership behaviors such as initiating structure and consideration. Leaders who allow character-driven ethics to steer their personal and professional actions have emerged as formidable influencers in enduring organizational changes (Shin, Seo, Shapiro, and Taylor 2015).

These learning leaders, motivated by personal beliefs based on solid ethical foundations, engage in self-reflection and continual scholarship to align current research outcomes with personal and professional pursuits as necessary. Transformational leaders must be willing to reassess their own beliefs in consideration of the transitional attributes of provisional knowledge. From this foundationally secure position, the leader is then able to foster change in the environment, motivating others and replicating themselves in the process (Gathondu, Nyambegera, and Kirubi 2018; Imran, Ilyas, and Aslam, 2016; Mezirow 1994).

The core objective of replicating leadership behavior in subordinates is at the heart of Transformational Leadership (Pater 2015). Both types of Transformational Leadership, Authentic Transformational Leadership and Pseudo-Transformational Leadership, intentionally or unwittingly replicate themselves in their subordinates. Additional research on the Pseudo-Transformational Leadership model, behavior, traits, and beliefs may provide insight on how to recognize its existence and circumvent its application and effects. A subordinate approach versus a leadership approach to Pseudo-Transformational Leadership is warranted since little research has been done on subordinates' perceptions of Transformational Leadership behavior in their leaders.

Organizational entrepreneurship. Teece (2016) advocated exploiting the capabilities of entrepreneurially-minded Transformational leaders to design new business models that transform the organization's goals into measurable results. Entrepreneurial orientation (Engelen, Gupta, Strenger, and Brettel 2015; Renko, El Tarabishy, Carsrud, and Brännback 2015; Shafique and Kalyar 2018) positively affects the performance of the organization. An entrepreneurial leadership style embodies accountability and ownership, traits that are reflected in Authentic Transformational Leadership. Innovation and creativity are hailed as being precedents to the complexities of organizational sustenance (Jaiswal and Dhar 2015).

Companies desiring to invest in growth do so by investing in the competencies and abilities of their Transformational leaders. Strategic renewal is the aim of capitalizing on entrepreneurial leadership in existing organizations (Blanka 2018). Organizational entrepreneurship leverages the capabilities of the Transformational leader in exploring opportunities and garnering consensus to pursue them (Koryak, Mole, Lockett, Hayton, Ucbarsaran, and Hodgkinson 2015). Organizational core competencies and capabilities are contingent on the transformational practices of leaders whose vision-driven organizations exploit entrepreneurial opportunities (Kuratko, Hornsby, and Hayton 2015).

One negative characteristic manifested in Pseudo-Transformational Leadership is what Gaddis and Foster (2015); Haynes, Hitt, and Campbell (2015); and Tourish (2013) called the *dark side* of leadership behavior that is influenced by organizational entrepreneurship. Haynes et al. (2015) maintained that greed and hubris have a detrimental effect on human and social capital; the pursuit of money coupled with an overblown self-confidence (hubris) can affect leaders who act independently of ethical constraints and who do so because of the desire for power, wealth, and recognition. Renko et al. (2015) agreed with Haynes et al.'s (2015) assertion that the organization's confidence in the leader's abilities to be proactive and take risks could backfire. The open-minded characteristic often seen in these leaders may be misrepresented when the leaders are engaged in single-minded pursuits that benefit them.

Organizational intrapreneurship. There is a positive correlation between organizational intrapreneurship and organizational growth; organizational intrapreneurship behavior by subordinates is seen as being decisively affected by Transformational Leadership (Valsania et al. 2016). Transformational leaders empower their subordinates to exercise intrapreneurial principles to drive innovation and promote collaboration (Deprez and Euwema 2017). Transformational practices of coaching and mentoring are instrumental in creating intrapreneurs; however, their presence in the organization is influenced by mentors who are either Authentic Transformational or Pseudo-Transformational leaders.

In contrast to organizational entrepreneurship, organizational intrapreneurs recognize and capitalize on existing organizational opportunities, while organizational entrepreneurs create new organizational opportunities (Blanka 2018). Atienza (2015) acknowledged that the dictates of global competition warranted diverse business practices, including intrapreneurship initiatives. Blanka (2018) agreed, citing innovativeness and the competitive advantage that intrapreneurial practices contribute to organizational success. Both Atienza and Blanka observed that individual-level initiatives that are influenced by Transformational Leadership are evidenced in subordinate performance.

Organizational entrepreneurship and organizational intrapreneurship work in tandem to support organizational learning. Organizational learning contributes to organizational knowledge, which can be leveraged as a core competence (Haase, Franco, and Félix 2015). Jeffcoat and Basnet (2015) asserted that subordinates engaging in intrapreneurship behavior share the load that is usually borne by the Transformational leader only and that load sharing is instrumental in producing efficiency, profitability, and sustainability in organizations that support this practice.

There are positive intrapreneurial influences on Authentic Transformational Leadership; however, intrapreneurship can also spawn Pseudo-Transformational Leadership behavior. This manifestation is predicated in part on a lack of research in proportion to that of Authentic Transformational Leadership evidenced in organizations. Achieving organizational goals is established by the Transformational leader's application of a holistic approach that collectively meets the needs of the organization and positively influences subordinates (Shafique and Kalyar 2018).

Restructuring organizational hierarchy. Resistance to change can obstruct proposed changes in the organizational structure; however, to lessen change impact, some approaches ensure participation and collaboration from affected stakeholders. Nørskov, Kesting, and Ulhøi (2017) found that despite traditional practices, change can occur in non-hierarchical settings and that such change is largely influenced by the Transformational leader. A positive correlation between organizational hierarchy and organizational capabilities was indicated by Li, Yuan, Ning, and Li-Ying (2015). Conversely, a negative correlation between structure and capability also exists.

Organizational leaders can perform assessments to identify the change impact on their subordinates. Formality and protocol will also present a significant issue. Pseudo-Transformational leaders who may be accustomed to insulation from subordinates in silo-based structures are now forced to interact in less formal and on-the-fly exchanges. To address this transition, the pros of this realignment were recommended: (a) reduction in meetings and emails, (b) concurrent task performance that reduces time, and (c) participatory decision-making, the latter also decreasing time (Masa'deh, Obeidat, and Tarhini 2016). These benefits of restructuring engage subordinates in collaborative and innovative practices rather than having it occur only in top-down scenarios.

Impact of organizational structure on Pseudo-Transformational Leadership. Pseudo-Transformational Leadership thrives in traditional organizational structures, where leaders reside in silos that prevent them from directly communicating with subordinates and vice versa. Restructuring the traditional organizational leadership hierarchy from the top-down authority in silo-based structures to structures based on interpersonal relations is paramount to effective Authentic Transformational Leadership. Such restructuring yields operational efficiencies such as knowledge sharing (Han, Seo, Yoon, and Yoon 2016). This practice, however, can decrease accountability from the leaders, who operate in a command-and-control environment and are insulated from the realities of organizational perception and practices.

Another negative by-product of siloed structures is territorialism. Safeguarding job security is prohibitive to knowledge sharing, which inhibits collaboration. The hierarchal structure that is in place hinders more than aids in the joint process that is indigenous to Authentic Transformational Leadership. Pseudo-Transformational Leadership manifests itself in territorialism. Thus, understanding the iterative cycles in collaboration and accountability, with frequent inspection, may yield insight on how to set and keep the organization and its leaders on the right course.

A traditional organizational structure exacerbates the lack of communication and creates incubated silos with only a vertical bi-directional flow of information (Mills and Boardley 2017). A more collaborative structure that fosters communications from various entities and exudes transparency is warranted to remedy the situation. Several alternatives to the traditional organizational structure exist that foster collaboration between subordinates and leaders. Some of these structures place leaders amid communications and eliminate the silo effect; Rosen (2013) noted constructive confrontation is preferred, and a structure that supports this is warranted.

The model of accountability embraces a collaborative culture where accountability is bi-directional. The perception of accessibility coupled with the visibility of leaders establishes trust and availability, two factors that enable effective collaboration. An all-access policy promotes spontaneous collaboration and subsequent real-time approaches to interaction. Insulation of leaders creates silos that generate level-consciousness and, at the very least, hampers communications. At its worst, the lack of communication can impact company performance, subordinate morale, and leadership efficacy (Brands, Menges, and Kilduff 2015; S. L. Choi, Goh, Adam, and Tan 2016).

Subordinates who were influential in taking the organization to its present state may not be the same that will take them into the future, and an organization's corporate culture can be the determining factor between success and failure. Not only is the structure of the organization important, but it is also a tool that can be used to motivate the subordinates. The type of organizational structure can also be a factor in the industry they operate in, as some may require a more rigid structure, while others, like the arts, tend to be more flexible. Organizations needing to be more responsive to market demands have to react quickly, and decision-making capability may be distributed throughout the organization, not just flow from the top-down, creating the collaborative model that they support (De Vries and Van der Poll 2016; Schenkel and Brazeal 2016; Strese, Meuer, Flatten, and Brettel 2016; X. Zhu and Bao 2017).

Synthesis of Research Findings

The authors within the review of literature provided an analysis of Authentic Transformational Leadership from which Pseudo-Transformational Leadership evolved or was contrasted (Northouse 2016). Characterization of both Authentic Transformational and Pseudo-Transformational Leadership behavior was evidenced. Some authors cited a balance between how both types of leaders managed self-regulation was telling, as imbalance signaled Pseudo-Transformational Leadership behavior (Collins and Jackson 2015). Proponents of Authentic Transformational Leadership cite its constructive virtues, such as ethical and moral foundations, which in turn fuel their behavior and decision-making (Riivari and Lämsä 2017). Leaders who demonstrate positive behavior tend to promote the same behavior in their subordinates (Ahmad et al. 2015; Khalili 2017; Meuser et al. 2016; Patterson et al. 2013; Reiley and Jacobs 2016). Also, negative behavior exhibited by Pseudo-Transformational leaders would produce the same in their subordinates (Caillier and Sa 2017; Christie, Barling, and Turner 2011; Cohen 2016; Cote 2017; DeShong, Grant, and Mullins-Sweatt 2015; Dussault and Frenette 2015).

Research findings on Transformational Leadership support the need for tools to measure the impact of the business leader's behavior on subordinates. The same character traits that propel Authentic Transformational leaders act as vehicles to launch evil, ineffective, and unproductive outcomes and gains inherent in Pseudo-Transformational Leadership (Schuh, Zhang, and Tian 2013). Northouse (2016) identified charisma as idealized influence because of the emulatable qualities of the leader. Idealized influence is exhibited by both Authentic Transformational and Pseudo-Transformational leaders. Authentic Transformational leaders, however, operate by integrity and high moral standards. Both types of leaders are charismatic, but the Pseudo-Transformational leader is deficient in the ethics and morals that define Authentic Transformational leaders.

According to Patterson et al. (2013), Pseudo-Transformational Leadership is likely to persist due to an individual's reticence to confront a business leader. A mental cost/benefit analysis influences a subordinate's decision on whether to confront unacceptable behavior in a leader and hold them accountable. Several factors prevent subordinates from being confrontational, including fear of repercussions, fear of the confrontation yielding non-beneficial returns, and fear of exacerbating the situation. In some cases, the thought of confronting a superior may bring up barriers to buttress job security or the relationship with the superior (Caillier and Sa 2017). The lack of confrontation may falsely lull a leader into thinking that they are doing everything right, which may result in further activities based on self-interest.

According to Chai, Hwang, and Joo (2017), Cikaliuk et al. (2015), and Cohen (2016), organizational commitment drives organizational outcomes, so subordinates' perceptions of the leaders' behaviors can lead to counterproductive work performance. Effelsberg and Solga (2015) and Einolander (2015) noted that conflicts between organizational interest and other interests affect how subordinates perceive the organization, which, in turn, affects their subsequent organizational commitment. The litmus test on organizational trust can provide insight into the type of leader present, as innovative organizations, although boasting positive facets, sometimes fall prey to Pseudo-Transformational practices.

Evidence of Pseudo-Transformational practices was usually indicated by the subordinate's perception of the leader's moral disengagement (Bonner et al. 2016). This perception, left unaddressed, can affect subordinates' commitment, attitudes, and behaviors, resulting in a negative association with the leadership model (Boon and Biron 2016; Buch et al. 2015). Subordinates work harder if they perceive an alignment with the leader's activities and the organization's mission (Carpenter and Gong 2016).

Pseudo-Transformational Leadership can influence organizational performance, credibility, and moral identity. Leadership integrity necessitates a consistency that transcends a moral identity designed to prescribe and solidify moral behavior. Since Pseudo-Transformational Leadership impacts the subordinate outcome, proactively understanding its triggers as well as its effects offers insights into employing countermeasures to eradicate the behavior and lessen its impact on the organization, its subordinates, partners, shareholders, and customers (Kim, Liden, Kim, and Lee 2015).

Self-regulation was offered as a panacea to redress a leader's Pseudo-Transformational behavior, particularly if there were economic ramifications to the behavior. This behavior often resulted from stressful conditions in the workplace (Zehnder et al. 2017). In the literature review, I examined the Pseudo-Transformational leader's effect on subordinate engagement and preventive measures such as hiring practices that identified and rejected prospective leaders with Pseudo-Transformational proclivities.

Binary depictions of Transformational Leadership as either Authentic Transformational or Pseudo-Transformational were evident in findings (Cooper 2015; Pandey, Davis, Pandey, and Peng 2016). Some authors, however, portrayed Pseudo-Transformational Leadership as a destination along the Transformational Leadership range that spanned the gamut from Authentic Transformational Leadership to Pseudo-Transformational Leadership (Hoch, Bommer, Dulebohn, and Wu 2018; Hughes and Harris 2017). This distinction was supported by claims that both Authentic Transformational leaders and Pseudo-Transformational leaders share the same foundational traits of inspiration, motivation, and charisma (Anderson and Sun 2017; Gebert, Heinitz, and Buengeler 2016; Graham et al. 2015; Miller 2015; Rosenbach 2018).

Critique of Previous Research

Findings from the literature review revealed a focus on the behavior versus the character of both Authentic Transformational and Pseudo-Transformational leaders. A Pseudo-Transformational leader was personified as highly motivational and inspirational despite hiding their true selfish intentions from their subordinates. The cognitive dissonance exhibited between character and behavior was found to be stressful for both the leaders and the subordinates (LePine, Zhang, Crawford, and Rich 2016; Liborius 2017). Stress caused by change initiatives was often a factor in realigning both leaders' and subordinates' behaviors and actions in moving the organization forward. An adoption of Pseudo-Transformational practices by an Authentic Transformational leader was deployed to implement the change, after which the Pseudo-Transformational leaders regressed to initial Authentic Transformational Leadership behavior (Law-Penrose et al. 2016).

Carlyle (1888) found early acceptance of the great man theory, especially as it seemingly corroborated Allport's (1937) trait theory. However, because of the gendered view on what constitutes an effective leader, it is more suitable to be a predictor of Pseudo-Transformational Leadership behavior. Comparing Authentic Transformational Leadership to Pseudo-Transformational Leadership unearthed the acceptable qualities and the antithesis of each. This comparison was necessary to further define Pseudo-Transformational Leadership due to the disproportion of Pseudo-Transformational research in comparison to Authentic Transformational Leadership.

Authentic Transformational leaders must simultaneously instill effective leadership practices while remediating ineffective leadership practices. Organizational success is incumbent on effective leadership (Cote 2017). Collaborative leadership that proceeds from transformational practices can be instrumental in remediating an organization, as in the case of Lee Iacocca (Malmendier and Tate 2015). Along with collaborative leadership is a trend toward entrepreneurial-orientated leadership (Engelen et al. 2015). However, greed and hubris can influence these entrepreneurial leaders driven in part by the confidence of the organization in their abilities. The results: entrepreneurial leaders single-mindedly pursue personally beneficial goals instead of organizationally responsible ones.

Intrapreneurship (Valsania et al. 2016) empowers subordinates to recognize and capitalize on existing growth or change opportunities in the organization. Although holistically beneficial, if subordinates are led by Pseudo-Transformational leaders, goals pursued will benefit their self-interest and not those of the organization. Finally, a call for a flattening and de-siloing of traditional organizational structures is warranted based on its environment being the breeding ground for Pseudo-Transformational Leadership.

Summary

I conducted the literature review with a focused search strategy on Authentic Transformational Leadership and Pseudo-Transformational Leadership behavior. Pseudo-transformational behavior constituted either a derivative of Authentic Transformational Leadership behavior or its antithesis. The conceptual framework for Pseudo-Transformational Leadership evolved from Burns's (1978) Transformational Leadership theory, Bass's (1985) transformational theory, and Barling's (2014) science of leadership. This framework provided the context from which Transformational Leadership was studied.

Burns (1978) positioned degrees of moral and ethical character traits as exemplifying either an Authentic Transformational leader or a Pseudo-Transformational leader. Bass (1985) expanded Burns's (1978) theory and introduced four principles governing those behaviors: (a) idealized influence, (b) inspirational motivation, (c) intellectual stimulation, and (d) individualized consideration. Barling (2014) presented the concept that Transformational Leadership occupies a continuum and leaders operate in varying degrees of Authentic Transformational and Pseudo-Transformational behavior.

Themes identified in the search included: (a) origins of effective leadership, (b) leadership behavior triggers, (c) economic effect of Pseudo-Transformational Leadership, (d) mechanisms for identifying transformational behavior, (e) transformational behavior versus transformational character, (f) leadership challenges and emerging trends, (g) effective and ineffective leadership effects and practices, and (h) the future of Transformational Leadership.

The future of Transformational Leadership includes behavior that engenders (a) change management, (b) organizational entrepreneurship, (c) organizational intrapreneurship, and (d) restructuring of organizational hierarchy.

In chapter 3, the intrinsic case study methodology is presented, and the research question is constructed. My role as the researcher is outlined to provide clarification and transparency to the participants and other stakeholders, including the Dissertation Committee and the Institutional Review Board. A research population and sampling method describing who the research population is and the process of obtaining a quality sample is presented. Also discussed are intentional participation logic, research instrumentation, data collection, and a data analysis plan. Finally, techniques are proposed to verify and validate the trustworthiness of the data collected.

CHAPTER 3

Research Method

Within this intrinsic case study, I explored subordinates' perceptions of their leaders' behaviors in a global company. Qualitative research promotes problem-solving and allows participants to describe their experiences (Creswell 2013). Insight into subordinates' perspectives can enlighten leadership practices, which may provide improvements in the organization (Tichy and Cohen 2007; Yin 2014). The problem is subordinates in a large global company are not allowed to anonymously convey their opinions, nor are they given a formal process to share their perceptions of their leaders' behaviors and how these behaviors affected them. The purpose of this intrinsic case study was to illustrate within a large global organization subordinates' perceptions of their leaders' behaviors as being Authentic Transformational or Pseudo-Transformational based on self-interest.

Research gaps in Pseudo-Transformational studies include the issue of only focusing on the leader's character rather than the subordinates' perceptions of the leader's actions. In the following section, I present the research question, define my role as a researcher, explain the purpose and design of the study, and describe the research population and selection logic. Also, instrumentation and data collection are specified, along with identifying the attributes, data analysis, and validation of the design. I then discuss issues of trustworthiness, ethical issues, my position as a researcher, and finally, a summary of chapter 3.

Research Question

The following research question was used within this intrinsic case study:

How do subordinates describe their perception of whether their leader's behavior was Authentic Transformational or Pseudo-Transformational based on self-interest?

Role of the Researcher

As a researcher, I wanted to uphold the rigor of the qualitative framework and perform the research in a manner that supported unbiased findings that emerged from the data collected. Wolcott (1994) presented criteria to ensure trustworthy research, advocating that the researcher pursues an inverse relationship between listening and talking; more listening forecasts a higher quality study. Exercising active listening helped to empower individuals to share their perceptions of their leaders' behaviors.

My role was to first obtain approval from the dissertation committee and the Institutional Review Board (IRB). Upon approval, I then secured approval from the study site. My role as the researcher entailed informing the volunteers of my function in the intrinsic case study to objectively interview and transcribe their responses and to assure them of the confidentiality and non-biased synthetization of the data collected. Establishing my role as a researcher served dual purposes: informing volunteers of how the study would be conducted and distinguishing that role from my other role as an employee of the study site. I maintained the role of an active listener during the process. I posed established questions, objectively asked subsequent questions, probed for clarification when necessary, recorded reflective notes, and respected the rights of the participants. I also transcribed responses within twenty-four hours of the interview.

Purpose and Design of the Study

The purpose of the intrinsic case study was to illustrate within a large global organization subordinates' perceptions of their leaders' behaviors as being Authentic Transformational or Pseudo-Transformational based on self-interest. The executive leaders of the organization were interested in exploring employee perception and in identifying gaps in communicating and implementing the organization's strategy. The leaders wanted to identify viable talking points, which would then equip them to directly address the subordinates' perceptions. Executive leaders were also interested in proactively crafting Authentic Transformational behavior and sought tools that were intentional, goal-oriented, and measurable. The leaders anticipated that results from the case study could serve as inputs into initiatives that would impact the level of commitment and propel them to mutually rewarding outcomes.

A case study research design was best suited for the study of the Transformational Leadership experiences in the organization. Other designs that did not fit the scope of the research were: (a) narrative—describing participants' life stories, (b) grounded theory—general theory driven by participants' views, (c) phenomenological—participants' experiences of phenomena, and (d) ethnography—observing participants in a cultural group over time (Creswell 2016). The case study design can supply comprehensive descriptions of the perception of leadership, including providing context, such as nonverbal behavior (McMillan 2012). A positivist approach to qualitative research relies on the causal relationship in the current case study and can also be applied to other studies (A. Lin 1998). Additionally, an intrinsic case study type allows for real-time observation and collection of data.

Research Population and Sampling Method

The research site was a global entity that delivers multiple solutions to different industries. The organization was comprised of 4,100 employees. Only the 171 employees who make up the North American division of the organization were invited to participate in the study. The North American division of the organization includes employees from both the United States and Canada. The North American executive leadership team was comprised of seven leaders. Seven functional areas in the North American division participated, allowing for a broad perspective of the organization's leadership behavior.

The following steps were taken to recruit participants: First, I created a list of activities that were needed before conducting the study. The North American executive leadership team sent an email to inform employees about the study and to solicit volunteers. Simultaneous with that communication, I prioritized, summarized, and filtered the organization's data provided to me by the Human Resources Department of the organization.

I reviewed the demographics of the North American population, then used this aggregated data to assess the demographics and other organizational classifications of the volunteer population. This aggregation was done to assess whether the volunteer participants constituted a relative sample of the organization's population, which would inform the quality of the research findings. I then employed intentional sampling to select volunteer participants.

Participant Selection Logic

Slavin (2008) and Stover (2007) advised against choosing participants unintentionally or without purpose, which may cloud objectivity and diminish the quality of the research. Subsequently, employing purposeful selection yielded a fair representation of the organization's leaders and subordinates, which may help to leverage the social capital to align with organizational strategies. Purposeful sampling allows for multiple perspectives of the research topic, yielding rich information, which adds to the credibility of the research (Patton 2002).

Following approval from the study site, the executive leaders of the organization sent an initial announcement via email to all employees, including a description of the proposed research, its value, and the need for volunteers for the study. They also explained the confidentiality of the study and that anonymization and aggregation of the data would be performed. The announcement also contained an off-site email address, which I created specifically for the study.

Individuals interested in participating in the study were instructed to contact me via the dedicated email address. Interested individuals were given two weeks to respond. Once the participants responded, I sent them a questionnaire to collect demographic information. I then conducted a review of their demographics to ensure the volunteer participants were diverse enough to relatively represent the organization's population.

This review was done to safeguard compliance with the predesigned purposeful sampling methodology. For example, male and female ratios and ethnically balanced criteria were sustained for a fair representation of the organization's demographics. The aggregated data provided by the Human Resources Department allowed me to identify the total numbers and ratios of different demographics, for example, the total number of male versus female employees. I then strove to ensure that the research sample represented the male-to-female ratio of the North American organization's employees.

In table 1 below, I showed the representative sample of the participants consisting of different citizenships, different ethnicities, employees who work from a corporate office and employees who work remotely, females and males, leaders, subordinates, varying ages, and varying tenures. I then showed their demographic correlation to the relative distribution of the research population. The participants represented seven functional areas in the division, which allowed for a broad perspective of the organization's leadership behavior.

	# of Participants	% of Research	% of Organization
Males	15	68%	62%
Females	7	32%	38%
Leaders	4	18%	27%
Subordinates	18	82%	73%
Remote	15	68%	49%
Non-Remote	7	32%	51%
Caucasian	17	77%	72%
Other	5	23%	28%
Canada	5	23%	29%
USA	17	77%	73%

Table 1: Demographic Distribution of Participants

The average tenure of the participants was four point six years, and the average age was forty-five. The sample consisted of twenty-two participants: eighteen subordinates and four leaders. Since the leaders also reported up the organizational chain of command to the executive leadership, they were also considered subordinates. I conducted a total of twenty-six interviews, comprising twenty-two interviews with subordinates and four interviews with leaders. First, fifteen males represented 68 percent of the participants, and seven females represented 32 percent of the same population.

The participants included four leaders who represented 18 percent of the participants, and eighteen subordinates represented 82 percent. A total of fifteen remote employees represented 68 percent of the participants, while seven employees constituting 32 percent of the participants, worked non-remotely. Those of a Caucasian ethnicity comprised seventeen participants and 77 percent of the ethnicities, and five non-Caucasian participants classified as other represented 23 percent. Finally, five Canadians represented 23 percent of the participants, while seventeen participants living in the United States represented 77 percent of the research population. The average age of the participants was forty-five, and their average tenure was four point six years.

A representative sample from each functional area in the North American division of the organization was selected to ensure a demographically balanced study. Intentional sampling included proportionate participation from the following demographics: male-to-female ratio, age range, ethnicity and race, leader to subordinate, remote versus on-site subordinates, age range, and tenure of employment (see figure 2).

Figure 2. Visual representation of research sample and organization population.

Instrumentation

The primary research instrument is the researcher. Additionally, a questionnaire and individual interviews were used during the study. The initial questionnaire was used to collect demographic information to compare with the aggregated demographic data received from the organization's Human Resource Department. I compared the data to ensure a demographically balanced study. After I had selected the participants, I conducted the interviews. I used a dedicated email address during the case study to facilitate communications between the study participants and myself. This dedicated email was also used to ensure confidentiality.

I took notes during and after the interviews to highlight certain responses and to perform additional follow up as necessary to clarify responses. I used Excel spreadsheet software to aggregate (filter and sort) the case study data. I also used a PowerPoint presentation constituting a slide deck containing explanations of the Transformational Leadership model. Zoom, a video conferencing tool, recorded and stored the interviews on my personal computer's hard drive. Participants also provided a pseudonym or were given one for the interviews to ensure confidentiality.

Data Collection

The importance of data collection and its validity in substantiating research results were the reasons why the interviews were recorded and subsequently transcribed (Creswell 2013). Data collected from participants in the interview sessions required quality collection processes. This collection entailed accurate measurements and valid instrumentation (Lingenfelter 2011). The yield of these quality processes led to subsequent quality research outcomes. Data were collected to the point of data saturation where no new themes or information was evident (Guest, Bunce, and Johnson 2006).

I selected the web conferencing tool Zoom to conduct the interviews because of its ability to perform video conferencing and record the sessions. The Zoom communications tool was also chosen to ensure the comfort and convenience of the participants during the interview stage. They were able to choose a location outside of work where they felt comfortable and at ease in expressing themselves. Video conferencing was also the standard in the organization for meetings and interviews. This familiarity was important because it can be a key component in informing an honest interaction and can aid in distinguishing between theory and practice (Safazadeh, Irajpour, Alimohammadi, and Haghani 2018). I performed note-taking using OneNote to transcribe the participants' comments.

I asked the participants nine structured interview questions to delve deeper into the perception of transformational behavior in their leaders and whether self-interest was a correlative driver. The different questions constituted the multiple lenses by which observers could frame their perceptions and answer the hows and whys predicated by case study research.

Identification of Attributes

Identifying which attributes would be considered behavior-defining was important because illustrating the perception of subordinates of their leaders' behaviors was the purpose of the case study. I used four attributes of Transformational Leadership as prescribed by Bass (1985). Subordinates rated their leaders on a scale of 1 to 10 to assess how these attributes characterized their leaders' behaviors. Leaders also rated themselves on those four behavioral attributes.

The first attribute of a leader is *idealized influence*, which is the governing connection between the subordinate and the leader. This leader is often characterized as being charismatic. *Inspirational motivation* is the leader's cogent communication of the organization's vision so that subordinates own it and are vested in its fruition. *Intellectual stimulation* is the ability of the leader to engage subordinates in problem-solving, critical thinking, risk-taking, idea generation, and facing challenges. Finally, *individualized consideration* denotes the leader's ability to emotionally connect with subordinates to understand them to better serve them. Coaching and mentoring are important aspects of individualized consideration, as they aid in solidifying the leader-subordinate relationship.

Data Analysis Procedures

Evidence-driven change is garnered from qualitative research, which is possible through concrete data analysis (Slavin 2008). Inductive data analysis allows for paradigm flexibility, allowing restructuring and progressive elaboration of the research framework as necessary (McMillan 2012). I employed inductive data analysis to inform the leaders of the business of how their behaviors were perceived by subordinates. Following the interviews, I transcribed the recordings verbatim. After entering phrases and sentences in an Excel spreadsheet, I analyzed the data by filtering and sorting to reveal themes, patterns, and trends. This analysis was used to identify emerging and subsequent patterns (Creswell 2013). Similar words and phrases began to appear, so I grouped them into categories. Data saturation was reached when no new patterns or categories appeared. From those categories, themes began to emerge.

Patterns included attributing certain behavior to a type of Transformational Leadership. These emerging patterns allowed for categorical aggregation and the construction of deeper meanings. During the initial round of coding, participants' responses were entered into a spreadsheet whose columns designated each of the four Transformational Leadership styles: (a) Authentic Transformational, (b) Transactional, (c) Laissez-Faire, and (d) Pseudo-Transformational. The columns were ordered relative to their effectiveness and prevalence, as indicated by the research I conducted. I then reviewed the responses to identify if certain words or phrases were used to describe the leadership behavior. Next, I searched all of the responses to find if they occurred in other interview responses. Multiple occurrences of similar responses were identified as a theme and assigned to a column alongside the responses. This process was used to ensure that natural human proclivity for subjectivity did not influence the data. Clark Pope (2017) stated that the researcher should constantly engage in a self-monitoring and auditing iteration to ensure that data analysis was conducted without bias. Any recognition of patterns was supported by data validation, which promoted objectivity and non-bias.

The participants' responses were given a code and classified utilizing Karlström and Runeson's (2006) chain of evidence. Based on Karlström and Runeson's (2006) chain of evidence model, (a) leadership behavior constituted actual events in the organization; (b) the intrinsic case study's subjects were interviewed and asked to provide their observations and experiences; (c) a sound recording of the interview was performed, with concurrent note-taking by the researcher; (d) the recording was then transcribed to further comprehend the statements and comments; (e) a research database was used to group quotes that represented and strengthened themes and patterns, and finally, (f) evidence-driven conclusions supported by the aggregation of the data reported was performed.

Once participants identified the primary style, I asked them to assign a percentage to each Transformational Leadership type. For example, a participant designated that out of 100 percent, X percent of the time their leader exhibited one of the four styles. I then asked them to be more specific to identify the degree to which the leader exhibited that style. This clarification was accomplished by showing them behavioral traits describing each style, and I asked them to rate those behaviors on a scale from 1 to 10. Finally, I asked them the interview questions and then aggregated the responses to reveal common themes.

The four-round approach was intentional in allowing a logical progression from a high-level identification of leadership behavior to a more granular classification of how that behavior was exhibited. This iterative approach allowed me to first assess whether Transformational Leadership was present and to what degree and assign qualifiers to the varying degrees. Data management and analysis were performed using Excel, a commercially available spreadsheet product that allowed for filtering, sorting, graphing, and pivoting of data to reveal key themes. The themes are closely aligned with the conceptual framework of Authentic Transformational Leadership and Pseudo-Transformational Leadership and the prescribed descriptors.

This prevailing methodology drove the cadence of moving from data to actionable information in my transcription of the interviews. Categorization of the interview responses provided informative and actionable meaning perspectives. At the culmination of the interviews, I established and corroborated themes, and I reached data saturation. I further examined the themes to note the similarity and significance of the alignment of consecutive data points.

Validation of the Research Design

The validity of the qualitative study was important, as it described the relationship between the study's design and outcome and the degree to which similar studies could be replicated (Creswell 2013). Both methodology and approach were used to validate the research design. Accurate data validation was instrumental in ensuring that the study was credible. This validation was accomplished by reviewing the interviews, notes, and subsequent categorization of the data.

I further engaged the participants as co-analysts in the research study by revisiting responses that needed clarification and answering questions before and following the data collection. Participants were prompted to freely communicate their position on the questions asked and seek clarification as necessary.

Assumptions

A researcher's worldview and approach to the inquiry are framed by assumptions (Levitt et al. 2018). An assumption within this study was that the research might be limited by participants' reluctance to report on their leaders' behavior for fear of retaliation. It was expected that some participants might not respond because of these fears, and further, if they did respond, they might not be as forthcoming with their answers. Another assumption was that the North American organization was experiencing changes that might affect the employees' perception of the leadership, who may temporarily adopt a Pseudo-Transformational Leadership style in the interim and resume transformational behavior once the change was implemented (Law-Penrose et al. 2016; Lee et al. 2018).

Delimitations

Delimitations are restrictions in the scope set by the researcher (Creswell 2016). I constrained the case study's scope to the North American division of the global organization, although there are several divisions in Europe and other continents. Including those participants was prohibitive for several reasons, including language barriers, cultural differences, and perception of research methodologies. The North American population includes both American and Canadian leaders and subordinates. Another delimitation was to limit the leadership styles to the Transformational Leadership model. Although there are other models, the research involved only Transformational Leadership.

Limitations

Factors that are outside of the control of the researcher are known as limitations (Creswell 2016). The participant pool was limited to those who were willing to be interviewed, which may limit the range, variety, and quality of data collected. Although participation selection logic was inclusive of achieving balance in data collection, for example, male/female ratio, age, tenure, and on-site versus virtual subordinates, this may not be representative of the respondents and participants in the intrinsic case study.

Newer subordinates, for example, may not want to participate in the survey, while more tenured subordinates may justifiably or unjustifiably exaggerate their views on their leaders' behaviors. Finally, subordinates who are virtual, working from their home offices, may not believe they are familiar enough with their leaders' style to participate in the research study.

Dependability

Research dependability was established by the repetitiveness of the data gathered. Dependability of data was critical to the research findings, so transcription of the field notes within twenty-four hours of the open-ended interviews as opposed to recounting the events later was necessary. My dual roles as the researcher and an employee of the research organization required taking steps to separate the two roles. When transcribing the notes, I was aware of the need to remain unbiased and not "go native" since doing so could skew the validity of the research.

Additionally, I presented myself as a trusted subject matter expert on the topic of Transformational Leadership. I relayed to participants the years of research that I conducted in addition to my occupying several Transformational Leadership roles. Findings from the study were the only input into evaluating the responses. Multiple audits of the data were performed to improve data accuracy. Any contradiction in earlier findings was examined to ensure quality. Finally, a data audit was performed at the end of the data analysis with the intent to review the data collection processes used and to objectively identify and eliminate any bias that may potentially skew the data collected and subsequent findings of the research.

Ethical Issues

Revisiting the conceptual framework was important to the integrity of the research to ensure that the questions followed a logical process. This process was undertaken to support the research question in addition to garnering quality results that would buttress the furtherance of the research and serve as a basis for decision-making. It was also important for me to be as specific and unambiguous as possible without leading the participants. Although the questions represented a hierarchy starting with descriptive, then progressing to evaluative, it was important to certify the answerability of the questions by keeping them unbiased and independent of each other (Creswell 2013).

Ethical considerations were submitted, and approval was obtained from the Institutional Review Board and Dissertation Committee. Additionally, I received permission from the president of the North American division of the study site organization to conduct the research. Consent forms were obtained from the participants of the research study, which included both leaders and subordinates. The forms contained requirements for consent for interviewing and recording the participants. The form's content also addressed the research purpose, the requirements of the participants, how the study will be conducted, and how the findings will be disseminated.

Conflict of Interest Assessment

The emotional and physical safety and well-being of the participants were of utmost concern. In my role as a researcher, guarding against going native was crucial to not obscure objectivity because I also worked for the organization for which I was conducting the research. The researcher's degree of going native can influence the variance of the field notes from being descriptive to a more in-depth interpretive analysis of the participants' behavior and could mean the difference between objective and subjectivity. My philosophical paradigm, creed, and beliefs could also affect the work and intentionally maintain objectivity to strengthen the research and thoroughly address the research question without presupposition (Glesne 2011).

Precautions were taken to ensure confidentiality and to prevent the disclosing of any related information and findings to unauthorized personnel in the organization. A Non-Disclosure Agreement was entered into between myself and the organization to ensure that confidentiality was maintained during my employment tenure. This precaution also addressed any inherent ethical issues that might be associated with the research and the use of the resulting outcomes. Finally, a Statement of Original Work form was submitted.

Researcher's Position

My position in the organization required that I maintained confidentiality, objectivity, and trust with the participants and the executive leaders of the organization. Because I was reporting on leadership behavior, it was important that I protected the confidentiality of the participants, ensured their emotional safety, and avoided exploitation of my position as a researcher. I reviewed with the participants the research tools that would accomplish this, including my personal and professional ethics, the Institutional Review Board, and the Non-Disclosure Agreement.

Clear and specific communications were employed to establish me as a subject matter expert on transformational behavior. Communication barriers (Kelly 2004) inhibit understanding of both the evaluation procedures and the results. Several factors prevent people from being confrontational, including fear of repercussions, fear of the confrontation yielding non-beneficial returns, and fear of exacerbating the situation. In some cases, the thought of confronting a superior may bring up barriers to buttress job security or the relationship (Patterson et al. 2013). My position as a researcher was to bridge the gap that will allow confrontation of leaders' behavioral issues without repercussions.

Summary

The purpose of this intrinsic case study was to illustrate within a large global organization subordinates' perceptions of their leaders' behaviors as being Authentic Transformational or Pseudo-Transformational based on self-interest. Accordingly, a thorough plan on how to design the study, recruit qualified participants, and explain my role as a competent researcher was presented. My role as a researcher was additionally important, as I am also employed with the organization where I conducted the study. Efforts were outlined to anonymize the identity of the participants to not be viewed as a liability, including the selection and refinement of the logic to secure qualified research participants. Participants were selected by demographics that fairly and accurately represented both the leadership and subordinate population of the organization.

The utilization of questionnaires and interviews were introduced as instruments for recruitment and for conducting the research. Various steps were outlined to protect both the participants and Concordia University to ensure confidentiality and validity of the research methodology and summarization of the findings. Rigorous steps were taken to conduct and report on a valid and substantive case study on subordinates' perceptions of their leaders' behaviors as being Authentic Transformational or Pseudo-Transformational based on self-interest. Accordingly, documents and artifacts, including consent forms and agreements, were used and are included in the appendices. In chapter 4, the data analysis and results will be presented along with a description of the research sample, methodology used in analyzing the data, a summary of the research findings, and a presentation of the data and results that were gathered.

CHAPTER 4

Data Analysis and Results

The purpose of this intrinsic case study was to illustrate within a large global organization subordinates' perceptions of their leaders' behaviors as being Authentic Transformational or Pseudo-Transformational based on self-interest. The Transformational Leadership models advanced by Burns (1978), Bass (1985), and Barling (2014) framed the research. I chose the qualitative case study, an inquiry strategy, as the best procedure to use for providing insight into the behavior of the study site's leaders. A comprehensive understanding of the issue resulted from in-depth, one-on-one interviews of the participants and subsequent synthesis of the themes and patterns in their responses.

An overview of the iterative and integrative process of data collection is presented, followed by the refinement process of data analysis, and the results that constitute associations with patterns and themes are presented in chapter 4. The sample population is identified and described. The methodology and analysis by which the findings were contrived are outlined, followed by a summary of the findings. The data is then presented with supporting results. Finally, the chapter is concluded with a cumulative summary.

Description of the Sample

The study site organization was a global entity that delivers multiple solutions to different industries. The organization was comprised of 4,100 employees. Only the 171 employees that make up the North American division of the organization were invited to participate in the study. The North American division of the organization included employees from both the United States and Canada. The participants represented seven functional areas in the division, which allowed for a broad perspective of the organization's leadership behavior.

The sample consisted of twenty-two participants: eighteen subordinates and four leaders. Since the leaders also reported up the organizational chain of command to the executive leadership, they were also considered subordinates. A total of twenty-six interviews were conducted, comprising twenty-two interviews with subordinates and four interviews with leaders. There were fifteen males and seven females; fifteen participants worked remotely; seven worked from an office; seventeen resided in the United States, and five resided in Canada. The average age of the participants was forty-five, and the average tenure of the participants was four point six years. Additionally, 77 percent of the population self-reported their ethnicity as Caucasian, while 23 percent reported their ethnicity as non-Caucasian. Although their ethnicity was identified, I provided a classification of "other" because identifying each ethnicity other than Caucasian may have led to the identification of the participants in that category. This aggregation allowed me to determine whether the participant sample demographically represented the organization.

The relationship between the participant sample and the organization's population is portrayed in table 2. In the research population: (a) 68 percent were male, and 62 percent of the organization's population were male; (b) 32 percent of the research population were females, and 38 percent of the organization's population were females; (c) 18 percent of the research population were leaders, and 27 percent of the organization's population were leaders; (d) 82 percent of the research population were subordinates, and 73 percent of the organization's population were subordinates; (e) 68 percent of the research population worked remotely, and 49 percent of the organization's population worked remotely; (f) 32 percent of the research population work in an office, and 51 percent of the organization's population work in an office; (g) 77 percent of the research population lived in the United States, and 72 percent of the organization's population lived in the United States; finally, (h) Canadian employees made up 23 percent of the research population and 28 percent of the organization's population.

Having relative demographic representation was important to validate the results of subordinates' perception of the effect of Transformational Leadership and the subsequent impact on behaviors and performance. Additionally, providing actionable empirical findings from the participants' responses was important for both the organization and the academic community. The North American organizational structure is fairly flat, with few levels of hierarchy. This allowed for more direct observation of Transformational Leadership behavior.

	Number of Participants	% of Research Population	% of Organization
Males	15	68%	62%
Females	7	32%	38%
Leaders	4	18%	27%
Subordinates	18	82%	73%
Remote	15	68%	49%
Non-Remote	7	32%	51%
United States	17	77%	72%
Canada	5	23%	28%

Table 2: Representative Sample of Organization Population

Methodology and Analysis

Examining contemporary issues to understand their root causes and to facilitate deeper understanding fits the intrinsic case study methodology (Stake 1995; Yin 1994). I used this methodology to understand how subordinates described their leaders' behaviors in the organization and to assess whether self-interest was a factor. This understanding was gained using the following tools: recruitment of the participants, the instrumentation used, and the data collection process. Inductive data analysis was used to identify themes and patterns from participants' responses (McMillan 2012). Data analysis was performed simultaneously with data collection to identify themes, patterns, and trends and to detect data saturation.

Summary of the Findings

Yin's (2017) technique, comprising a linear-analytic structure, includes problem, related work, methods, analysis, and conclusions. I used this technique to present the synthesized data and results. The structured pre-planned approach undertaken for this intrinsic case study comprised a chain of events yielding answers to the following research question: How do subordinates describe their perception of whether their leader's behavior was Authentic Transformational or Pseudo-Transformational based on self-interest?

Using the positivist approach allowed me to ascribe meaning and understanding to the subordinates' perceptions of their leaders' behaviors. Using questionnaires and interviews to collect data, later aggregated and summarized, I observed themes emerging that described the leaders' behaviors. The findings from the research question are provided below.

Question #1: How do subordinates describe their leader's behavior as being Authentic Transformational or Pseudo-Transformational based on self-interest?

Organized findings supported the participants' interpretation of Transformational Leadership behavior and its impact on subordinate behavior. To establish if Pseudo-Transformational behavior was driven by self-interest, I had to first ascertain that Pseudo-Transformational Leadership was present. Accordingly, data from the one-on-one interviews were amalgamated to inform: (a) the perception of the type of leadership behavior exhibited in the organization, (b) the presence of Pseudo-Transformational behavior, (c) the degree of Pseudo-Transformational Leadership, and (d) the extent to which it was observed by subordinates as being driven by self-interest.

Data sources used included an initial questionnaire and one-on-one interviews. Contextual implications from the first round of coding and synthesis revealed that all four types of Transformational Leadership behavior were present:

1. Authentic Transformational,
2. Transactional,
3. Laissez-Faire, and
4. Pseudo-Transformational.

Participants were shown the four types of leadership styles and informed of the behavioral traits of each style to confidently establish the presence of Pseudo-Transformational Leadership. The educational component of the study was important in extrapolating the occurrence of Transformational Leadership behavior and establishing credibility and supporting confidence in the research findings. Many participants were already knowledgeable about the Transformational Leadership model.

Participants were then asked to assign a percentage to each of the leadership styles exhibited by their leader. They were instructed to assign the highest percentage to the style exhibited most of the time. They were further instructed to assign the remaining percentage to the remaining styles, to aggregate the assignment to equal 100 percent. The assignment to each leadership was aggregated, yielding the following representation of Transformational Leadership behavior: Authentic Transformational, 45 percent; Laissez-Faire, 29 percent; Transactional, 14 percent; and Pseudo-Transformational, 12 percent. Figure 3 depicts the percentage assigned by the participants to each type of leadership behavior observed in the organization:

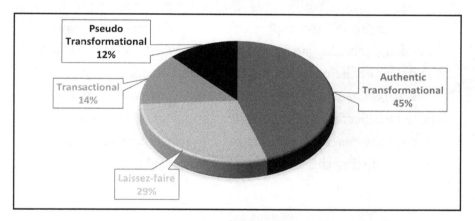

Figure 3. Percentage assigned by the participants to each type of leadership behavior observed in the organization.

Of importance was that out of the 22 participants interviewed, only one indicated that the leader or the participant himself demonstrated a singular type of leadership behavior all of the time. That behavioral type was Authentic Transformational Leadership. The elasticity of Transformational Leadership behavior to include all four types—Authentic Transformational, Transactional, Laissez-Faire, and Pseudo-Transformational—seemed to be a common thread in the subordinates' describing their leaders' Transformational Leadership behaviors and will be outlined further in the "Discussion" and "Conclusion" sections of chapter 5. Four leaders participated in the study, three males and one female. The research findings indicated that the female leader rated herself lower in her Authentic Transformational Leadership behavior than her male counterparts.

Presentation of the Data and Results

A case study is both process and product, according to Stake (1995). An important aspect of case study research requires knowledge sharing and disseminating results clearly so that the voices of the participants are heard (Chandler, Anstey, and Ross 2015; Creswell 2013). Data-driven results emerged from the data collection and synthetization processes used in interviewing the research participants. Results supported by data collected during the interviews are presented as follows.

Questionnaire

A questionnaire was sent out to the organization's population after they were apprised of the intended case study. The use of the questionnaire was to solicit demographic information to compare with the demographics of the organization's population. The information from the questionnaires was used for the intentional selection of the participants to relatively represent the organization's population. The demographic information collected from the participants is listed in table 1.

Interviews

Data collection was conducted using one-on-one structured interviews with the participants. Zoom, a web-based videoconferencing tool, was used to conduct and record interviews. The interviews entailed nine questions tailored to prompt participants to describe the Transformational Leadership behaviors of leaders.

Question #1: How do subordinates perceive the transformational behavior of leaders?

Six participants indicated a culture of Authentic Transformational Leadership by responding by pseudonym as follows. Joe, "Leaders are honest and transparent." Roy, "Leaders had an overarching view of how their team can help the organization as a whole." Una, "Leaders are engaged in purposeful behavior." Three participants described the communications style of their leaders: Kim, "clear in communication"; Ben, "organized in thought and process"; Tara, "forthright and transparent." Others assessed the communications process they observed, established their credibility with the leaders, and helped to build a strong team. Collaboration was cited by two participants as important: Claude noted that the leader "gets in a foxhole with the team." David described the collaboration as the leader "has skin in the game."

Participants reported Laissez-Faire Leadership behavior in the organization, stating that the absence of leadership empowered them to be "CEOs of their organization." Tara appreciated the lack of leadership and indicated how it made her feel, stating said her leader was "self-motivated" and "instilled confidence." Wally and Nancy criticized the lack of leadership, arguing that it marginalized their contributions to the organization. Wally noted that she was "only being measured by utilization." Nancy said the leader was "myopic and not holistic." David recommended how objective evaluations should be conducted: "driven by customer success and satisfaction." The hands-off approach is detrimental to growth, according to Larry, who cited a "lack of leading by example." Others noticed that because both them and their leaders worked remotely, it fostered Laissez-Faire Leadership; points of contact were few since subordinates were empowered to perform with little supervision.

Roy, Sally, and Vera reported the practice of Transactional Leadership at the organization. They noticed a cascading effect to that behavior in that their leader's supervisor also exhibited Transactional Leadership behavior. David and Opal remarked that Transactional Leadership was effective, as a "bonus is tied to it." Others indicated that in that type of environment, they were only acknowledged by their leader if they "win deals" (Kim, Opal, Claude, Mimi, Roy). Others (Zelda, Quincy) noticed that high performers were preferred by their leaders and that if there was conflict, their leader would side with the high performer without vetting the information they received.

Some participants indicated that leaders were intentionally pursuing goals that would allow them to reflect positively in the eyes of the executive leadership and, in essence, compete with the subordinates. To that end, Paula stated, "Ego is present...can't admit when wrong." Zelda stated:

"It seems like there is some self-praising the manager likes to do; it's happened every time I've asked. I was told, 'Send it out to the group and see if somebody can answer it,' so I send it out to the group, and the manager is the first person to respond with an answer. Why couldn't you just tell me that in the email specifically to you, asking you if you knew the answer?"

David stated:

"There's been a couple of projects that the manager was working on and had passed those off to somebody else on the team, finding out from the team that the project is problematic and challenging. What I see is the manager is keeping projects that they like or feel can do good for them in their career and passing off the ones that are more challenging and problematic."

Una reported:

"It seems that management is driving a lot of things by self-interest…a lot of innovations were started to make us shiny, but they don't work." Kim: "It's more of 'this is what we are going to do, so do it,' without consideration of what the impact will be."

Other participants (Zelda, Una, Frank, Quincy) indicated that individuals' abilities were downplayed for the leaders to "look good" without consideration of the subordinates. There was a sense of disconnectedness between subordinates and their leaders. Specifically, Ben reported, "There's a disconnect between him and upper management and us." Further, Larry noted, "People [are] not utilized to their full potential." Several noticed a disconnection between their leaders and their leaders' superiors. For example, Claude stated, "Ego is related to fear of upper management." Also, Paula said, "I hope this research doesn't fall on deaf ears and that it works because it needs to." Wally added, "Pseudo-transformational culture is prevalent, that 'yes man' and keeping upper management happy." Whereas Amy reported, "Information is siloed, segregated, and piecemealed: that drives the culture to appease upper management only."

Question #2: *How do subordinates perceive the Pseudo-Transformational behavior of leaders?*

The self-interested Pseudo-Transformational behavior of the leaders was viewed to be sustainably aligned with creating an environment inundated with fear, frustration, and a survivalist mentality. Some participants commented that self-interest had dual drivers: ego and fear. Particularly, Amy said, "We are losing knowledge because of the self-interests of some of those executives." Erin stated, "It's Pseudo-Transformational, and it points upwards, so it's basically when someone is watching, not for the benefit of the organization necessarily but to save face." Xavier added, "Leadership behavior is driven by self-interest and ego." Joe noted, "Leadership is driven by fear." Kim commented about leadership being "driven by ego and self-interest." Opal shared the "leader is not open to different views." Finally, Travis said the "leader exhibits fear of confrontation and consequences."

Question #3: *Is a leader's self-interest positively and significantly related to Pseudo-Transformational Leadership?*

Most of the responses indicated that a leader's self-interest was positively and significantly correlated to Pseudo-Transformational Leadership. Of the twenty-two participants, only one indicated that a healthy amount of self-interest was needed to pursue career aspirations and promotion. Specifically, Larry stated, "I tend to think that you need some of that self-interest to succeed in your goals and selfishly get your advantage so that you can take your team with you."

Contemplative comments included Quincy, saying subordinates "don't have a say; if the manager says you did something, that's all." David added, "He can't admit when he is wrong; even though he is wrong so many times, he won't admit it...it's sad." Mimi said the leader was "driven by self-interest and fear." Nancy noted, "Self-interest and fear drive leader." Claude stated the "leader picks good projects and passes on problematic projects to someone else and keeps the projects they like."

Question #4: Does self-interest explain the variability in Pseudo-Transformational Leadership practices?

Authentic Transformational Leadership was reported to be evidenced by a high degree of collaboration and positive reinforcement; however, it was not evident in Pseudo-Transformational Leadership. Vera stated, "It is always regarding how it's perceived as to how they are doing their job." Value was placed in accepting input and feedback and vetting out information. Mimi said, "It seemed that if ideas came up that was different from the manager's, they didn't seem to be weighted, so they seemed to be kind of discarded." Joe noted, "...reactive leadership, taking something in and acting on it."

Frustration was communicated regarding the absence of Authentic Transformational Leadership, shrouded by the prevalent practice of Pseudo-Transformational behavior. For example, Frank stated:

"If there is a one-on-one conversation, usually those feel quite sincere and motivating, but in a group setting or meeting where others are invited or included, the feeling kind of goes down a little bit, and sometimes I feel, not just myself but others, experience talking down to rather than talking to us or encouraging us."

Erin added, "Eye service only when politics can work in your favor, not the greater good for staff."

Question #5: What is the correlation between a leader's interest and effective leadership?

Participants repeatedly described an environment where the leaders' interest in remaining employed or being promoted superseded that of being responsive to the needs of the subordinates they led and engaging them in creative and innovative practices. The real or imagined fear of castigation or retaliation from the leader often translated to frustration by the subordinates. The one-directional fixation by leaders on how they were perceived by executive leadership was a source of frustration, as evidenced in the following responses. Amy shared, "There seems to be constant punishment coming out of nowhere, and it seems to be quite personal, and it makes for a very stressful environment." Ben noted, "Lots of self-praise." Xavier suggested the leader "should look at the person, not the resource."

Question #6: How does a leader's Pseudo-Transformational behavior affect subordinates?

Attrition leading to organizational knowledge leaking was cited most often as the impact of Pseudo-Transformational behavior. For example, Wally said, "We have a lot of brilliant people here, and some I don't think are utilized to their full potential because they are not allowed to think out of the box." Travis commented about the "attrition and loss of good subordinates." Tara noted, "We have lost a lot of good subordinates because they feel that the work they are doing is falling on lost ears." The downstream impact of the behavior was seen as being easily replicated; subordinates often repeated the behavior of leaders by adopting a self-serving stance and operating in a survivalist mode.

The survivalist mentality exhibited the same self-interested behavior that participants cited as being Pseudo-Transformational and not effective. Joe commented, "More negative qualities are easily replicated." Nancy noted, "They engage in information holding to show they know more than they do." Larry said, "Covering his [redact], doesn't want to put himself on the line." Erin shared, "Information is siloed, segregated, and piecemealed that drives the culture to appease upper management only." Ben added, "People will talk about bad experiences before they talk about the good ones."

Question #7: How is the adoption of Pseudo-Transformational Leadership influenced by self-interest?

Participants reported that the environment of change causes uncertainty. They further reported that lack of information sharing greatly accelerated that uncertainty, leading to leaps in speculative conversations and activities. In addition, there was a shutdown of communication from subordinates, who do "just enough" to survive (Amy). These individuals cited often that a sales environment was not sustainable due to unrealistic sales targets and that incentive-based performance appraisal was insufficient to motivate and galvanize subordinates. They also noted that self-interested-based Pseudo-Transformational Leadership lacked high levels of engagement, which was negatively correlated with possessing emotional intelligence. Particularly, Travis said, "We're in a sales environment, where everything is related to protecting yourself." Paula reported, "I can play dumb well; don't question my ability and intellect on certain things." Amy suggested, "There need to be three types of managers: HR manager, team manager, and product manager."

Question #8: Is there a trade-off between self-interest and optimizing organizational gains?

Knowledge management and sharing were cited as being critical as an organization pursues Authentic Transformational Leadership. Knowledge hoarding, the antithesis of sharing, was seen to be prevalent and instrumental in creating not only gaps between leaders and subordinates but among subordinates as well. Knowledge hoarding created horizontal silos in place of the vertical ones that were removed. Frank observed:

"There's definitely some self-interest there. There is a lot of information holding, from my perception, to be the owner of that information so that way it needs to go through that person so they become more, I guess, needed, which causes a lack of information sharing."

Question #9: What impact does the perception of Pseudo-Transformational Leadership have on subordinates' behaviors?

Subordinates reported that a shared vision was not present, and a disconnect that fostered misunderstanding was present.

Notably absent were the principles of Authentic Transformational Leadership, which include idealized influence, inspirational motivation, intellectual stimulation, and individualized consideration. The negative connection to the subordinates exhibited by Pseudo-Transformational behavior translated to the subordinates emulating the leaders' behaviors instead of individualized consideration and intellectual stimulation. Joe said, "The most negative leadership qualities can be replicated through bad attitudes and the passing on of negative emotions. Good qualities are not as easily replicated as the negative ones." Paula added, "It's easier to adopt bad attitudes than the good ones; you can subconsciously slip into bad attitudes."

Interview responses were reviewed, and common themes were identified in the participants' responses. Research findings supported the presence of both Authentic Transformational Leadership and Pseudo-Transformational Leadership. Pseudo-Transformational Leadership, it was reported, was primarily driven by self-interest, secondarily by fear, and thirdly by ego. Fear, the second driver of Pseudo-Transformational behavior, it was reported, is comprised of two states: (a) a leader whose behavior was driven by fear and (b) the leader instilling fear in subordinates.

The underlying observations stated in the responses were that self-interest-based Pseudo-Transformational Leadership was first driven by the sales cycle; secondly, the maturity of the product, and thirdly, the uncertainty about the product's competitive viability to similar offerings in the marketplace. The overall uncertainty in the environment, it was perceived, instigated a leadership behavior that was driven largely by the product's condition, instilling an atmosphere of self-interest-driven Pseudo-Transformational behavior to protect oneself and to survive in the face of uncertainties. This is common in the product life cycle at the introduction and growth apex, which is influenced by change, rate of change, product maturity, and market and external conditions.

In conducting the case study, I first determined if Transformational Leadership behavior was present. Considerable attention was taken to establish the presence of Transformational Leadership. This negated the presence of any outliers that may prevent a true assessment of the correlation between Pseudo-Transformational behavior and self-interest. The first analysis confirmed the presence of four types of Transformational Leadership: Authentic Transformational, Transactional, Laissez-Faire, and Pseudo-Transformational.

Nine participants in the intrinsic case study indicated that Pseudo-Transformational Leadership was present. Thirteen participants did not observe the practice of Pseudo-Transformational behavior. Seven out of the nine participants who reported Pseudo-Transformational reported self-interest as a driver in exhibiting that behavior, strengthening confidence in the construct of the research questions.

Comments establishing supporting evidence of Pseudo-Transformational Leadership behavior influenced by self-interest are present in the following participants' comments. Repeated similar comments revealed common themes that included leaders being unable to express mistakes, being dictatorial, hoarding knowledge, being territorial, exhibiting self-centeredness, focusing on personal gains, favoring competitiveness over collaboration, being divisive, having pernicious tendencies, emoting and exercising detrimental manipulation over empowering subordinates.

Some comments were as follows: Vera stated, "To him, everything he does is perfect; he doesn't mess up. He was driven by his self-interest rather than what my needs were." Ben reported, "Pseudo-Transformational Leadership is based on self-interest and ego, based on tenure, high stress, and high profile." Paula stated, "He's been doing this for a long time, so definitely there's a lot of self-interest." Sally noted, "In one-on-one sessions, talked about himself for twenty minutes." Una stated, "Career aspirations promote self-interest." Ben observed the leader "does not utilize and empower the team to handle things." Mimi said, "Self-interest is when politics can work in your favor rather than for the greater good of the company." David cautioned, "Be careful; they will throw you under the bus."

Comments supporting the question on the impact that self-interested Pseudo-Transformational Leadership has had on subordinates' behavior are presented as follows: Larry said, "It's very much a cascading effect that's causing these leadership issues to appear." Joe noted a "disconnect between upper and lower management." Kim commented, "Don't see the ability to move up." Amy shared, "The direct report above my manager is driven by fear, and it is not positive. It's cascading downhill and making it difficult and affecting how things are being done. It's detrimental within the team." Tara cautioned, "You have to make sure that you are not rubbing up against that gray area because then you run out of people that are going to trust you." Roy said, "Pseudo-Transformational Leadership replicates itself." Nancy claimed, "Pseudo-Transformational Leadership is toxic." Larry stated, "Pseudo-Transformational leaders don't see how it impacts others." Frank said, "They have lost people who have a lot of knowledge, and they just let them walk out the door; you can't get that back, and they don't get that." Amy was just "resigned to 'it is what it is.'" Una shared, "I experienced fear constantly, and more often than not, looking back, I had good results." Xavier added, "Pseudo-Transformational Leadership is cascading as pressure from upper management to provide success without given the tools to do so."

Summary

The research question for this case study was: How do the subordinates perceive their leaders' transformational behaviors as being Authentic Transformational or Pseudo-Transformational based on self-interest? A majority of the participants, 45 percent, described their leaders' behavior as Authentic Transformational, while 12 percent described Pseudo-Transformational behavior. Of the 12 percent who identified Pseudo-Transformational behavior, 76 percent perceived the Pseudo-Transformational behavior to be driven by self-interest. In chapter 5, I will discuss the conclusions, examine and summarize the results of the literature, and present limitations and their implications.

CHAPTER 5

Discussion and Conclusion

The purpose of the intrinsic case study was to illustrate within a large global organization subordinates' perceptions of their leaders' behaviors as being Authentic Transformational or Pseudo-Transformational based on self-interest. One-on-one interviews and subsequent analysis of data collected revealed themes, patterns, and trends that served to answer the research question: How do subordinates describe their perception of their leaders' behaviors as Authentic Transformational or Pseudo-Transformational based on self-interest? In chapter 5, I present a summary and discussion of the research study results, then I consider the results about the literature on Transformational Leadership. Limitations and implications on practice, policy, and theory are assessed, followed by recommendations for further research. Finally, a conclusion of the research is presented.

Summary of the Results

More than 50 percent of participants in the case study expressed appreciation that the organization was interested in hearing them voice their opinions about leadership behavior. They indicated they were hopeful their ideas would be heard and changes would follow. Participants also conveyed their desire to participate in future studies on Transformational Leadership. Among the participants, seventeen delivered emotionally charged responses due, in part, to being able to express themselves freely without fear of retaliation and being able to contribute to an endeavor to strengthen communications in the organization. For this reason, I remained objective not to be governed by the prior responses that could influence me to "go native" as I collected more data from participants. Following is a summary of participants' perceptions of the four types of Transformational Leadership behavior in the organization: Authentic Transformational, Laissez-Faire, Transactional, and Pseudo-Transformational.

Authentic Transformational Leadership Behavior

Authentic Transformational leaders act as role models who communicate a clear vision, provide mentorship, and engage their subordinates in creativity, innovation, and critical thinking. Forty-five percent of the participants reported that leaders exhibited Authentic Transformational behavior. They cited the selfless, organizationally-focused, and ethically- and morally-based behavior of those leaders. Additionally, they viewed their leaders as being role models and observed that strength in communicating the organization's vision and gaining buy-in were some of the qualities they admired the most.

Of the twenty-two participants, eight observed the collaborative style of their leaders, which they claimed engendered teamwork. A few reported that not only was their leader organizationally focused, but the leader also had a strategic vision for the team. Some participants also indicated that although they did not view their leaders as being role models, they were satisfied in ranking their behavior as being Authentic Transformational because their leader exhibited behavior that was indicative of both leadership and followership.

Strong communicating abilities were quoted most often as being a desirable behavior in their leaders. Forthright, honest, and transparent communications, five participants mentioned, were important to establishing credibility and building a strong team. The interviews revealed four participants believed their leader had an overarching view of how their team could help the organization as a whole and had a focused view on how to accomplish it. Furthermore, six participants mentioned the positive aspects of Authentic Transformational Leadership tended to replicate. Moreover, eight participants indicated that goal-oriented leaders were able to provide a clear, easy-to-follow framework from which each team member could contribute to organizational goals. A process-oriented leader with the ability to take input was admired by participants. Leaders who were vested in doing the right thing and doing right by people were also identified by participants as being Authentic Transformational.

Empowering subordinates was also ranked high by twelve participants in describing their leaders. Of the twenty-two, three participants communicated they saw their leaders' behaviors as trending toward Authentic Transformational Leadership, although currently, they did not see it being expressed fully. Participants witnessing the positive aspects of leaders who were able to strike a balance between the conceptual and the actual were reported to be Authentic Transformational leaders.

Laissez-Faire Leadership Behavior

Laissez-Faire leaders provide little or no leadership to their subordinates. These leaders usually oversee high-performing teams and individuals. Of the participants, 29 percent indicated their leaders exhibited Laissez-Faire Leadership. Some participants perceived the flat, non-hierarchical organizational structure contributed to this type of leadership. They expressed concern, however, that Laissez-Faire Leadership was effective for the more tenured employees. The less tenured required Authentic Transformational Leadership. Participants cited that under this type of leadership, the team was high functioning without micromanagement. Participants note this Laissez-Faire Leadership allowed for independent thought.

Among the participants, eight described the presence of Laissez-Faire Leadership as a function of global directives flowing down. Little or no leadership was needed, they said, since everyone was doing as told. Participants opined that their roles under this leadership model were self-designed, with no clear-cut guidelines. Furthermore, five participants perceived some Laissez-Faire leaders as not doing any work and possessing an uncaring attitude. They expressed frustration in some leaders' lack of experience and not being able to communicate with them readily.

High-performing and self-managed teams thrived under their leaders' Laissez-Faire style. According to 90 percent of the participants, self-motivated individuals instilled confidence in the Laissez-Faire leader. These individuals believed that this type of leadership was ideal. They also thought this type of leadership was the easiest to replicate since the leader did not have to do much. Specifically, ten participants noted that the lack of coaching or leading by example was a missing and necessary component not exhibited in Laissez-Faire Leadership.

Of the twenty-two participants, eleven noted that high-performing individuals were left alone, and those individuals who were not high performers did not benefit from Laissez-Faire Leadership. For example, eight participants found that when there was no directional leadership, they tended to overperform. The downside of Laissez-Faire Leadership, as confirmed by eleven participants, was that leaders were not in tune with the individuals they led, and they did not get to know them. Additionally, eight participants stated these leaders were not versed in assessing the nuances of their team's functional dynamics, and, therefore, they're unable to establish a culture that prizes interpersonal relationships. Another drawback participants perceived was not obtaining support as needed, especially in areas where they considered themselves to be weak.

Lack of goal setting was also indicated by participants when describing their leaders' Laissez-Faire behavior. Furthermore, participants expressed frustration in the absence of an established career path. Specifically, five participants voiced the lack of a clear path to promotion and frustration at being kept in the same position because they performed well in their jobs. These individuals were considered to be subject matter experts in their roles. The absence of feedback was also frustrating to some participants. Participants expressed that under Laissez-Faire Leadership, they witnessed the presence of active knowledge hoarding by leaders, and passive information silos were being constructed.

Of the twenty-two participants, ten noted that Laissez-Faire Leadership behavior was attributed to hiring practices. Participants regarded the organization's hiring of professionals who were experienced in the industry and, therefore, needed little to no leadership as contributing to Laissez-Faire Leadership behavior. Participants noticed Laissez-Faire leaders lead professionals who do not require handholding. They surmised that the time-sensitive nature of the industry led to hiring very competent and mature professionals. Laissez-Faire leaders gave them resources and then got out of their way.

Participants insisted they wanted direction, assignments, and constructive feedback without the micromanagement. They desired professional development and felt that the lack of involvement communicated that the leaders were not invested in them. They also conveyed that the Laissez-Faire leaders were following the path of the least resistance. Furthermore, five participants viewed this expertise-driven leadership as being attributable to trust; others felt that the leaders did not care. Participants noted less tenured leaders tended to demonstrate Laissez-Faire Leadership. Moreover, three participants reflected that this hands-off approach led to a lack of direction. Lack of input was also observed in the less experienced Laissez-Faire leaders.

Transactional Leadership Behavior

Transactional Leadership was identified as leadership that was contingency-based. Participants indicated that 14 percent of their leaders exhibited Transactional behavior. Participants described their experiences as being performance based on rewards or lack of rewards. Participants described Transactional Leadership as positioning unrealistic commission plans and targets. Some also claimed that the Transactional culture was adopted from the global organization's culture.

The lack of coaching opportunities was also seen as prohibitive in Transactional Leadership. Four participants noted they were acknowledged only when they won deals and not at other times. Some participants indicated in the case of conflicts, the Transactional leader tended to side with these deal winners and not get the full story. On the contrary, five participants reported a militaristic aspect of Transactional Leadership. Other participants believed this type of leadership flowed from the top down.

The pressure their leaders were experiencing from their supervisors was reflected in their behavior toward the participants. Notably, four participants recognized that when a bonus was tied to performance, it was effective; however, they wondered about individuals who were not driven by financial incentives. They identified other performance-driven incentives such as recognition, company parties, and the ability to interact with other employees who were not physically in the same office as themselves.

Pseudo-Transformational Leadership Behavior

Pseudo-Transformational leaders exhibit behavior most opposite to that of an Authentic Transformational leader. Their behavior tends to serve their interests and is sometimes masked as Authentic Transformational Leadership. Of the twenty-two participants, 12 percent observed that their leaders exhibited Pseudo-Transformational behavior. Some participants noted that for-profit businesses drive Pseudo-Transformational behavior. Participants expressed suspicion about these leaders and feared they would undermine their subordinates if the opportunity arose to make themselves look good.

Among the participants, four remarked that their leader was not collaborative, and if they were assigned a task, they had to perform whether they expressed objections or not. Some objections, they claimed, were morally based. Pseudo-Transformational leaders were seen by some of the participants as lacking self-awareness; they did not appear to be cognizant of how their behavior affected others. Career aspirations seemed to drive Pseudo-Transformational behavior, as seen by twelve participants. Some participants observed that Pseudo-Transformational behavior resulted from pressure from the leaders' supervisor to provide success without having the necessary tools to do so.

Factors that contributed to Pseudo-Transformational behavior, according to seven participants, include revenue and profit-driven initiatives, difficulty in selling the product, deadlines not being met, and clients either leaving the company or being litigious. Ninety-two percent of the participants noted that self-interest, ego, and fear were present in their Pseudo-Transformational leaders. They noticed that leaders were engaged in information holding and seemed to fear if their subordinates knew more than they did. When these leaders felt threatened, they exerted their authority. Participants perceived that fear more than ethics was the motivation for their behavior.

Pseudo-Transformational leaders were seen to be task-oriented and reactive by nine participants. These leaders feared confrontation, and information was not vetted before their acting on it, as many participants experienced. Often the information was acted on based on how it was perceived rather than how it was. Pseudo-Transformational leaders operated in fear of getting caught not having the proper skills for their job. Further, Pseudo-Transformational leaders were also seen as influencing organizational politics to work in their favor, many participants experienced.

Of the participants who observed Pseudo-Transformational behavior in their leaders, 76 percent believed the behavior was being influenced by self-interest. They cited self-interest based on lack of tenure and operating in a high profile, high-stress environment as contributors. Also, fear was exhibited when difficult decisions needed to be made. Some participants reported leaders driven by self-interest were not sure about organizational goals and were more concerned about presenting a good image rather than being that image. Participants noted that Pseudo-Transformational leaders were prone to self-praise, not open to different views, and passed off difficult and complex projects to their subordinates while keeping the easy ones to themselves, ensuring an easy win.

Discussion of the Results

Participants described the existence of the following Transformational Leadership behavior in the organization: Authentic Transformational (45 percent), Laissez-Faire (29 percent), Transactional (14 percent), and Pseudo-Transformational (12 percent). A relationship existed between leaders' behavior and their respective supervisor's behavior. Participants who reported Transactional and Pseudo-Transformational behavior believed the maturity of the organization's product was the motivator for both types of behavior. The product was in the introduction stage of the product life cycle.

A majority of participants indicated their leaders' behaviors were Authentic Transformational. Participants believed that the leaders were adept at communicating the organization's vision and engaging their subordinates in pursuing the vision through collaboration, innovation, and critical thinking. The leaders further acted as role models and, at times, coached and mentored subordinates. Participants perceived these leaders as displaying proficiency in emotional intelligence, which fostered connectedness with their subordinates. Authentic Transformational Leadership was cited as being the most desirable type of leadership behavior by all of the participants.

Laissez-Faire Leadership, according to the research results, was optimal for high-performing teams and individuals. Participants conveyed that the organization's hiring policy was in part responsible for Laissez-Faire Leadership behavior. Participants cited both pros and cons of Laissez-Faire Leadership behavior. Some enjoyed the lack of micromanagement and that their leaders entrusted them to work independently. Others pointed out the lack of constructive feedback, growth, career development, and interactions with their leader. Many viewed Laissez-Faire Leadership as being optimal for more tenured subordinates. Several believed that Laissez-Faire Leadership was exhibited by inexperienced leaders.

The culture at the study site also exhibited Transactional Leadership behavior, as reported by participants. Transactional Leadership behavior was found to be driven by the sales cycle, the maturity of the product, and uncertainty about its competitive viability. The contingency-based leadership behavior was seen by many participants as lacking other non-monetary incentives. Participants disclosed that some of them were not motivated by monetary recognition only, and several observed their leaders siding with the top performers instead of vetting information before making decisions.

Of the 12 percent of participants who reported Pseudo-Transformational behavior in their leaders, 76 percent believed their leaders' Pseudo-Transformational behavior was driven by self-interest. Self-interest was driven by fear, ego, and a survivalist mentality that was largely attributable to the maturity of the product. Many participants maintained the product was driving the leadership behavior. Participants expressed uncertainty about the future of the product and believed their leaders were also uncertain, which in turn affected their behavior.

Discussion of the Results of the Literature

Pseudo-Transformational behavior can be transient and a driver for change, after which the leader resumes Authentic Transformational behavior (Law-Penrose et al. 2016; Lee et al.

2018; Pater 2015; Lee, Wang, and Piccolo 2018). This is common in the product life cycle at the introduction and growth apex, which is influenced by change, rate of change, product maturity, and market and external conditions. The research study site was a company that was experiencing multiple simultaneous changes. The changes included a product that was fairly new and was being introduced to the market.

Barling, Fullagar, and Kelloway (1992) purported that Transformational Leadership occupies a continuum that spans Authentic Transformational Leadership, Laissez-Faire Leadership, and Pseudo-Transformational Leadership. This continuum, Barling et al. asserted, is a vacillation from morality-centered behavior to egoism and narcissism-centered behavior. The research study results support this assertion, as participants expressed that all three types of behavior were present in their leaders. Barling et al.'s (1992) assertion supported the transient transformational behavior model expressed by Law-Penrose et al. (2016).

The frequency of transformational behavior is what determines the identification of Authentic Transformational behavior or Pseudo-Transformational behavior (Bass and Steidlmeier 1999). They indicated that leaders practice both types of transformational behavior, and the behavior that is practiced the most is the primary descriptor of the leader. This finding was upheld by the analysis of the research data; participants described their leaders as displaying varying degrees of the four types of transformational behavior: Authentic, Transactional, Laissez-Faire, and Pseudo-Transformational.

Pseudo-Transformational Leadership behavior is the opposite of Authentic Transformational Leadership behavior

(Bass 1985; Burns 1978). Participants were asked to describe their leaders' behaviors form a scale of 0 percent to 100 percent. The Transformational Leadership behaviors included: Authentic Transformational, Laissez-Faire, Transactional, and Pseudo-Transformational behavior. Four participants assigned a score of 0 percent to the practice of Pseudo-Transformational behavior by their leader and a score of 100 percent to Authentic Transformational Leadership behavior. The reverse assignment also found five participants assigned a score of 0 percent to their leaders' Authentic Transformational Leadership behavior and a score of 100 percent to their Pseudo-Transformational Leadership behavior.

Limitations

Limitations to the intrinsic case study included participants not truthfully responding about their leaders' behavior for fear of retribution. Another limitation was that since only the North American division of the organization participated in the study, the results would not describe the organizational leadership as a whole. Not all of the volunteers participated in the case study, which may leave elements of leadership perception that were not explored in the case study. Participants who were new to the organization may not have had enough interaction with their leader, which may affect their opinion about their leadership style.

The intrinsic case study's scope was limited to the North American division of the global organization, although there were several divisions in Europe and other continents. Including participants from other divisions were prohibitive for several reasons: language barriers, cultural differences, and perception of research methodologies. Less-tenured subordinates, for example, may not want to participate in the survey, while more tenured subordinates may justifiably or unjustifiably exaggerate their views on their leaders' behaviors. Finally, subordinates who were virtual, working from their home offices, may not have believed they were familiar enough with their leaders' style to participate in the research study.

Implications of the Results for Transformation

The effects of Transformational Leadership behavior on subordinates' perceptions were illustrated from the research findings. The educational component of research results can influence transformation in different areas. These results have implications for transformational practice, policy, and theory. Research-identified outcomes can pinpoint gaps in leadership behavior and subordinate perception, indicating areas of opportunities for leaders to improve communications and accountability, which can facilitate future positive engagements between both communities (Stake 1995; Yin 2003).

Leadership behavior can be interpreted from the data analysis and reported to the leadership, who, in turn, can use the verified and validated results as inputs into broader initiatives that are inclusive of transformational sustainability. The qualitative analysis was supported by examining the different data points that revealed the perception of self-interest-based Pseudo-Transformational Leadership. Implications on Transformational Leadership practice, policy, and theory are examined in the following sections.

Implications on Practice

Leadership should be fluid, according to de Haan (2016). Additionally, transformation occurs when organizations have upward feedback and clear lines of communication. The leaders' nurturing of relationships with subordinates and other leaders are the basis for self-reflection. Northouse (2016) observed a need to move from transformational knowledge to practice. The case study results can be used to educate leaders on how their behavior was perceived and provide practical and actionable support for pursuing effective leadership.

Implications on Policy

Evidence-based transformations affect policy, drive change, and solve critical problems (Slavin 2008). Lingenfelter (2011) called for an alliance between the scholarship of researchers and policymakers to capitalize on each other's strengths. Stover (2007) attributed technological innovations to the contraction of the time frame between research and publishing while alternatively promoting the packaging of research via marketing efforts to affect public policy. The research results can be used to influence the organization's human resources policies, including hiring practices and professional development.

Implications on Theory

Knowledge acquired from the results of this descriptive research can be used as input to subsequent studies, broadening the effect of the research and its ability to be practically applied. The research results have supported theories on Authentic Transformational Leadership behavior and Pseudo-Transformational Leadership behavior by correlating the behaviors ascribed to each type. The study of Pseudo-Transformational behavior has been extended by identifying specific contributors to this behavior. Carlyle's (1888) intent in advocating the great man theory to describe effective male leaders can also be used to support the Pseudo-Transformational theory. The gendered view of leaders is one of the chief contributors to the propensity for Pseudo-Transformational behavior.

Recommendations for Further Research

The evaluative structure of research presents opportunities for ongoing research. Four leaders participated in the case study: three males and one female. The research findings indicated that the female leader rated herself lower in her Authentic Transformational Leadership behavior than her male counterparts. Comparative studies to understand female Transformational leaders and self-assessment would be beneficial. Furthermore, virtual leadership represents an area where additional research would be valuable. The proximity of the subordinates to the leader may influence their perception of the type of Transformational Leadership behavior being practiced. Future studies should be conducted on the global organization to assess the full scope of Transformational Leadership. Also, research on how technology impacts Transformational Leadership would constitute valuable research.

Conclusion

In this intrinsic case, study participants reported that (a) 45 percent of their leaders exhibited Authentic Transformational behavior, and (b) 12 percent exhibited Pseudo-Transformational behavior based on self-interest. Multiple data tools were used for data collection, including interviews and a questionnaire. I analyzed the data using Creswell's (2013) qualitative research methodology to identify emerging themes and subsequent patterns. I collected data to the point of saturation, where consistent patterns emerged, allowing for categorical aggregation and the construction of deeper meanings.

Overall findings from the aggregating of the participants fulfilled the case study's purpose of answering the research question. Participants stated that 45 percent of their leaders practiced Authentic Transformational Leadership, and 12 percent practiced Pseudo-Transformational Leadership behavior based on self-interest. Participants also identified two other types of Transformational Leadership behavior in the organization: Laissez-Faire and Transactional.

All of the participants expressed that Authentic Transformational Leadership was the optimal type of leadership and that addressing areas of opportunities would help to make the transition from the current leadership practice. Many of the participants articulated that they felt the maturity of the product was driving the leaders' Pseudo-Transformational behavior based on self-interest.

The findings from this intrinsic case study may contribute to the existing literature on Transformational Leadership by providing insight into how leader behavior is perceived by subordinates. The findings also extend the studies on Pseudo-Transformational Leadership behavior by isolating this behavior from other types of Transformational Leadership behavior and identifying that participants perceived self-interest as the contributing factor. Findings from this study may help to drive changes and improvement in organizational leadership culture.

Executive Readout

Research Objective

Is Transformational Leadership visible, and what is the impact on employee perception and performance?

The case study was undertaken to:

- measure the impact of business leaders' behavior on others within the organization,
- identify any gaps that may exist in communicating business strategy across the organization, and
- strengthen communications and enablement to thrive in a competitive environment.

Findings support Authentic Transformational Leadership DNA supported by Laissez-Faire Leadership, indicating organizationally focused leaders and high-performing teams and individuals. There is also a positive correlation between a manager's leadership style and their respective manager's leadership style. This culture is nuanced by task-oriented leadership (Transactional) and Pseudo-Transformational, which is driven by the sales cycle, the maturity of the product, and uncertainty about its competitive viability. This is common in the product life cycle at the introduction and growth apex, which is influenced by change, rate of change, product maturity, and market and external conditions.

As we approach the inception of the growth cycle, employees are actively engaged in driving the transformational strategy forward; however, the maturity of the product raises concern about competitive intelligence and internal process management. A triangulation of Authentic Transformational, Laissez-Faire, and Transactional Leadership during the different phases of the product life cycle is recommended. Additionally, a focus group with managers, driven by the findings of the case study, is beneficial to sustainable change. Further, replicating the case study globally will close the loop in measuring leaders' impact, identifying and strengthening communication gaps.

An excerpt of note from the executive leadership team of the research organization:

"On behalf of the leadership team, I want to thank you for the time and energy you have put into this case study. We all appreciate it! The artifacts are useful, and we will be discussing the outcomes/recommendations at a future leaders' meeting. Thank you for the great work and dedication to the company you have shown. Your contribution has been invaluable in moving us forward."

References

Ahmad, A. R., A. G. Abdul-Rahman, and N. K. Soon. "The Effects of Transformational and Transactional Leadership Styles on Job Satisfaction." *Advanced Science Letters* 21, no. 5 (May 2015): 1505–1508. https://doi.org/10.1166/asl.2015.6087.

Alavi, S., and C. Gill. "Leading Change Authentically." *Journal of Leadership and Organizational Studies* 24, no. 2 (2017): 157–171. https://doi.org/10.1177/2F1548051816664681.

Ali, N. M., R. Jangga, M. Ismail, S. N. I. M. Kamal, and M. N. Ali. "Influence of Leadership Styles in Creating Quality Work Culture." *Procedia Economics and Finance* 31 (2015): 161–169. https://doi.org/10.1016/S2212-5671(15)01143-0.

Allport, G. W. *Personality: A psychological interpretation.* Oxford: Holt, 1937.

Anand, S., P. Vidyarthi, and S. Rolnicki. "Leader-member Exchange and Organizational Citizenship Behaviors: Contextual Effects of Leader Power Distance and Group Task Interdependence." *The Leadership Quarterly* 29, no. 4 (2018): 489–500. https://doi.org/10.1016/j.leaqua.2017.11.002.

Anderson, M. H., and P. Y. Sun. "Reviewing Leadership Styles: Overlaps and the Need for a New 'Full-Range' Theory." *International Journal of Management Reviews* 19, no. 1 (2017): 76–96. https://doi.org/10.1111/ijmr.12082.

Aras, G., and C. Ingley, eds. *Corporate Behavior and Sustainability: Doing Well by Being Good (Finance, Governance and Sustainability)*. Burlington: Gower, 2016.

Ardichvili, A., K. Natt och Dag, and S. Manderscheid. "Leadership Development: Current and Emerging Models and Practices." *Advances in Developing Human Resources* 18, no. 3 (2016): 275–285. https://doi.org/10.1177/2F1523422316645506.

Arnten, A. A., B. Jansson, K. Olsen, and T. Archer. "Self-reported Attributes of Police-Chiefs Compared to Civil Leadership: Inner Drive, Tolerance to Stress and Enterprise." *Journal of Forensic Research* 8, no. 1 (2017): 367–370. https://doi.org/10.4172/2157-7145.1000367.

Ashikali, T., and S. Groeneveld. "Diversity Management in Public Organizations and Its Effect on Employees' Affective Commitment: The Role of Transformational Leadership and the Inclusiveness of the Organizational Culture." *Review of Public Personnel Administration* 35, no. 2 (2015): 146–168. https://doi.org/10.1177/2F0734371X13511088.

Atienza, C. "Organizational Culture as a Key Enabler of Intrapreneurship: A Critical Review of Literature." *Journal of Asia Entrepreneurship and Sustainability* 11, no. 3 (2015): 85–128. https://www.academia.edu/19847391/Organizational_Culture_as_a_Key_Enabler_of_Intrapreneurship_A_Critical_Review_of_Literature.

Atmojo, M. "The Influence of Transformational Leadership on Job Satisfaction, Organizational Commitment, and Employee Performance." *International Research Journal of Business Studies* 5, no. 2 (2015): 113–128. https://doi.org/10.21632/irjbs.5.2.113-128.

Avolio, B. J., and B. M. Bass. *Developing Potential Across a Full Range of Leadership: Cases on Transactional and Transformational Leadership.* Hove: Psychology Press, 2004.

Avolio, B. J., and W. L. Gardner. "Authentic Leadership Development: Getting to the Root of Positive Forms of Leadership." *The Leadership Quarterly* 16, no. 3 (June 2005): 315–338. https://doi.org/10.1016/j.leaqua.2005.03.001.

Babalola, M., J. Stouten, and M. Euwema. "Frequent Change and Turnover Intentions: The Moderating Role of Ethical Leadership." *Journal of Business Ethics* 132, no. 2 (2016): 311–322. https://doi.org/10.1007/s10551-014-2433-z.

Balogun, J., J. M. Bartunek, and B. Do. "Senior Managers' Sensemaking and Responses to Strategic Change." *Organization Science* 26, no. 4 (June 2015): 960–979. https://doi.org/10.1287/orsc.2015.0985.

Barling, J. *The Science of Leadership: Lessons from Research for Organizational Leaders.* New York: Oxford University Press, 2014.

Barling, J., A. Akers, and D. Beiko. "The Impact of Positive and Negative Intraoperative Surgeons' Leadership Behaviors on Surgical Team Performance." *The American Journal of Surgery* 215, no. 1 (January 2018): 14–18. https://doi.org/10.1016/j.amjsurg.2017.07.006.

Barling, J., and C. L. Cooper. *The SAGE Handbook of Organizational Behavior.* Los Angeles: SAGE Publications, 2008.

Barling, J., C. Fullagar, and K. K. Kelloway. *The Union and Its Members: A Psychological Approach.* Oxford: Oxford University Press, 1992.

Barrick, M. R., G. R. Thurgood, T. A. Smith, and S. H. Courtright. "Collective Organizational Engagement: Linking Motivational Antecedents, Strategic Implementation, and Firm Performance." *Academy of Management Journal* 58, no. 1 (2015): 111–135. https://doi.org/10.5465/amj.2013.0227.

Barth, A., and P. Benoliel. "School Religious-Cultural Attributes and School Principals' Leadership Styles in Israel." *Religious Education* 114, no. 4 (2019): 470–485. https://doi.org/10.1080/00344087.2019.1581873.

Bass, B. M. *Organizational Decision Making.* Homewood: R. D. Irwin, 1983.

———. *Leadership and Performance Beyond Expectation.* New York: Free Press, 1985.

———. *Transformational Leadership: Industrial, Military, and Educational Impact.* Mahwah: Laurence Erlbaum, 1998.

Bass, B. M., and B. J. Avolio, eds. *Improving Organizational Effectiveness through Transformational Leadership.* Thousand Oaks: SAGE Publications, 1994.

Bass, B. M., and P. Steidlmeier. "Ethics, Character, and Authentic Transformational Leadership Behavior." *The Leadership Quarterly* 10, no. 2 (Summer 1999): 181–217. https://doi.org/10.1016/S1048-9843(99)00016-8.

Bass, B. M, and R. Bass. *The Bass Handbook of Leadership: Theory, Research, and Managerial Applications,* 4th ed. New York: Free Press, 2008.

Bedi, A., C. Alpaslan, and S. Green. "A Meta-Analytic Review of Ethical Leadership Outcomes and Moderators." *Journal of Business Ethics* 139, no. 3 (2016): 517–536. https://doi.org/10.1007/s10551-015-2625-1.

Belschak, F. D., D. N. Den Hartog, and K. Kalshoven. "Leading Machiavellians: How to Translate Machiavellians' Selfishness into Pro-Organizational Behavior." *Journal of Management* 41, no. 7 (2015): 1934–1956. https://psycnet.apa.org/doi/10.1177/0149206313484513.

Bergethon, K. P., and D. C. Davis. "Emotional Leadership: Leadership Styles and Emotional Intelligence," in M. Khosrow-Pour, ed., Social Issues in the Workplace: Breakthroughs in Research and Practice (pp. 229–244). Hershey: Information Resources Management Association (USA), 2018. https://doi.org/10.4018/978-1-5225-3917-9.

Birkás, B., and Á. Csathó. "Size the Day: The Time Perspectives of the Dark Triad." *Personality and Individual Differences* 86 (November 2015): 318–320. https://doi.org/10.1016/j.paid.2015.06.035.

Blair, C. A., K. Helland, and B. Walton. "Leaders Behaving Badly: The Relationship Between Narcissism and Unethical Leadership." *Leadership and Organization Development Journal* 38, no. 2 (April 2017): 333–346. https://doi.org/10.1108/LODJ-09-2015-0209.

Blanka, C. "An Individual-Level Perspective on Intrapreneurship: A Review and Ways Forward." *Review of Managerial Science* 12, no. 1 (2018): 1–43. https://www.springerprofessional.de/en/an-individual-level-perspective-on-intrapreneurship-a-review-and/15456984.

Boje, D. M, G. A. Rosile, J. Saylors, and R. Saylors. "Using Storytelling Theatrics for Leadership Training." *Advances in Developing Human Resources* 17, no. 3 (2015): 348–362. https://doi.org/10.1177/2F1523422315587899.

Bolman, L. G., and T. E. Deal. *Reframing Organizations: Artistry, Choice, and Leadership*. Hoboken: John Wiley and Sons, 2017.

Bonner, J. M., R. L. Greenbaum, and D. M. Mayer. "My Boss Is Morally Disengaged: The Role of Ethical Leadership in Explaining the Interactive Effect of Supervisor and Employee Moral Disengagement on Employee Behaviors." *Journal of Business Ethics* 137, no. 4 (2016): 731–742. https://doi.org/10.1007/s10551-014-2366-6.

Boon, C., and M. Biron. "Temporal issues in Person–Organization Fit, Person–Job Fit and Turnover: The Role of Leader–Member Exchange." *Human Relations* 69, no. 12 (May 2016): 2177–2200. https://doi.org/10.1177/2F0018726716636945.

Brands, R. A., J. I. Menges, and M. Kilduff. "The Leader-in-Social-Network Schema: Perceptions of Network Structure Affect Gendered Attributions of Charisma." *Organization Science* 26, no. 4 (March 2015): 1210–1225. https://doi.org/10.1287/orsc.2015.0965.

Buch, R., Ø. L. Martinsen, and B. Kuvaas. "The Destructiveness of Laissez-Faire Leadership Behavior: The Mediating Role of Economic Leader–Member Exchange Relationships." *Journal of Leadership and Organizational Studies* 22, no. 1 (2015): 115–124. https://doi.org/10.1177/2F1548051813515302.

Bucklin, B. R., A. M. Alvero, A. M. Dickinson, J. Austin, and A. K. Jackson. "Industrial-Organizational Psychology and Organizational Behavior Management: An Objective Comparison." *Journal of Organizational Behavior Management* 20, no. 2 (2000): 27–75. https://doi.org/10.1300/J075v20n02_03.

Burkholder, G. J., K. A. Cox, L. M. Crawford, and J. H. Hitchcock, eds. *Research Design and Methods: An Applied Guide for the Scholar-Practitioner.* Thousand Oaks: SAGE Publications, 2019.

Burns, J. M. *Leadership.* New York: Harper and Row Books, 1978.

———. *The Power to Lead: The Crisis of the American Presidency.* New York: Simon and Schuster, 1985.

———. *Transforming Leadership: A New Pursuit of Happiness*, vol. 213. Broadway, NY: Grove Press, 2004.

———. *Fire and Light: How the Enlightenment Transformed Our World.* New York: St. Martin's Press, 2013.

Caillier, J. G. "Can Changes in Transformational-Oriented and Transactional-Oriented Leadership Impact Turnover Over Time?" *International Journal of Public Administration* 41, no. 12 (2018): 935–945. https://doi.org/10.1080/01900692.2017.1300918.

Caillier, J. G., and Y. Sa. "Do Transformational-Oriented Leadership and Transactional-Oriented Leadership Have an Impact on Whistle-Blowing Attitudes? A Longitudinal Examination Conducted in US Federal Agencies." *Public Management Review* 19, no. 4 (2017): 406–422. https://doi.org/10.1080/14719037.2016.1177109.

Carlyle, T. *On Heroes, Hero-Worship and the Heroic in History.* New York: Fredrick A. Stokes and Brother, 1888.

Carpenter, J., and E. Gong. "Motivating Agents: How Much Does the Mission Matter?" *Journal of Labor Economics* 34, no.1 (2016): 211–236. https://doi.org/10.1086/682345.

Chai, D. S., S. J. Hwang, and B. Joo. Transformational Leadership and Organizational Commitment in Teams: The Mediating Roles of Shared Vision and Team-Goal Commitment. *Performance Improvement Quarterly* 30, no. 2 (2017): 137–158. https://doi.org/10.1002/piq.21244.

Chandler, R., E. Anstey, and H. Ross. "Listening to Voices and Visualizing Data in Qualitative Research: Hypermodal Dissemination Possibilities." *SAGE Open* 5, no. 2 (June 2015). https://doi.org/10.1177/2F2158244015592166.

Chen, X., W. He, and L. Weng. "What Is Wrong with Treating Followers Differently? The Basis of Leader–Member Exchange Differentiation Matters." *Journal of Management* 44, no. 3 (2018): 946–971. https://doi.org/10.1177/2F0149206315598372.

Choi, S. B., K. Kim, and S.W. Kang. "Effects of transformational and Shared Leadership Styles on Employees' Perception of Team Effectiveness." *Social Behavior and Personality: an International Journal* 45, no. 3 (April 2017): 377–386. https://doi.org/10.2224/sbp.5805.

Choi, S. L., C. F. Goh, M. B. H. Adam, and O. K. Tan. "Transformational Leadership, Empowerment, and Job Satisfaction: The Mediating Role of Employee Empowerment." *Human Resources for Health* 14, no. 1 (2016): 73. https://doi.org/10.1186/s12960-016-0171-2.

Christie, A., J. Barling, and N. Turner. "Pseudo-Transformational Leadership: Model Specification and Outcomes." *Journal of Applied Social Psychology* 41, no. 12 (2011): 2943–2984. https://doi.org/10.1111/j.1559-1816.2011.00858.x.

Cikaliuk, M., L. Erakovic, B. Jackson, C. Noonan, and S. Watson. "Governance and Leadership by Board Chairs: Relationships and Their Effects." *International Conference on Management, Leadership and Governance* (2015): 57–64. Academic Conferences and Publishing Limited.

Clark Pope, D. *Increasing Validity in Qualitative Research*. London: SAGE Publications, 2017.

Cohen, A. "Are They Among Us? A Conceptual Framework of the Relationship Between the Dark Triad Personality and Counterproductive Work Behaviors (CWBs)." *Human Resource Management Review* 26, no. 1 (2016): 69–85. https://doi.org/10.1016/j.hrmr.2015.07.003.

Collins, M. D. and C. J. Jackson. "A Process Model of Self-Regulation and Leadership: How Attentional Resource Capacity and Negative Emotions Influence Constructive and Destructive Leadership." *The Leadership Quarterly* 26, no. 3 (2015): 386–401. https://doi.org/10.1016/j.leaqua.2015.02.005.

Cooper, D. "Effective Safety Leadership: Understanding Types and Styles that Improve Safety Performance." *Professional Safety* 60, no. 02 (2015): 49–53. https://www.proquest.com/docview/1659755225.

Copeland, M. "The Impact of Authentic, Ethical, Transformational Leadership on Leader Effectiveness." *Journal of Leadership, Accountability and Ethics* 13, no. 3 (2016): 79–97. https://fisherpub.sjfc.edu/business_facpub/38/.

Cote, R. "Vision of Effective Leadership." Journal of Leadership, *Accountability and Ethics* 14, no. 4 (2017): 52–63. https://doi.org/10.33423/jlae.v14i4.1486.

Creswell, J. W. *Qualitative Inquiry and Research Design: Choosing among Five Approaches*, 3rd ed. Los Angeles: SAGE Publications, 2013.

———. *Qualitative Inquiry and Research Design: Choosing Among Five Approaches*, 5th ed. Los Angeles: SAGE Publications, 2016.

Cuadrado, I., C. García-Ael, and F. Molero. "Gender-Typing of Leadership: Evaluations of Real and Ideal Managers." *Scandinavian Journal of Psychology* 56, no. 2 (January 2015): 236–244. https://doi.org/10.1111/sjop.12187.

Damij, N., Z. Levnajić, V. Rejec Skrt, and J. Suklan. "What Motivates Us for Work? Intricate Web of Factors beyond Money and Prestige." *Plos ONE* 10, no. 7 (2015): 1–13. https://doi.org/10.1371/journal.pone.0132641.

Dartey-Baah, K. "Resilient Leadership: A Transformational-Transactional Leadership Mix." *Journal of Global Responsibility* 6, no. 1 (May 2015): 99–112. https://doi.org/10.1108/JGR-07-2014-0026.

Dashborough, M. T., and N. M. Ashkanasy. "Emotion and Attribution of Intentionality in Leader–Member Relations." *Leadership Quarterly* 13, no. 5 (October 2002): 615–634. https://doi.org/10.1016/S1048-9843(02)00147-9.

de Haan, E. "The Leadership Shadow: How to Recognise and Avoid Derailment, Hubris and Overdrive." *Leadership* 12, no. 4 (2016): 504–512. https://doi.org/10.1177/2F1742715015572526.

De Vries, H., and H. M. Van der Poll. "The Influence of Lean thinking on Organisational Structure and Behaviour in the Discrete Manufacturing Industry." *Journal of Contemporary Management* 13, no. 1 (January 2016): 55–89. https://journals.co.za/content/jcman/13/1/EJC185650.

Delegach, M., R. Kark, T. Katz-Navon, and D. Van Dijk. "A Focus on Commitment: The Roles of Transformational and Transactional Leadership and Self-Regulatory Focus in Fostering Organizational and Safety Commitment." *European Journal of Work and Organizational Psychology* 26, no. 5 (June 2017): 724–740. https://doi.org/10.1080/1359432X.2017.1345884.

Deprez, J., and M. Euwema. "You Can't Always Get What You Want? Leadership Expectations of Intrapreneurs." *Journal of Managerial Psychology* 32, no. 6 (2017): 430–444. https://doi.org/10.1108/JMP-04-2016-0107.

DeShong, H. L., D. M. Grant, and S. N. Mullins-Sweatt. "Comparing Models of Counterproductive Workplace Behaviors: The Five-Factor Model and the Dark Triad." *Personality and Individual Differences* 74 (February 2015): 55–60. https://doi.org/10.1016/j.paid.2014.10.001.

DuBois, M., J. Koch, J. Hanlon, B. Nyatuga, and N. Kerr. "Leadership Styles of Effective Project Managers: Techniques and Traits to Lead High Performance Teams." *Journal of Economic Development, Management, IT, Finance and Marketing* 7, no. 1 (2015): 30–46. https://www.academia.edu/43503667/Leadership_Styles_of_Effective_Project_Managers_Techniques_and_Traits_to_Lead_High_Performance_Teams.

Duneier, M. *Slim's Table: Race, Respectability, and Masculinity.* Chicago: University of Chicago Press, 2015.

Dussault, M., and E. Frenette. "Supervisors' Transformational Leadership and Bullying in the Workplace." *Psychological Reports* 117, no. 3 (December 2015): 724–733. https://doi.org/10.2466/2F01.PR0.117c30z2.

Effelsberg, D., and M. Solga. "Transformational Leaders' In-Group versus Out-Group Orientation: Testing the Link between Leaders' Organizational Identification, Their Willingness to Engage in Unethical Pro-Organizational Behavior, and Follower -Perceived Transformational Leadership." *Journal of Business Ethics* 126, no. 4 (February 2015): 581–590. https://doi.org/10.1007/s10551-013-1972-z.

Einarsen, S., M. S. Aasland, and A. Skogstad. *The Nature and Outcomes of Destructive Leadership Behavior in Organizations*. New York: Gower, 2016.

Einolander, J. "Evaluating Organizational Commitment in Support of Organizational Leadership." *Procedia Manufacturing* 3 (2015): 668–673. https://doi.org/10.1016/j.promfg.2015.07.300.

Eklund, K. E., E. S. Barry, and N. E. Grunberg. "Gender and Leadership," in A. Alvinius, ed. *Gender Differences in Different Contexts* (pp.129–150). Rijeka: Intech Open Science, 2017. http://dx.doi.org/10.5772/63040.

Engelen, A., V. Gupta, L. Strenger, and M. Brettel. "Entrepreneurial Orientation, Firm Performance, and the Moderating Role of Transformational Leadership Behaviors." *Journal of Management* 41, no. 4 (2015): 1069–1097. https://doi.org/10.1177/2F0149206312455244.

Etikan, I., S. A. Musa, and R. S. Alkassim. "Comparison of Convenience Sampling and Purposive Sampling." *American Journal of Theoretical and Applied Statistics* 5, no. 1 (January 2016): 1–4. https://doi.org/10.11648/j.ajtas.20160501.11.

Ford, J., and N. Harding. "Followers in Leadership Theory: Fiction, Fantasy and Illusion." *Leadership* 14, no. 1 (2018): 3–24. https://doi.org/10.1177%2F1742715015621372.

Fowler, D. J., R. A. Posthuma., and W. C. Tsai. "Hiring Transformational Leaders in Education: Lessons Learned from Structured Employment Interviews." *International Online*

Journal of Education and Teaching 3, no. 4 (October 2016): 240–260. http://iojet.org/index.php/IOJET/article/view/136.

Gaddis, B. H., and J. L. Foster. "Meta-Analysis of Dark Side Personality Characteristics and Critical Work Behaviors among Leaders across the Globe: Findings and Implications for Leadership Development and Executive Coaching." *Applied Psychology* 64, no. 1 (2015): 25–54. https://doi.org/10.1111/apps.12017.

Garretsen, H., J. Stoker, and R. Weber. "Economics and Leadership." *The Leadership Quarterly* 27, no. 6 (December 2016): 912–913. https://doi.org/10.1016/j.leaqua.2016.11.004.

Gathondu, P. G., S. M. Nyambegera, and M. Kirubi. "Influence of Learning as an Outcome of Transformational Leadership on Performance of Staff of Kenyan Microfinance Institutions." *Journal of Strategic Management* 2, no. 1 (2018): 15–33. https://stratfordjournals.org/journals/index.php/journal-of-strategic-management/article/view/123.

Gebert, D., K. Heinitz, and C. Buengeler. "Leaders' Charismatic Leadership and Followers' Commitment—The Moderating Dynamics of Value Erosion at the Societal Level." *The Leadership Quarterly* 27, no. 1 (2016): 98–108. https://doi.org/10.1016/j.leaqua.2015.08.006.

Ghoshal, S. "Bad Management Theories Are Destroying Good Management Practices." *Academy of Management Learning and Education* 4, no. 1 (2005), 75–91. https://doi.org/10.5465/amle.2005.16132558.

Glesne, C. *Becoming Qualitative Researchers: An Introduction*, 4th ed. Boston: Pearson, 2011.

Graham, K. A., J. C. Ziegert, and J. Capitano. "The Effect of Leadership Style, Framing, and Promotion Regulatory Focus on Unethical Pro-Organizational Behavior." *Journal of Business Ethics* 126, no. 3 (February 2015): 423–436. https://doi.org/10.1007/s10551-013-1952-3.

Guest, G., A. Bunce, and L. Johnson. "How Many Interviews Are Enough? An Experiment with Data Saturation and Variability." *Field Methods* 18, no. 1 (February 2006): 59–82. https://doi.org/10.1177%2F1525822X05279903.

Haase, H., M. Franco, and M. Félix. "Organisational Learning and Intrapreneurship: Evidence of Interrelated Concepts." *Leadership and Organization Development Journal* 36, no. 8 (2015): 906–926. https://doi.org/10.1108/LODJ-03-2014-0053.

Han, S. H., G. Seo, S. W. Yoon, and D. Y. Yoon. "Transformational Leadership and Knowledge Sharing: Mediating Roles of Employee's Empowerment, Commitment, and Citizenship Behaviors." *Journal of Workplace Learning* 28, no. 3 (April 2016): 130–149. https://doi.org/10.1108/JWL-09-2015-0066.

Hancock, D. R., and B. Algozzine. *Doing Case Study Research: A Practical Guide for Beginning Researchers*. New York: Teachers College Press, 2016.

Harish, J. "Leadership for a New Paradigm in Human Development." *Cadmus* 2, no. 4 (April-May 2015): 88–104. http://www.cadmusjournal.org/files/journalpdf/Vol2Issue4/Vol2_Issue4_Part2.pdf.

Haynes, K. T., M. A. Hitt, and J. T. Campbell. "The Dark Side of Leadership: Towards a Mid-Range Theory of Hubris and Greed in Entrepreneurial Contexts." *Journal of Management*

Studies 52, no. 4 (2015): 479–505. https://doi.org/10.1111/joms.12127.

Henry, P. A. "An Examination of Murder and Suicide in Guyana." *Issues in Social Science* 4, no. 1 (2016): 28–40. https://doi.org/10.5296/iss.v4i1.8892.

Hentrich, S., A. Zimber, S. F. Garbade, S. Gregersen, A. Nienhaus, and F. Petermann. "Relationships between Transformational Leadership and Health: The Mediating Role of Perceived Job Demands and Occupational Self-Efficacy." *International Journal of Stress Management* 24, no. 1 (2017): 34–61. https://doi.org/10.1037/str0000027.

Hetland, J., H. Hetland, A. B. Bakker, and E. Demerouti. "Daily Transformational Leadership and Employee Job Crafting: The Role of Promotion Focus." *European Management Journal* 36, no. 6 (December 2018): 746–756. https://doi.org/10.1016/j.emj.2018.01.002.

Hoch, J. E., W.H. Bommer, J. H. Dulebohn, and D. Wu. "Do Ethical, Authentic, and Servant Leadership Explain Variance above and beyond Transformational Leadership? A meta-analysis." *Journal of Management* 44, no. 2 (2018): 501–529. https://doi.org/10.1177/2F0149206316665461.

Holmes, M. "The Leadership Shadow: How to Recognise and Avoid Derailment, Hubris and Overdrive." *Action Learning: Research and Practice* 12, no. 1 (March 2015): 117–121. https://doi.org/10.1080/14767333.2015.1006920.

House, R. J. "A Path Goal Theory of Leader Effectiveness." *Administrative Science Quarterly* 16, no. 3 (September 1971): 321–339. https://doi.org/10.2307/2391905.

Hughes, P., and M. Harris. "Organizational Laundering: A Case Study of Pseudo-Transformational Leadership." *Organization Development Journal* 35, no. 2 (2017): 59–77. https://www.academia.edu/32669238/Organizational_Laundering_A_Case_Study_of_Pseudo-Transformational_Leadership.

Imran, M. K., M. Ilyas, and U. Aslam. "Organizational Learning through Transformational Leadership." *The Learning Organization* 23, no. 4 (May 2016): 232–248. https://doi.org/10.1108/TLO-09-2015-0053.

Jaiswal, N. K., and R. L. Dhar. "Transformational Leadership, Innovation Climate, Creative Self-Efficacy and Employee Creativity: A Multilevel Study. *International Journal of Hospitality Management* 51 (October 2015): 30–41. https://doi.org/10.1016/j.ijhm.2015.07.002.

Jakobwitz, S., and V. Egan. "The Dark Triad and Normal Personality Traits." *Personality and Individual Differences* 40, no. 2 (January 2006): 331–339. https://doi.org/10.1016/j.paid.2005.07.006.

Jeffcoat, G., and C. Basnet. "Horizontal Cooperation in the New Zealand Road Transport Industry: Can Sharing the Load Deliver Efficiency, Profitability, and Sustainability?" *Journal of Asia Entrepreneurship and Sustainability* 11, no. 5 (November 2015): 97–140. http://www.asiaentrepreneurshipjournal.com/JAESVolXINov2015.pdf.

Jensen, U. "Does Perceived Societal Impact Moderate the Effect of Transformational Leadership on Value Congruence? Evidence from a Field Experiment." *Public Administration Review* 78, no. 1 (2018): 48–57. https://doi.org/10.1111/puar.12852.

Johnson, R. B., and L. Christensen. *Educational Research: Quantitative, Qualitative, and Mixed Approaches.* Thousand Oaks: SAGE Publications, Incorporated, 2019.

Judge, T. A., and R. F. Piccolo. "Transformational and Transactional Leadership: a Meta-Analytic Test of Their Relative Validity." *Journal of Applied Psychology* 89, no. 5 (2004), 755–768. https://doi.org/10.1037/0021-9010.89.5.755.

Karadağ, E. *Leadership and Organizational Outcomes: Meta-Analysis of Empirical Studies.* New York: Springer, 2015.

Kark, R., D. Van Dijk, and D. R. Vashdi. "Motivated or Demotivated to Be Creative: The Role of Self-Regulatory Focus in Transformational and Transactional Leadership Processes." *Applied Psychology* 67, no. 1 (2018): 186–224. https://doi.org/10.1111/apps.12122.

Karlström, D., and P. Runeson. "Integrating Agile Software Development into Stage-Gate Managed Product Development." *Empirical Software Engineering* 11, no. 2 (June 2006): 203–225. https://doi.org/10.1007/s10664-006-6402-8.

Kelly, M. J. *Qualitative Research Practice.* Thousand Oaks: SAGE Publications, 2004.

Khalili, A. "Transformational Leadership and Organizational Citizenship Behavior: The Moderating Role of Emotional Intelligence." *Leadership and Organization Development Journal* 38, no. 7 (September 2017): 1004–1015. https://doi.org/10.1108/LODJ-11-2016-0269.

Kim, D., D. Choi, and C. Vandenberghe. "Goal-Focused Leadership, Leader-Member Exchange, and Task Performance: The Moderating Effects of Goal Orientations and Emotional Exhaustion." *Journal of Business and Psychology* 33, no. 5 (September 2017): 645–660. https://doi.org/10.1007/s10869-017-9516-7.

Kim, T. Y., C. R. Liden, S. P. Kim, D. R. and Lee. "The Interplay Between Employee Core Self-Evaluation and Transformational Leadership: Effects on Employee Outcomes." *Journal of Business and Psychology* 30, no. 2 (2015): 345–355. https://doi.org/10.1007/s10869-014-9364-7.

Klein, H. K., and M. D. Myers. "A Set of Principles for Conducting and Evaluating Interpretive Field Studies in Information Systems." *MIS quarterly* 23, no. 1 (March 1999): 67–94.

Klenke, K. *Women's Leadership in Context*. Bingley: Emerald Publishing Limited, 2017.

Koryak, O., K. F. Mole, A. Lockett, J. C. Hayton, D. Ucbasaran, and G. P. Hodgkinson. "Entrepreneurial Leadership, Capabilities and Firm Growth." *International Small Business Journal* 33, no. 1 (January 2015): 89–105. https://doi.org/10.1177/2F0266242614558315.

Kossek, E. E., R. J. Petty, T. E. Bodner, M. B. Perrigino, L. B. Hammer, N. L. Yragui, and J. S. Michel. "Lasting Impression: Transformational Leadership and Family Supportive Supervision as Resources for Well-Being and Performance." *Occupational Health Science* 2, no. 1 (March 2018): 1–24. https://doi.org/10.1007/s41542-018-0012-x.

Kranabetter, C., and C. Niessen. "Managers as Role Models for Health: Moderators of the Relationship of Transformational Leadership with Employee Exhaustion and Cynicism." *Journal of Occupational Health Psychology* 22, no. 4 (October 2017): 492–502. https://doi.org/10.1037/ocp0000044.

Kuratko, D. F., J. S. Hornsby, and J. Hayton. "Corporate Entrepreneurship: the Innovative Challenge for a New Global Economic Reality." *Small Business Economics* 45, no. 2 (January 2015): 245–253. https://doi.org/10.1007/s11187-015-9630-8.

Landsberger, H. A. "The Behavioral Sciences in Industry." *Industrial Relations: A Journal of Economy and Society* 7, no. 1 (October 1967): 1–19. https://doi.org/10.1111/j.1468-232X.1967.tb01059.x.

Lauretto, M. D. S., F. Nakano, C. A. D. B. Pereira, and J. M. Stern. "Intentional Sampling by Goal Optimization with Decoupling by Stochastic Perturbation." *AIP Conference Proceedings* 1490, no. 1 (October 2012): 189–201. https://doi.org/10.1063/1.4759603.

Law-Penrose, J. C., K. S. Wilson, and D. L. Taylor. "Leader–Member Exchange (LMX) from the Resource Exchange Perspective: Beyond Resource Predictors and Outcomes of LMX." *The Oxford Handbook of Leader-Member Exchange* (October 2015): 55–56. https://doi.org/10.1093/oxfordhb/9780199326174.013.17.

Lee, J., G. Wang, and R. F. Piccolo. "Jekyll and Hyde Leadership: A Multilevel, Multisample Examination of Charisma and Abuse on Follower and Team Outcomes." *Journal of Leadership and Organizational Studies* 25, no. 4 (February 2018): 399–415. https://doi.org/10.1177%2F1548051818757692.

LePine, M. A., Y. Zhang, E. R. Crawford, B. L. and Rich. "Turning Their Pain to Gain: Charismatic Leader Influence on Follower Stress Appraisal and Job Performance." *Academy of Management Journal* 59, no. 3 (2016): 1036–1059. https://doi.org/10.5465/amj.2013.0778.

Levitt, H. M., M. Bamberg, J. W. Creswell, D. M. Frost, R. Josselson, and C. Suárez-Orozco. "Journal Article Reporting Standards for Qualitative Research in Psychology: The APA Publications and Communications Board Task Force Report." *American Psychologist* 73, no. 1 (January 2018): 26–46. https://doi.org/10.1037/amp0000151.

Lewin, K. "The Dynamics of Group Action." *Educational Leadership* 1, no. 4 (1944): 195–200. https://files.ascd.org/staticfiles/ascd/pdf/journals/ed_lead/el_194401_lewin.pdf.

Li, J., L. Yuan, L. Ning, and J. Li-Ying. "Knowledge Sharing and Affective Commitment: The Mediating Role of Psychological Ownership." *Journal of Knowledge Management* 19, no. 6 (October 2015): 1146–1166. https://doi.org/10.1108/JKM-01-2015-0043.

Liborius, P. "What Does Leaders' Character Add to Transformational Leadership?" *The Journal of Psychology* 151, no. 3 (January 2017): 299–320.

Lin, A. C. "Bridging Positivist and Interpretivist Approaches to Qualitative Methods." *Policy Studies Journal* 26, no. 1 (1998): 162–180. https://doi.org/10.1111/j.1541-0072.1998.tb01931.x.

Lin, C., P. Huang, S. Chen, and L. Huang. "Pseudo-Transformational Leadership Is in the Eyes of the Subordinates." *Journal of Business Ethics* 141, no. 1 (March 2017): 179–190. https://doi.org/10.1007/s10551-015-2739-5.

Lingenfelter, P. E. "Evidence and Impact: How Scholarship Can Improve Policy and Practice." *Change: The Magazine of Higher Learning* 43, no. 3 (May 2011): 44–49. https://doi.org/10.1080/00091383.2011.569260.

Loewenstein, M. J. "Agency Law and the New Economy." *Business Lawyer* 72, no. 4 (2017): 1009–1045. https://www.americanbar.org/digital-asset-abstract.html/content/dam/aba/publications/business_lawyer/2017/72_4/article-agency-law-201709.pdf.

Machi, L. A., and B. T. McEvoy. *The Literature Review: Six Steps to Success*, 3rd ed. Thousand Oaks: Corwin, 2016.

Majeed, N., T. Ramayah, N. Mustamil, M. Nazri, and S. Jamshed. "Transformational Leadership and Organizational Citizenship Behavior: Modeling Emotional Intelligence as Mediator." *Management and Marketing* 12, no. 4 (December 2017): 571–590. https://doi.org/10.1515/mmcks-2017-0034.

Malmendier, U., and G. Tate. "Behavioral CEOs: The Role of Managerial Overconfidence." *Journal of Economic Perspectives* 29, no. 4 (Fall 2015): 37–60. https://doi.org/10.1257/jep.29.4.37

Masa'deh, R. E., B. Y. Obeidat, and A. Tarhini. "A Jordanian Empirical Study of the Associations among Transformational Leadership, Transactional Leadership, Knowledge Sharing, Job Performance, and Firm Performance: A Structural Equation Modelling Approach." *Journal of Management Development* 35, no. 5 (June 2016): 681–705. https://doi.org/10.1108/JMD-09-2015-0134.

Matthew, M., and K. S. Gupta. "Transformational Leadership: Emotional Intelligence." *SCMS Journal of Indian Management* 12, no. 2 (April-June 2015): 75. https://www.academia.edu/31082876/Transformational_Leadership_Emotional_Intelligence.

McMillan, J. H. *Educational Research: Fundamentals for the Consumer*, 6th ed. Boston: Pearson Education, 2012.

Meuser, J. D., W. L. Gardner, J. E. Dinh, J. Hu, R. C. Liden, and R. G. Lord. "A Network Analysis of Leadership Theory." *Journal of Management 42, no. 5 (May 2016): 1374–1403. https://doi.org/10.1177/2F0149206316647099.

Mezirow, J. "Understanding Transformation Theory." *Adult Education Quarterly* 44, no. 4 (Summer 1994): 222–232. https://doi.org/10.1177/2F074171369404400403.

Miller, M. "The Persona of Charismatic versus Transformational Leaders." *Global Conversations* 3, no. 1 (2015): 43–58. https://pdfs.semanticscholar.org/e6f0/ea9a3bcfde4cb58b9d4c0d-81f7454711edfe.pdf.

Mills, J. P., and I. D. Boardley. "Advancing Leadership in Sport: Time to 'Actually' Take the Blinkers Off?" *Sports Medicine* 47, no. 3 (March 2017): 565–570. https://doi.org/10.1007/s40279-016-0661-3.

Nohe, C., and G. Hertel. "Transformational Leadership and Organizational Citizenship Behavior: A Meta-Analytic Test of Underlying Mechanisms." *Frontiers in Psychology* 8 (2017): 1364. https://doi.org/10.3389/fpsyg.2017.01364.

Nørskov, S., P. Kesting, and J. Ulhøi. "Deliberate Change Without Hierarchical Influence? The Case of Collaborative OSS Communities." *International Journal of Organizational Analysis* 25, no. 2 (May 2017): 346–374. https://doi.org/10.1108/IJOA-08-2016-1050.

Northouse, P. G. *Leadership: Theory and Practice*. Thousand Oaks: SAGE Publications, 2016.

Nübold, A., J. Bader, N. Bozin, R. Depala, H. Eidast, E. A. Johannessen, and G. Prinz. "Developing a Taxonomy of Dark Triad Triggers at Work–a Grounded Theory Study Protocol." *Frontiers in Psychology* 8 (March 2017): 293. https://doi.org/10.3389/fpsyg.2017.00293.

Obeidat, B. Y., R. M. T. Masa'deh, D. S. Zyod, and A. A. H. Gharaibeh. "The Associations Among Transformational Leadership, Transactional Leadership, Knowledge Sharing, Job Performance, and Firm Performance: A Theoretical Model." *Journal of Social Sciences* 4, no. 2 (April 2015): 848–866. https://doi.org/10.25255/jss.2015.4.2.848.866.

Ogbonnaya, C., K. Daniels, S. Connolly, M. van Veldhoven, and K. Nielsen. "Employees, Managers, and High Performance Work Practices: A 'Win-Win' or the Transformational Leader's Exploitative Approach to Organizational Performance." *Understanding the High Performance Workplace* 2016, no. 1 (January 2016): 57–80. https://www.researchgate.net/publication/278963469_Employees_managers_and_high_performance_work_practices_A_'win-win'_or_the_transformational_leader's_exploitative_approach_to_organizational_performance.

Ola, B. "A Critique of Conceptual Leadership Styles," in P. Godbole, D. Burke, and J. Aylott, eds. *Why Hospitals Fail* (pp. 57–68). New York: Springer International Publishing AG, 2017. https://doi.org/10.1007/978-3-319-56224-7_5.

Otchere-Ankrah, B., E. S. Tenakwah, and E. J. Tenakwah. "Organisational Reputation and Impact on Employee Attitude: A Case Study of MTN Ghana Limited and Vodafon Ghana Limited." *Journal of Public Affairs* 16, no. 1 (2016): 66–74. https://doi.org/10.1002/pa.1566.

Özbağ, G. "The Role of Personality in Leadership: Five Factor Personality Traits and Ethical Leadership." *Procedia - Social and Behavioral Sciences* 235 (November 2016): 235–242. https://doi.org/10.1016/j.sbspro.2016.11.019.

Pandey, S. K., R. S. Davis, S. Pandey, and S. Peng. "Transformational Leadership and the Use of Normative Public Values: Can Employees Be Inspired to Serve Larger Public Purposes?" *Public Administration* 94, no. 1 (2016): 204–222. https://doi.org/10.1111/padm.12214.

Para-González, L., D. Jiménez-Jiménez, and A. R. Martínez-Lorente. "Exploring the Mediating Effects between Transformational Leadership and Organizational Performance." *Employee Relations* 40, no. 2 (February 2018): 412–432. https://doi.org/10.1108/ER-10-2016-0190.

Pater, R. "Recasting Leadership to Change Culture." *Professional Safety* 60, no. 4 (2015): 22–24. https://www.proquest.com/docview/1671206153.

Patterson, K., J. Grenny, R. McMillan, A. Switzler, and D. Maxwell. *Crucial Accountability: Tools for Resolving Violated Expectations, Broken Commitments, and Bad Behavior*. New York: McGraw-Hill, 2013.

Patton, M. Q. *Qualitative Research and Evaluation Methods*. Thousand Oaks: SAGE Publications, 2002.

Paulhus, D. L., and K. M. Williams. "The Dark Triad of Personality: Narcissism, Machiavellianism, and Psychopathy." *Journal of Research in Personality* 36, no. 6 (December 2002): 556–563. https://doi.org/10.1016/S0092-6566(02)00505-6.

Peck, J. A, and M. Hogue. "Acting with the Best of Intentions… or Not: A Typology and Model of Impression Management in Leadership." *The Leadership Quarterly* 29, no. 1 (2018): 123–134. https://doi.org/10.1016/j.leaqua.2017.10.001.

Peters, L. H., D. D. Hartke, and J. T. Pohlmann. "Fiedler's Contingency Theory of Leadership: An Application of the

Meta-Analysis Procedures of Schmidt and Hunter." *Psychological Bulletin* 97, no. 2 (1985): 274–285. https://doi.org/10.1037/0033-2909.97.2.274.

Pitts, J. N. *Transactional Leader: Religion and John F. Kennedy's 1960 Presidential Campaign*. 2017. http://search.proquest.com/docview/1933776430/.

Politis, J., and N. Politis. "Does Personality Influence Agency Problems? The Role of the 'Big Five' Personality Dimensions," in F. Pinzaru and C. Bratianu, eds. *ECMLG 2016 - Proceedings for the 12th European Conference on Management, Leadership and Governance* (pp. 231–239). Bucharest: ACPIL, 2016. https://researchers.cdu.edu.au/en/publications/does-personality-influence-agency-problems-the-role-of-the-big-fi.

Price, T. L. "The Ethics of Authentic Transformational Leadership." *The Leadership Quarterly* 14, no. 1 (February 2003): 67–81. https://doi.org/10.1016/S1048-9843(02)00187-X.

Ravitch, S. M., and N. M. Carl. *Qualitative Research: Bridging the Conceptual, Theoretical, and Methodological*. Thousand Oaks: SAGE Publications, 2015.

Ravitch, S. M., and M. Riggan. *Reason & Rigor: How Conceptual Frameworks Guide Research*. Thousand Oaks: SAGE Publications, 2016.

Reiley, P. J., and R. R. Jacobs. "Ethics Matter: Moderating Leaders' Power Use and Followers' Citizenship Behaviors." *Journal of Business Ethics* 134, no. 1 (March 2016): 69–81. https://doi.org/10.1007/s10551-014-2416-0.

Renko, M., A. El Tarabishy, A. L. Carsrud, and M. Brännback. "Understanding and Measuring Entrepreneurial Leadership Style." *Journal of Small Business Management* 53, no. 1 (2015): 54–74. https://doi.org/10.1111/jsbm.12086.

Richards, L., and J. Morse. *Readme First for a User's Guide to Qualitative Methods*, 3rd ed. Thousand Oaks: SAGE Publications, 2013.

Riivari, E., and A. M. Lämsä. "Organizational Ethical Virtues of Innovativeness." *Journal of Business Ethics* 155 (March 2017): 1–18. https://doi.org/10.1007/s10551-017-3486-6.

Rosen, E. *The Bounty Effect: 7 Steps to the Culture of Collaboration*. San Francisco: Red Ape Publishing, 2013.

Rosenbach, W. E. *Contemporary Issues in Leadership*. New York: Routledge, 2018.

Salehzadeh, R., A. Shahin, A. Kazemi, and A. S. Barzoki. "Proposing a New Approach for Evaluating the Situational Leadership Theory Based on the Kano Model." *International Journal of Public Leadership* 11, no. 1 (February 2015): 4–20. https://doi.org/10.1108/IJPL-05-2014-0003.

Safazadeh, S., A. Irajpour, N. Alimohammadi, and F. Haghani. "Exploring the Reasons for Theory-Practice Gap in Emergency Nursing Education: A Qualitative Research." *Journal of Education and Health Promotion* 7 (October 2018). https://doi.org/10.4103/jehp.jehp_25_18.

Salovey, P., and J. D. Mayer. "Emotional intelligence." *Imagination, Cognition and Personality* 9, no. 3 (March 1990): 185–211. https://doi.org/10.2190%2FDUGG-P24E-52WK-6CDG.

Sayadi, Y. "The Effect of Dimensions of Transformational, Transactional, and Non-Leadership on the Job Satisfaction and Organizational Commitment of Teachers in Iran." *Man-*

agement in Education 30, no. 2 (May 2016): 57–65. https://doi.org/10.1177%2F0892020615625363.

Schenkel, M., and D. V. Brazeal. "The Effect of Pro-Entrepreneurial Architectures and Relational Influences on Innovative Behavior in a Flat Organizational Structure." *Journal of Business and Entrepreneurship* 27, no. 2 (Spring 2016): 93–118. https://www.proquest.com/docview/1814126920?pq-origsite=gscholar&fromopenview=true.

Schmitt, A., D. N. Den Hartog, and F. D. Belschak. "Transformational Leadership and Proactive Work Behaviour: A Moderated Mediation Model Including Work Engagement and Job Strain." *Journal of Occupational and Organizational Psychology* 89, no. 3 (January 2016): 588–610. https://doi.org/10.1111/joop.12143.

Schuh, S. C., X. A. Zhang, and P. Tian. "For the Good or the Bad? Interactive Effects of Transformational Leadership with Moral and Authoritarian Leadership Behaviors." *Journal of Business Ethics* 116, no. 3 (September 2013): 629–640. https://doi.org/10.1007/s10551-012-1486-0.

Shafique, I., and M. N. Kalyar. "Linking Transformational Leadership, Absorptive Capacity, and Corporate Entrepreneurship." *Administrative Sciences* 8, no. 2 (March 2018): 9. https://doi.org/10.3390/admsci8020009.

Sharma, P. N., and M. J. Pearsall. "Leading under Adversity: Interactive Effects of Acute Stressors and Upper-Level Supportive Leadership Climate on Lower-Level Supportive Leadership Climate." *The Leadership Quarterly* 27, no. 6 (December 2016): 856–868. https://doi.org/10.1016/j.leaqua.2016.08.003.

Shin, J., M. G. Seo, D. L. Shapiro, and M. S. Taylor. "Maintaining Employees' Commitment to Organizational Change: The Role of Leaders' Informational Justice and Transformational Leadership." *The Journal of Applied Behavioral Science* 51, no. 4 (September 2015): 501–528. https://doi.org/10.1177/2F0021886315603123.

Silva, A. "What Is Leadership?" *Journal of Business Studies Quarterly* 8, no. 1 (2016): 1. https://www.semanticscholar.org/paper/What-is-Leadership-Silva/e09ef0ec879806b040cf8126dec54a6938573158.

Skinner, B. F. *About Behaviorism.* New York: Vintage Books, 1976.

Skubinn, R., and L. Herzog "Internalized Moral Identity in Ethical Leadership." *Journal of Business Ethics* 133, no. 2 (January 2016): 249–260. https://doi.org/10.1007/s10551-014-2369-3.

Slavin, R. E. "Evidence-Based Reform in Education: Which Evidence Counts?" *Educational Researcher* 37, no. 1 (2008): 47–50. https://doi.org/10.3102/0013189X08315082.

Sowcik, M., A. C. Andenoro, M. McNutt, and S. E. Murphy. *Leadership 2050: Critical Challenges, Key Contexts, and Emerging Trends.* Bingley: Emerald Group Publishing, 2015.

Staats, B. "The Adaptable Emphasis Leadership Model: A More Full Range of Leadership." *Servant Leadership: Theory and Practice* 2, no. 2 (2016): 2. https://www.semanticscholar.org/paper/The-Adaptable-Emphasis-Leadership-Model%3A-A-More-Staats/0c2109bb2393e374736eaa90b9521f23cf44a099.

Stake, R. E. *The Art of Case Study Research.* Newbury Park: SAGE Publications, 1995.

Stover, D. "Politics and Research: As a Deluge of Reports Offers Commentary on Everything from Abstinence to Vouchers, Is Today's Information Credible, or Rooted in Ideology?" *American School Board Journal* 194, no. 11 (2007): 18.

Strese, S., M. W. Meuer, T. C. Flatten, and M. Brettel. "Organizational Antecedents of Cross-Functional Coopetition: The Impact of Leadership and Organizational Structure on Cross-Functional Coopetition." *Industrial Marketing Management* 53 (February 2016), 42–55. https://doi.org/10.1016/j.indmarman.2015.11.006.

Teece, D. J. "Dynamic Capabilities and Entrepreneurial Management in Large Organizations: Toward a Theory of the (Entrepreneurial) Firm." *European Economic Review* 86 (July 2016): 202–216. https://doi.org/10.1016/j.euroecorev.2015.11.006.

Tetteh-Opai, A. A., and P. O. Omoregie. "Influence of Transactional Leadership Style on Administrative Effectiveness in Sports Organisations in Ghana." *IFE Psychology: An International Journal* 23, no. 2 (January 2015): 64–70. https://journals.co.za/content/ifepsyc/23/2/EJC183852.

Thompson, G., and L. Glasø. "Situational Leadership Theory: A Test from Three Perspectives." *Leadership and Organization Development Journal* 36, no. 5 (July 2015): 527–544. https://doi.org/10.1108/LODJ-10-2013-0130.

Tichy, N. M., and E. Cohen. *The Leadership Engine*. New York: HarperCollins, 2007.

Tourish, D. *The Dark Side of Transformational Leadership: A Critical Perspective*. New York: Routledge, 2013.

Triana, M. D. C., O. C. Richard, and İ. Yücel. "Status Incongruence and Supervisor Gender as Moderators of the Transformational Leadership to Subordinate Affective Organizational Commitment Relationship." *Personnel Psychology* 70, no. 2 (2017): 429–467. https://doi.org/10.1111/peps.12154.

Valsania, S. E., J. A. Moriano, and F. Molero. "Authentic Leadership and Intrapreneurial Behavior: Cross-Level Analysis of the Mediator Effect of Organizational Identification and Empowerment." *International Entrepreneurship and Management Journal* 12, no. 1 (March 2016): 131–152. https://doi.org/10.1007/s11365-014-0333-4.

Vernon, R. "International Investment and International Trade in the Product Cycle," in J. M. Letiche, ed. *International Economic Policies and Their Theoretical Foundations*, 2nd ed. (pp. 415–435). Cambridge: Academic Press, 1992. https://doi.org/10.1016/B978-0-12-444281-8.50024-6.

Viding, E., E. McCrory, and A. Seara-Cardoso. "Psychopathy." *Current Biology* 24, no. 18 (September 2014): R871-R874. https://doi.org/10.1016/j.cub.2014.06.055.

Wall, T., L. Bellamy, V. Evans, and S. Hopkins. "Revisiting Impact in the Context of Workplace Research: A Review and Possible Directions." *Journal of Work-Applied Management* 9, no. 2 (December 2017): 95–109. https://doi.org/10.1108/JWAM-07-2017-0018.

Wang, H. J., E. Demerouti, and P. Le Blanc. "Transformational Leadership, Adaptability, and Job Crafting: The Moderating Role of Organizational Identification." *Journal of Vocational Behavior* 100 (June 2017): 185–195. https://doi.org/10.1016/j.jvb.2017.03.009.

Wolcott, H. F. *Transforming Qualitative Data: Description, Analysis, and Interpretation.* Newbury Park: SAGE Publications, 1994.

Wolfe, B. L., and P. P. Dilworth. "Transitioning Normalcy: Organizational Culture, African American Administrators, and Diversity Leadership in Higher Education." *Review of Educational Research* 85, no. 4 (December 2015): 667–697. https://doi.org/10.3102%2F0034654314565667.

Yasir, M., and N. Mohamad. "Ethics and Morality: Comparing Ethical Leadership with Servant, Authentic and Transformational Leadership Styles." *International Review of Management and Marketing* 6, no. 4S (2016): 310–316. https://www.econjournals.com/index.php/irmm/article/view/2504.

Yin, R. K. *Case Study Research and Applications: Design and Methods.* Newbury Park: SAGE Publications, 1994.

Zehnder, C., H. Herz, and J. Bonardi. "A Productive Clash of Cultures: Injecting Economics into Leadership Research." *The Leadership Quarterly* 28, no. 1 (2017): 65–85. https://doi.org/10.1016/j.leaqua.2016.10.004.

Zhao, H. H., S. E. Seibert, M. S. Taylor, C. Lee, and W. Lam. "Not Even the Past: The Joint Influence of Former Leader and New Leader During Leader Succession in the Midst of Organizational Change." *Journal of Applied Psychology* 101, no. 12 (2016): 1730–1738. https://doi.org/10.1037/apl0000149.

Zhu, W., X. Zheng, R. E. Riggio, and X. Zhang. "A Critical Review of Theories and Measures of Ethics-Related Leadership." *New Directions for Student Leadership* 2015, no. 146 (May 2015): 81–96. https://doi.org/10.1002/yd.20137.

Zhu, X., and M. Bao. "Substitutes or Complements? Individual-Focused and Group-Focused Transformational Leadership in Different Organizational Structures in New Firms."

Leadership and Organization Development Journal 38, no. 5 (July 2017): 699–718. https://doi.org/10.1108/LODJ-04-2016-0097.

CPSIA information can be obtained
at www.ICGtesting.com
Printed in the USA
BVHW061904041122
651162BV00013B/540